The Pacific Northwest Gardener's
Book of Lists

The Pacific Northwest Gardener's

BOOK OF
LISTS

Jan and Ray McNeilan

Taylor Publishing Company
Dallas, Texas

This book is dedicated to Jim and Marje Luce,
who helped us lay the foundation for
our most rewarding lifelong partnership.

Copyright © 1997 Jan and Ray McNeilan

All rights reserved.
No part of this book may be reproduced in any form or by any means—including photocopying and electronic
reproduction—without written permission from the publisher.

Designed by David Timmons
Illustrations p. 66 and p. 87 by Georgene Wood

Published by   Taylor Publishing Company
                     1550 West Mockingbird Lane
                     Dallas, Texas 75235
                     www.taylorpub.com

Library of Congress Cataloging-in-Publication Data

McNeilan, Jan.
    Pacific Northwest gardener's book of lists / Jan and Ray McNeilan.
        P.   cm.
    Includes index
    ISBN 0-87833-956-6
    1. Landscape plants—Northwest, Pacific. 2. Landscape gardening—Northwest, Pacific
I. McNeilan, Ray A. II. Title.
SB408.M37   1997
     9'09795—dc21   96-52183
                                                                      CIP

              nited States of America
              6   5   4

CONTENTS

Acknowledgments

Our sincere thanks go to the gardeners, nursery people, extension service professionals, horticulturists, and ardent plant society members who helped us develop lists that will help gardeners throughout the Pacific Northwest.

A LETTER TO THE READERS

Dear Pacific Northwest Gardeners,

The original *Book of Lists*, by Lois Trigg Chaplin, is the source book and idea-starter for Southern gardeners. Now gardeners in the Pacific Northwest have a *Book of Lists*, patterned along the same lines. If you have ever begun a landscaping project and found your thought processes devoid of any but the most common of plants, this book is for you. If you have looked critically at your bed of roses, or your border of irises, and felt it was time to replace something—but with what?—this book is for you. Here you will find lists of plants to fit specific environmental conditions or to supply special features to a landscape or to avoid because of their bad habits. You will learn that the wealth of ornamental plants available to gardeners provides something for nearly any growing situation.

This book's purpose is to stimulate your desire for more information. We hope that you will want to read further about your plant likes and dislikes, and learn to make better selections in your landscapes and gardens. We called upon the generous advice of many plant experts as we developed this book and its lists. You will find tips and hints scattered throughout. You will also find a list of gardening-related books that we feel are important to the Northwest gardener. You may notice that not every plant in the world is listed. We left some for you to add to the lists as you work your way through a garden center, or as you browse the books about specific plants. Education happens more easily when you experience something, and adding to our lists can help you to learn more about the world of ornamentals.

Learn who the plant experts are in your community, and seek them out for more information about how to successfully grow plants in your local microclimate. The local retail nursery manager, the plant society, the garden club, your local extension agent, and Master Gardener volunteers, can all assist you. We hope this book will encourage you to explore the world of plants and paint your landscape with color and interest.

Good luck and good gardening,

Jan and Ray McNeilan

INTRODUCTION

You would think that to start a book, the author(s) would begin with an introduction. In reality, it is the last thing written, once the book is in its final stages of preparation. We have learned a lot more about our own region in the process of developing the chapters and many lists for this book, and we want to give our knowledge to you in short lists. No need to blow your mind reading the entire book at one sitting: instead use the book as a guide as you need it. First we would like to give our thanks to Lois Trigg Chaplin, who wrote *The Southern Gardener's Book of Lists*, and who made the suggestion for this book. It is a great idea that she had, and we commend her for providing this resource to the gardener seeking that perfect plant for that exact place in the landscape.

Here is how the *Book of Lists* works. Each chapter is composed of lists of plants that would fit a particular situation, either in a landscape (for example, a list of annuals for moist and cool situations) or in a region (for example, groundcovers for windy seaside gardens or ornamental grasses for high desert conditions). The lists are never complete. We could write this book forever, adding new hybrids and discoveries and developing new categories almost daily. But we would like for you to do that as you use this book. Add to the lists, pencil in new findings, make notes of what you like or don't like or how something might be used differently. Make this book a garden-planning resource that you can build on. We have offered you some challenges, as some of the plants found in our lists may be hard to find, but we think they are worthy of your search.

What a difference your microclimate makes. Whether your plants survive and thrive or wither and die in your garden is determined more by your own microclimate than by the overall hardiness zone. Your overall zone is fixed by whomever decides what boundaries of temperature extremes will be used. As Dr. Michael Colt of Idaho says about plant zones, "Actually the specific zone rating of a given herbaceous perennial cultivar should be considered as only a rough guideline rather than a mandatory factor. When in doubt, just do it!" You have the ability within your own zone to provide windbreaks and shelters to protect against drying winds, change shade and sun exposures to provide whatever the plant needs, mulch with different colors to absorb or reflect heat. In short, you can do much to make your own garden conditions receptive to plants you would like to try.

Soil also makes a great difference in whether a particular plant will grow in your locale. Across the Pacific Northwest, soils range from coastal sand to low valley silty clay to high desert silt, and across a pH scale from extremely acid in parts of the rainy northwest area to extremely alkaline in some of the southeastern areas. Learn what your own soil conditions will allow and which plants will best fit your conditions. Use the regions given in this book as a guide, but ask locally about the plants that interest you.

The scientific names that we have used have been checked with *Hortus Third* and other reference books to be as correct as possible. However, plant taxonomists continue to find reasons to change things every now and then and about every ten years come out with a new list, which causes all writers to check every reference at least twice when writing a book about plant materials. In cases where we were not sure, we used the newest reference available.

Where did all the plants come from in our lists? From nursery industry people, from many gardener friends, from a large network of garden information journalists, from almost any source of new plant material, and from at least sixty-five years of combined experience between the two of us. Before using a plant in a list, we checked against at least two references to make sure it was something available to the gardening public.

In the lists we have used common names for simplicity, followed by the botanical names of genus and species, and in some cases listed cultivars or varieties where a particular individual plant was best suited for the listing. In the chapter on roses we used almost entirely the cultivar names; in the chapter on trees we give you mostly the genus and species names. Unless a specific cultivar/variety was felt to be the exact plant needed for a particular list, only the genus and species names were listed. This does not mean that blind selection of cultivars will give you the expected result; instead it gives you a general listing so you can find locally suited cultivars that would be suggested by your nursery person, extension agent, or other plant expert.

We do not want to give you the idea that by blindly following these lists you will come up with the best selections in the world. There are too many variables, both in life and in landscaping. As Jan Behrs, editor and publisher of *Pacific Northwest Gardener Newsletter* says, "Gardening is not for the timid. You can't read a rulebook, then go out and follow a bunch of formulas. It's more like falling in love. A few marigolds, a few tomatoes, and pretty soon you're head-over-heels in the dirt, staying up all hours, lusting after new plants, spending all your hard-earned pay, singing in the rain. Don't worry. Before you know it, both your yard and your life will be blossoming."

As you look around your own neighborhood, you can see examples of how plant development can vary according to how they are managed, or in the way they respond to differing microclimates. In simple terms, you cannot assume that a particular plant in your yard is going to grow or look like the one in your neighbor's yard. Dr. Ray Maleike, Washington State Extension Horticulturist, has this to say about a normally assumed plant characteristic, dormancy, "Recent research by Dr. Les Fuchigami, Deptartment of Horticulture, Oregon State University, has shown that if a plant is subjected to a sub-lethal stress (a stress that does not quite kill the plant, as for example lack of sufficient water during a critical part of the growing season), the plant may not go into dormancy, or the stress may break the dormancy that the plant has acquired. If the plant is not dormant, it may not be hardy and the plant may suffer cold injury at a much higher temperature and the plant may be killed." Meanwhile, your neighbor's plant, which was kept well watered during the growing season, lives through the cold winter and blooms gloriously the following spring.

BOOKS YOU SHOULD KNOW ABOUT

The supply of gardening books will amaze you when you step into a modern bookstore. There are books on nearly every subject imaginable, and in some cases three or four written on the same topic. It is up to you to sort through this plethora of composition and harvest the kernels of wisdom that will help you in your gardening endeavors. Here are the books we would suggest that can help you to avoid costly mistakes in your choices of plants, or in the development of your gardens.

Must have for basic reference
Gardening with Native Plants of the Pacific Northwest, second edition, Dr. Arthur Kruckeberg, University of Washington Press, Seattle, 1996.
Hortus Northwest: A Pacific Northwest Native Plant Directory and Journal, Dale Shank (issued bi-annually), PO Box 955, Canby, Oregon 97013.
Manual of Woody Landscape Plants, fourth edition, Michael Dirr, Stipes Publishing Co., Champaign, Illinois, 1990.
The Random House Book of Perennials, volumes 1 and 2, Roger Phillips and Martyn Rix, Random House, Inc., New York, 1991.
Sunset Western Garden Book, Sunset Publishing Co., Menlo Park, California (a must for any gardener in the western part of the US).
Trees (Eyewitness Handbooks), Allen J. Coombes, Dorling Kindersley, Inc., New York, 1992.
Trees and Shrubs for Pacific Northwest Gardens, second edition, John and Carol Grant, Timber Press, Portland, 1990.

Should have
The American Mixed Border, Ann Lovejoy, Macmillan, New York, 1993.
Gardening with Roses, Patrick Taylor, Timber Press, Portland, 1995.
Great Garden Sources of the Pacific Northwest, Nan Booth Simpson, TACT, 1994.
Greer's Guidebook to Available Rhododendrons, Species and Hybrids, third edition, Harold E. Greer, Offshoot Publications, Eugene, Oregon, Library of Congress cat. # 95-067367, revised.
Hortus Third, Staff of the L. H. Bailey Hortorium, Cornell University, Macmillan, New York, 1996.
Ornamental Grasses: The Amber Wave, Carole Ottesen, McGraw-Hill Publishing Co, 1989.
Pacific Northwest Guide to Home Gardening, McNeilan and Ronningen, Timber Press, Portland, 1989.
Peonies, Allan Rogers, Timber Press, Portland, 1995.
Rhododendrons in America, Ted Van Veen, Sweeney, Krist & Dimm, 1976.
Winter Gardening in the Maritime Northwest, Binda Colebrook, Sasquatch Books, Seattle, 1989.

Others for specific needs
The Complete Shade Gardener, George Schenk, Houghton Mifflin Co., New York, 1984.
Designing with Perennials, Pamela J. Harper, Macmillan, New York, 1991.
Flowering, Fruiting and Foliage Vines, Chuck Crandall and Barbara Crandall, Sterling Publishing Co., Inc., New York, 1995.

Fragrance in Bloom, Ann Lovejoy, Sasquatch Books, Seattle, 1996.
The Garden in Winter, Rosemary Verey, Little, Brown, Boston, 1988.
Gardening with Color, Mary Keen, Random House, New York, 1991.
The Hosta Book, Paul Aden, Timber Press, Portland, 1988.
Landscaping with Container Plants, Jim Wilson, Houghton Mifflin Co., New York, 1990.
Trees of Greater Portland, Phyllis C. Reynolds and Elizabeth F. Dimon, Timber Press, Portland, 1993.
Trees of Seattle, Arthur Lee Jacombson, Sasquatch Books, Seattle, 1989.

ABOUT ZONES

In the Pacific Northwest gardeners generally are referred to zones defined by USDA or Sunset, both of which give a good broad definition of plant zones. However, most gardeners, whether neophyte or beyond dedication, will have amended their landscapes with microclimates that extend well outside their defined plant zones. While the concept of *microclimate* includes the general sunlight, temperature ranges, air movement patterns, rainfall, growing season typical of the region, it specifically focuses on the conditions in one's own gardening space that allow plant growth. To avoid the pitfall of classifying each plant to an exact temperature regime, we have taken the liberty of giving a broad brush to categories that are acceptable to our plant suggestions. To make the categories understandable, here is our rating system.

Coastal (C) means just that; the garden is on the coast or influenced by the coastal environment. It is subject to wind, salt air, drizzle, and has enormous differences in microclimates. It has the mildest of the growing season temperatures. Includes Zone 5 Sunset, Zone 9 and 8 USDA.

Low Mountains (LM) includes the uplands having a mild, medium-length growing season and may have snow for short periods in the winter. Includes Zone 3 and 4 Sunset, Zone 7 USDA.

Low Valleys (LV) describes the Willamette Valley in Oregon, the Columbia Valley up to the Cascade Range, and the river valleys that lead in to Puget Sound. The growing seasons are lengthy and the winters are varied, often marked by freezing rain and cold wintery winds that can shrivel the hardiest of plants. Includes Zone 6 Sunset, Zone 8 USDA.

Dry Valleys (DV) describes the climate found in Medford and Grants Pass and the upper portions of the Columbia River Valley. The summers are dry and the growing season long enough to produce fabulous fruit crops, and the winters are cold enough to satisfy the dormancy requirements of any perennial. Includes Zone 7 Sunset, Zone 6 USDA.

High Desert (HD) describes much of the eastern portion of the Pacific Northwest. This zone could also be described as high mountain. Growing seasons are short, and temperatures can be more extreme than those of the other climatic zones of the region. Includes Zone 1 and 2 Sunset, Zone 5 USDA.

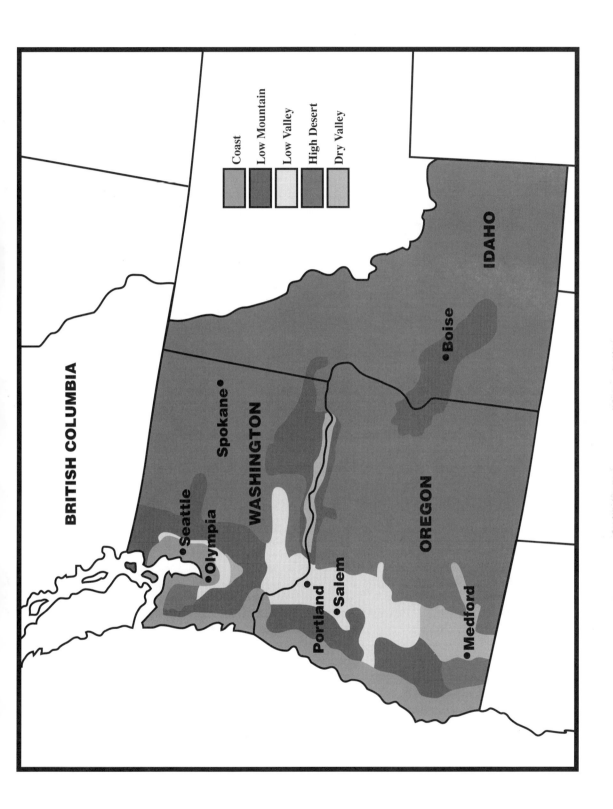

Coast
Low Mountain
Low Valley
High Desert
Dry Valley

BRITISH COLUMBIA

IDAHO

•Boise

Spokane•

WASHINGTON

•Seattle

•Olympia

OREGON

Portland •

•Salem

•Medford

TREES

Trees are woody plants that generally have one main stem, called a trunk, and are over twenty feet tall at maturity. Shrubs are woody plants that typically have multiple stems and are usually less than twenty feet tall at maturity. Although there are exceptions to this statement, it is a good rule of thumb.

Trees in the Pacific Northwest fit into two major groups, the conifers and the broadleaves. The conifers are the firs, pines, and cedars, along with spruce, hemlock, redwoods, and yews. The broadleaf group includes maples, ash, locust, dogwood, willows, cottonwoods, and a whole pageful of others. There are more types of broadleaf trees here than there are conifers, but there are many conifer forests in this region with millions of conifer trees.

The gardener who is planning and planting his/her first landscape can find a bewildering array of trees at any retail nursery or garden center. Some will be wide-spreading shade trees when they are mature, others may be tall spires that accent a place in the yard. The conifers supply green color year around, while the leafy types may provide flowers, change color through their growing season, and shed leaves in the fall for your compost pile. Select carefully, dear gardener, for the tree takes a long while to reach maturity, and it may remain in the landscape long after you have moved on.

When planting the landscape, the trees should be the first to be selected and planted, for they will take ten years or more to become a truly integral part of the landscape. Large trees can be purchased from nurseries that specialize in growing the "instant tree." Plant your tree properly, siting it where the tree fits the environmental conditions best; in other words in well-drained, fertile soils, away from windy sites (unless you are planting a windbreak), and in areas where the roots can grow naturally.

The first growing season is the most important in the life of your new tree. Trees can generally be planted in early to mid spring throughout the Pacific Northwest, and can also be planted in the autumn in Coastal and Low Valley areas in the western part of the region. During the summer, see that the tree is deeply watered at least every three weeks if rainfall is not forthcoming. In new planting areas apply a complete type fertilizer to the area before planting. In already-established landscapes the tree will usually get quite enough fertilizer from the lawn or flower and shrub beds. Let the tree's growth guide you in its need for fertilizer. In most cases the only element needed, or that gives a growth response, is nitrogen, and it should be used sparingly.

In the following lists we have identified trees that fit many conditions you might encounter as you begin planning the tree population for your yard. The lists are by no means complete, but can serve to guide you as you investigate this woody world and begin your tree education. Good luck.

EVERGREEN TREES WITH COLUMNAR (FASTIGATE) CHARACTER

Columnar trees fit in the landscape where there is not enough space for a standard tree with spreading habit. Their columnar form can be used in smaller gardens, or as fence lines, hedgerows, or to mark a focal point. A columnar plant serves as an exclamation point that says, "Hey, look what happens at this place."

Incense cedar (*Calocedrus decurrens*)	All PNW
Italian cypress (*Cupressus sempervirens*)	C, LV, LM, DV
Blue Italian cypress (*Cupressus sempervirens* 'Glauca')	C, LV, LM, DV
Serbian spruce (*Picea omorika*)	All PNW
Hoops blue spruce (*Picea pungens* 'Hoopsii')	All PNW
Bosnian pine (*Pinus heldreichii* 'Leucodermis')	All PNW
Columnar eastern white pine (*Pinus strobus* 'Fastigiata')	C, LV, LM, DV
Columnar Scotch pine (*Pinus sylvestris* 'Fastigiata')	All PNW
Irish yew (*Taxus baccata* 'Fastigiata')	C, LV, LM, DV
Gold Irish yew (*Taxus baccata* 'Fastigiata Aurea')	C, LV, LM, DV
Hogan red cedar (*Thuja plicata* 'Fastigiata')	All PNW
Western red cedar (*Thuja plicata* vars.)	All PNW

TREES THAT WILL SURVIVE AND THRIVE IN HEAVY SOILS

Many of us garden in soil that consists largely of clay and silt particles, both of which are very small and packed tightly together. We amend these soils with organic matter, or sometimes with ground limestone, to separate the particles and provide a little air for the roots of plants that we try to grow in these soils. In spite of what we do to correct the soil conditions, eventually it returns to its normal tight and heavy state. The alternative to trying to correct the everlasting problem of heavy soil drainage is to find plants that will be happy in those soils—and there actually are some that fit. Here are a few to use in your selection process.

Black Locust

Maple (*Acer* spp.)	All PNW
Red alder (*Alnus oregana*)	C, LV, LM
European white birch (*Betula pendula*)	All PNW
Hornbeam (*Carpinus* spp.)	C, LV, LM, DV
Eastern redbud (*Cercis canadensis*)	LM, DV, HD
Hawthorn (*Crataegus* spp.)	All PNW
Ash (*Fraxinus* spp.)	All PNW
Sourgum (*Nyssa sylvatica*)	C, LV, LM, DV
White poplar (*Populus alba*)	All PNW
Pear (*Pyrus* spp.)	C, LV, LM, DV

English oak (*Quercus robur*)	C, LV, LM, DV
Black locust (*Robinia pseudoacacia*)	All PNW
Staghorn sumac (*Rhus typhina*)	All PNW
Willow (*Salix* spp.)	All PNW

"In most respects, the Puget Sound region seems like tree heaven with its gentle climate, ample rainfall, and lush vegetation. Tree huggers from most parts of the country envy us. But landscape trees do encounter a few problems in getting established here. First, many parts of our region have glacial till for soil as a result of the last ice age. That translates into scant topsoil and compacted subsoil. Second, our summers can be deceptively dry. While Seattle averages forty inches of rain annually, only five inches of that falls between May 1 and August 31! Since many of our landscape trees come from areas with wetter, more humid summers, careful attention must be given to summer irrigation for several years after planting."—Van Bobbitt, Community Horticulture Coordinator, Washington State University

TREES FOR DRY SITES

While the Pacific Northwest is noted for its rainfall and damp climate (on the west side of the Cascade Range), the rain does not generally fall during the summer growing season, so irrigation becomes a must for newly planted trees. Whether they will thrive after their first year depends on their own hardiness, depth of rooting, and the type of soil in which they have been planted. Here are a few that you can depend on, once they have been assisted past that so-important first growing season.

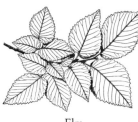

Red horsechestnut (*Aesculus × carnea* 'Briotti')	All PNW
Madrone (*Arbutus menziesii*)	All PNW
Incense cedar (*Calocedrus decurrens*)	All PNW
Siberian peashrub (*Caragana arborescens*)	LV, LM, DV, HD
Hackberry (*Celtis occidentalis*)	LM, DV, HD
Eastern redbud (*Cercis canadensis*)	LM, DV, HD
Hawthorn (*Crataegus* spp.)	All PNW
Russian olive (*Elaeagnus angustifolia*)	LM, DV, HD
Ash (*Fraxinus* spp.)	All PNW
Coffee tree (*Gymnocladus dioicus* 'Espresso')	All PNW
Goldenrain tree (*Koelreuteria paniculata*)	LV, LM, DV, HD
Crape myrtle (*Lagerstroemia indica*)	C, LV, LM, DV
Flowering crabapple (*Malus* spp.)	All PNW
Ponderosa pine (*Pinus ponderosa*)	LM, DV, HD
Scotch pine (*Pinus sylvestris*)	All PNW
Locust (*Robinia* spp.)	LV, LM, DV, HD
Staghorn sumac (*Rhus typhina*)	All PNW
Mountain ash (*Sorbus aucuparia*)	All PNW
American elm (*Ulmus americana*)	All PNW
Camperdown elm (*Ulmus glabra* 'Camperdownii')	All PNW

Elm

TREES WITH WEEPING CHARACTER

Weepers are normally used as specimen trees in the landscape. They can be utilized in the center of a shrub bed as a focal point or at the end of a large bed as a visual anchor. In the rainy winters of the Pacific Northwest, the weeping forms reflect the nature of the territory. If, as you peruse nursery plant labels, you come upon the word *pendula*, this means that the plant's branches have a pendant, or weeping, character.

Weeping birch (*Betula pendula*)	All PNW
Burgundy wine weeping birch (*Betula pendula* 'Purpurea')	All PNW
Weeping katsura tree (*Cercidiphyllum japonicum* 'Pendulum')	All PNW
Weeping blue atlas cedar (*Cedrus atlantica* 'Glauca Pendula')	C, LV, LM, DV
Atlas cedar (*Cedrus atlantica pendula*)	C, LV, LM, DV
Deodar cedar (*Cedrus deodora* 'Pendula')	C, LV, LM, DV
Weeping cedar of Lebanon (*Cedrus libani* 'Pendula')	C, LV, LM, DV
Weeping Lawson cypress (*Chamaecyparis lawsoniana* 'Pendula')	C, LV, LM, DV
Weeping Nootka cypress (*Chamaecyparis nootkatensis* 'Pendula')	C, LV, LM, DV
Weeping beech (*Fagus sylvatica* 'Pendula')	All PNW
Purple fountain beech (*Fagus sylvatica* 'Purple Fountain')	All PNW
Purple weeping beech (*Fagus sylvatica* 'Purpurea Pendula')	All PNW
Weeping European larch (*Larix decidua* 'Pendula')	All PNW
Chaparral common mulberry (*Morus alba* 'Chaparral')	All PNW
Weeping Norway spruce (*Picea abies* 'Pendula')	All PNW
Weeping pine (*Pinus densiflora* 'Pendula')	All PNW
Weeping Japanese red pine (*Pinus densiflora* 'Pendula')	C, LV, LM, DV
Weeping white pine (*Pinus strobus* 'Pendula')	C, LV, LM, DV
Weeping flowering cherry (*Prunus* spp.)	Varies
Weeping willow-leafed pear (*Pyrus salicifolia* 'Pendula')	C, LV, LM, DV
Weeping pussy willow (*Salix babylonica*)	All PNW
Weeping French pussy willow (*Salix caprea* 'Pendula')	All PNW
Weeping sequoia (*Sequoiadendron giganteum* 'Pendulum')	All PNW
Weeping Japanese snowbell (*Styrax japonicus* 'Pendula')	C, LV, LM, DV
Weeping hemlock (*Tsuga canadensis* 'Pendula')	C, LV, LM, DV

TREES FOR NATURESCAPING

A new word has come into use where naturalists and the landscape industry come into contact. Naturescaping is defined by its authors as a way of turning "normal yards" into sanctuaries for wildlife and for people. As structures and industry have taken the place of fields, forests, and wilderness, wildlife has had to adapt to the growth of cities. Naturescaping is seeking to give back something that will provide an interface for wildlife and people. The trees in this list are those well suited to providing cover, nesting sites, food, and shelter for wildlife. Use this list as a starter for your own list, scout out native groves, and list the trees which seem to attract birds or that provide some of the needs for animal life.

Big-leaf maple (*Acer macrophyllum*)	All PNW
Red alder (*Alnus oregona*)	C, LV, LM
Hazelnut (*Corylus cornuta*)	C, LV, LM
Hawthorn (*Crataegus* spp.)	All PNW

Oregon ash (*Fraxinus latifolia*)   All PNW
Crabapple (*Malus* spp.)   All PNW
Indian plum (*Osmaronia cerasiformis*)   C, LV, LM
Douglas fir (*Pseudotsuga menziesii*)   All PNW
Oregon white oak (*Quercus garryana*)   LV, LM, DV
Cascara (*Rhamnus purshiana*)   C, LV, LM
Idaho locust (*Robinia ambigua* 'Idahoensis')   All PNW
Red elderberry (*Sambucus callicarpa*)   C, LV, LM, DV
Black elderberry (*Sambucus melanocarpa*)   DV, HD
Blue elderberry (*Sambucus mexicana*)   All PNW
Purple elderberry (*Sambucus nigra* 'Purpurea')   C, LV, LM, DV
Mountain ash (*Sorbus aucuparia*)   C, LV, LM, DV
Western red cedar (*Thuja plicata*)   C, LV, LM

A hedgerow planting of hawthorn, crabapple, red alder, or western red cedar along the side of your property is a great way to help wildlife and also provide a screen between you and your neighbors. Not only does a hedgerow offer cover and nesting areas, it can also be a year-round bird buffet. The more diverse your plantings, the more species of wildlife you can expect to attract.—Naturescaping, A Place For Wildlife, Oregon Dept. of Fish & Wildlife

DECIDUOUS TREES WITH COLUMNAR CHARACTER

A columnar deciduous tree could serve as a summertime windbreak, as an autumn color spot, or where a spreading tree wouldn't fit. Many of these trees are used in parking strips as street trees. They stay in bounds and are less likely to raise the sidewalk. An added benefit from using columnar trees is the interesting winter silhouettes offered by their bare branches.

Armstrong red maple (*Acer* × *freemanii* 'Armstrong')   All PNW
Greencolumn maple (*Acer nigrum* 'Greencolumn')   All PNW
Columnar Norway maple (*Acer platanoides* 'Columnar')   All PNW
Bowhall red maple (*Acer rubrum* 'Bowhall')   All PNW
Columnar red maple (*Acer rubrum* 'Columnare')   All PNW
Scarlet Sentinel maple (*Acer rubrum* 'Scarlet Sentinel')   All PNW
Columnar hornbeam (*Carpinus betulus* 'Fastigiata')   C, LV, LM, DV
Dawyck beech (*Fagus sylvatica* 'Fastigiata')   All PNW
Dawyck Purple beech (*Fagus sylvatica* 'Dawyck Purple')   All PNW
Princeton Sentry ginkgo (*Ginkgo biloba* 'Princeton Sentry')   All PNW
Goldenrain tree (*Koelreuteria paniculata* 'Fastigiata')   C, LV, LM, DV
Tulip tree (*Liriodendron tulipifera*)   All PNW
Swedish columnar aspen (*Populus tremula* 'Erecta')   All PNW
Spire cherry (*Prunus hillieri* 'Spire')   All PNW
Columnar Sargent cherry (*Prunus sargentii* 'Columnaris')   All PNW
Amanogawa cherry (*Prunus serrulata* 'Amanogawa')   All PNW
Capital pear (*Pyrus calleryana* 'Capital')   C, LV, LM, DV
Crimson spire oak (*Quercus* 'Crimschmidt')   C, LV, LM, DV
Skyrocket oak (*Quercus robur* 'Fastigiata')   C, LV, LM, DV
Tallhedge buckthorn (*Rhamnus frangula* 'Tallcole')   All PNW
Corinthian linden (*Tilia cordata* 'Corzam')   All PNW

TREES FOR TOUGH URBAN SITES

Trees growing in urban sites must sometimes tolerate conditions that are not fit for man nor beast, nor we might add, for trees and other plants. Intolerable soils, soil-compacting traffic, paving and sidewalks, plus the fact that few receive the care that a normal self-respecting tree should expect. Luckily, many cities now have street-tree ordinances that suggest the proper type of tree to be planted, and there are many volunteers who are interested in keeping street trees in good condition. However, in spite of all of the help and advice that is available, mistakes can be made in placing the right plant in the right situation. The list below is made of trees that tolerate city conditions such as air pollution, reflected heat, and limited open soil surface for air and water.

Maple (*Acer* spp.)	All PNW
Red horsechestnut (*Aesculus carnea*)	C, LV, LM
Hornbeam (*Carpinus betulus*)	C, LV, LM, DV
Hackberry (*Celtis* spp.)	C, LV, LM, DV
Hawthorn (*Crataegus* spp.)	All PNW
Ash (*Fraxinus* spp.)	C, LV, LM, DV
Marshall green ash (*Fraxinus pennsylvanica* 'Marshall')	All PNW
Maidenhair tree (*Ginkgo biloba*)	All PNW
Thornless honey locust (*Gleditsia triacanthos* vars.)	All PNW
Goldenrain tree (*Koelreuteria paniculata*)	C, LV, LM, DV
Sweetgum (*Liquidambar styraciflua*)	All PNW
Flowering crabapple (*Malus* spp.)	All PNW
Sour gum (*Nyssa sylvatica*)	C, LV, LM, DV
Callery pear (*Pyrus calleryana* 'Bradford')	C, LV, LM, DV
Oak (*Quercus* spp.)	C, LV, LM, DV
Linden (*Tilia* spp.)	C, LV, LM, DV
Lacebark elm (*Ulmus parvifolia*)	C, LV, LM
Japanese zelkova (*Zelkova serrata*)	C, LV, LM

Maidenhair Tree

> *Tree shape and growth habit change as a tree grows. Young trees are often upright, while older ones of the same cultivar may become spreading. "Mature" size of a tree varies by climate, landscape site characteristics and how long the tree lives. City trees rarely reach the size and age of their counterparts in native forest stands.—J. Frank Schmidt & Son Co., Boring, Oregon*

TREES FOR CONTAINERS

Landscapes can be created on decks and patios with containerized trees blended with containers of shrubs, vines, perennials, and flowering annuals. Plantings in containers allow you the freedom of movement to change the configuration of the landscape plan or to take advantage of sun, shade, or areas protected from wind.

Vine maple (*Acer circinatum*)	All PNW
Amur maple (*Acer ginnala*)	All PNW

Japanese maple (*Acer palmatum* vars.)	All PNW
Eastern redbud (*Cercis canadensis*)	LM, DV, HD
Hinoki cypress (*Chamaecyparis obtusa* 'Gracilis')	All PNW
Flowering dogwood (*Cornus* spp.)	Varies
Contorted filbert (*Corylus avellana* 'Contorta')	C, LV, LM, DV
European beech (*Fagus sylvatica* varieties)	All PNW
English holly (*Ilex* spp.)	C, LV, LM, DV
Crape myrtle (*Lagerstroemia indica*)	C, LV, LM, DV
Sourwood (*Oxydendrum arboreum*)	C, LV, LM, DV
Dwarf Alberta spruce (*Picea glauca* 'Conica')	All PNW
Black Hills spruce (*Picea glauca densata*)	All PNW
Japanese black pine (*Pinus thunbergiana*)	All PNW
Flowering plum (*Prunus* spp.)	C, LV, LM, DV
Smooth sumac (*Rhus glabra*)	All PNW
Deerhorn cedar (*Thujopsis dolabrata* 'Nana')	C, LV, LM, DV
Camperdown elm (*Ulmus glabra* 'Camperdownii')	All PNW

Maples are subject to a soil-borne disease called verticillium wilt. **This fungus disease is often carried by potatoes or other members of the Solanaceae family, and can remain in the soil for many years. Learn what you can about the history of your soil before planting maples, otherwise you may find an unwanted problem that is difficult, if not impossible, to control.**

SMALL TREES WITH SOMETHING FOR WINTER INTEREST

Some trees simply shed their leaves in the fall and become a part of the landscape background. Others present a picture of colorful twigs, retained and interesting fruits, and vibrant colors and help to overcome your winter "blahs." Here are a few of them to help you start your own list.

Paperbark maple (*Acer griseum*)	All PNW
Coral bark Japanese maple (*Acer palmatum* 'Sango Kaku')	All PNW
Columnar hornbeam (*Carpinus betulus* 'Fastigiata')	C, LV, LM, DV
Glorybower tree (*Clerodendrum trichotomum*)	C, LV, LM
Bloodtwig dogwood (*Cornus sanguinea*)	All PNW
Red-twig dogwood (*Cornus stolonifera*)	All PNW
Yellow-twig dogwood (*Cornus stolonifera* 'Flaviramea')	All PNW
Washington hawthorn (*Crataegus phaenopyrum*)	All PNW
Birch bark cherry (*Prunus serrula*)	All PNW
Pin oak (*Quercus palustris*)	All PNW
Contorted willow (*Salix matsudana* 'Tortuosa')	All PNW
Camperdown elm (*Ulmus glabra*)	All PNW

About Bloodtwig dogwood: "It is not fussy but likes damp locations best. For the best winter color, we suggest that you prune hard every couple of years, keeping the height to under six feet."—Sam Benowitz, Raintree Nursery, Morton, Washington

TREES THAT ARE ADAPTABLE FOR BONSAI

The ancient Oriental art of growing trees and shrubs in small containers is attractive to many gardeners who like the idea of manipulating the growth of a plant to fit such a growing condition. Specialty shops sell ready-made bonsai plants that have been grown in traditional pots. Many retail nurseries sell plants that lend themselves to the bonsai role, being perhaps not properly formed for a normal sort of landscape tree, but with the form that would permit the training and pruning necessary to make a good bonsai candidate. Here are some trees that would fit the bill admirably. Be prepared to give these dwarf gems constant care once you have committed them to the bonsai container. You may even decide to take them on vacation with you.

Trident maple (*Acer buergeranum*)
Japanese maple (*Acer palmatum*)
Hornbeam (*Carpinus* spp.)
Katsura tree (*Cercidiphyllum japonicum*)
Hawthorn (*Crataegus* spp.)
Beech (*Fagus* spp.)
Honey locust (*Gleditsia triacanthos*)
Japanese larch (*Larix kaempferi*)
Pines (*Pinus* spp.)

Japanese pagoda tree (*Sophora japonica*)
Little leaf linden (*Tilia cordata*)
Cork bark elm (*Ulmus parvifolia*)
Japanese zelkova (*Zelkova serrata*)

Hedge maple (*Acer campestre*)
Vine maple (*Acer circinatum*)
Korean hornbeam (*Carpinus koreana*)
Redbud (*Cercis* spp.)
Japanese persimmon (*Diospyros kaki*)
Maidenhair tree (*Ginkgo biloba*)
Crape myrtle (*Lagerstroemia indica*)
Crabapple (*Malus* spp.)
Dwarf weeping willows (*Salix lindleyana,
    S. myrtilloides, S. repens*)
Japanese snowbell (*Styrax japonica*)
Canadian hemlock (*Tsuga canadensis*)
Siberian elm (*Ulmus pumila*)

"The Acers, particularly the small-leafed Japanese maples, are by far the easiest to develop into bonsai, and they are the easiest to maintain. The most important factor in growing bonsai plants is the soil mix. Put them in a media that will hold onto the moisture needed to keep the plant supplied but that will also contain enough air to keep the roots alive. Too often people who are trying to grow bonsai plants kill them by overwatering. I use hemlock bark, ground to a medium fineness, and my plants do well."—Ed Wood, Bonsai Village, Wilsonville, Oregon

TREES WITH "UNUSUAL" CHARACTERISTICS

There exists throughout this wonderful planet of green plants, many that have startling things to show at various times of the year. Here are a few examples, some that you might want to place in that special part of the landscape where you can look out the kitchen window every morning and see something so unusual that it just starts your day off right!

Tree	What Makes it Unique
Striped bark maple (*Acer capillipes, A. davidii*)	White bark stripes
Monkey-puzzle tree (*Araucaria araucana*)	Foliage, ropelike branches
Redbud (*Cercis* spp.)	Flowers before leaves

Harlequin glorybower (*Clerodendrum trichotomum*)	Winter star-shaped sepals
Kousa dogwood (*Cornus Kousa*)	Winter fruits
Contorted filbert (*Corylus avellana* 'Contorta")	Curled branches and catkins
Korean sweetheart (*Euscaphis japonica*)	Bark chocolate-striped white
Ginkgo (*Ginkgo biloba*)	Yellow fall leaves
Osage orange (*Maclura pomifera*)	Very unusual fruit
Medlar (*Mespilus germanica*)	Odd-shaped edible fruit
Hondo spruce (*Picea jezoensis hondoensis*)	Red/purple spring female cones
Birchbark cherry (*Prunus serrula*)	Mahogany bark
Pin oak (*Quercus palustris*)	Leaves hang on all winter
Contorted willow (*Salix matsudana* 'Tortuosa')	Curled branches
Japanese umbrella pine (*Sciadopitys verticillata*)	Needlelike waxy leaves
Japanese stewartia (*Stewartia pseudocamellia*)	Flowers, winter nutlets
Deerhorn cedar (*Thujopsis dolabrata*)	Foliage

Pin Oak

The pin oak, a fine lawn tree prized for its rich fall color, is deciduous, but you will see it hanging onto its leaves until they are finally pushed off by new growth in the spring. This reasonably rapid-growing tree, whose lower limbs droop nearly to the ground, has the ability to keep its brown leaves through the winter. Its long, slender, and horizontally layered limbs give this large tree an elegant appearance.

TREES FOR WET SITES

Not everyone is blessed with deep, well-drained soil. Some gardeners manage their landscapes where water may stand periodically. The first "wet area" tree that crosses most minds is willow or those knobby cypresses that are shown in *National Geographic* amongst alligators and snakes. However, there are more than a few that work well in soils too wet to be called damp.

Red maple (*Acer rubrum*)	All PNW
Black alder (*Alnus glutinosa*)	All PNW
Red alder (*Alnus oregona*)	C, LV, LM
White alder (*Alnus rhombifolia*)	LV, LM, HD
Birch (*Betula* spp.)	All PNW
Red-twig dogwood (*Cornus stolonifera*)	All PNW
White ash (*Fraxinus americana*)	C, LV, LM
Oregon ash (*Fraxinus latifolia*)	C, LV, LM, HD
Marshall green ash (*Fraxinus pennsylvanica* 'Marshall')	All PNW
Sweetgum (*Liquidambar styraciflua*)	LV, LM
Sour gum (*Nyssa sylvatica*)	C, LV, LM
Sitka spruce (*Picea sitchensis*)	C, LV
Aspen (*Populus tremuloides*)	LV, LM, HD
Black cottonwood (*Populus trichocarpa*)	LV, LM, DV, HD
Willows (*Salix* spp.)	All PNW
Coast redwood (*Sequoia sempervirens*)	C, LV, LM, DV

TREES FOR THE HIGH AND DRY GARDENS OF EASTERN WASHINGTON, IDAHO, AND OREGON

These sites are generally dry overall with cold winters. However, even the neophyte gardener can adjust the microclimate of his or her own yard and garden so that a rather large list of plants will grow and thrive in that locale. Here are a few that are noted for their hardiness and ability to grow where water may be limited and where the soil may be slightly alkaline.

Amur maple (*Acer ginnala*)	Striking red fall color
Box elder (*Acer negundo*)	May become a weed tree
Madrone (*Arbutus menziesii*)	Needs excellent drainage
Northern catalpa (*Catalpa speciosa*)	Well adapted to heat and cold
Tartarian dogwood (*Cornus alba*)	Small tree to 10 feet
Smoke tree (*Cotinus Coggygria*)	At its best in poor soils
Hawthorn (*Crataegus* spp.)	Tends to become twiggy
Russian olive (*Eleagnus angustifolia*)	Brown bark with silver leaves
Maidenhair tree (*Ginkgo biloba*)	Bright gold fall color
Honey locust (*Gleditsia triacanthos*)	Tolerant and hardy
Coffee tree (*Gymnocladus dioicus* 'Espresso')	Huge leaves, good fall color
Colorado spruce (*Picea pungens*)	Dense, strong tree
Austrian pine (*Pinus nigra*)	Strong, durable
Chokecherry (*Prunus virginiana*)	Good autumn color
Sumac (*Rhus* spp.)	Most have rich fall color
Idaho locust (*Robinia ambigua* 'Idahoensis')	Showiest of locust trees
Black locust (*Robinia pseudoacacia*)	Commonly overlooked
Japanese pagoda tree (*Sophora japonica*)	Spreading tree for patio and lawn
Mountain ash (*Sorbus* spp.)	Bright red fruit through winter
Japanese zelkova (*Zelkova serrata*)	Excellent wide shade tree

"Austrian pine is one of the most durable evergreen trees for this area and farther east. Once established, it will take drought and is strong in the wind. It seems to like our alkaline soils."—Phil Pashek, Nurseryman, The Dalles, Oregon

SAMPLER OF TREES WITH COLORFUL AND/OR UNUSUAL BARK

Striped, white, peeling, and exfoliating are descriptive terms given to some of the suggested trees in this list. Any of them can provide a landscape with something out of the ordinary, something that is interesting in the dead of winter or during the growing season. Some invite your exploratory touch, some encourage a caress of interest, some are just fun to peel off.

Striped bark maple (*Acer capillipes*)	All PNW	white vertical stripes
David maple (*Acer davidii*)	All PNW	white vertical stripes
Paperbark maple (*Acer griseum*)	All PNW	cinnamon-brown, exfoliating

Coral bark Japanese maple (*Acer palmatum* 'Sango Kaku')	All PNW	bark of newest growth intense red
Madrone (*Arbutus menziesii*)	All PNW	older bark splits to reveal new, green bark that matures to a sleek mahogany
Monarch birch (*Betula maximowicziana*)	C, LV, LM, DV	flaking bark changes from orange-brown to light gray or white
River birch (*Betula nigra*)	All PNW	exfoliation exposes contrasting tan-orange bark
White birch (*Betula pendula*)	All PNW	chalk-white
Incense cedar (*Calocedrus decurrens*)	All PNW	mahogany bark on older trunks invites you to peel off the old
Crape myrtle (*Lagerstroemia indica*)	C, LV, LM, DV	smooth, gray bark flakes away to reveal pink new bark
Persian Parrotia (*Parrotia persica*)	C, LV, LM	smooth, gray bark flakes off, leaving white patches
Vanessa Persian Parrotia (*Parrotia persica* 'Vanessa')	C, LV, LM	mottled brown and white
Sycamore (*Platanus* spp.)	C, LV, LM, DV	shedding bark creates dappled brown and cream pattern
Aspen (*Populus tremuloides*)	All PNW	smooth, silvery gray
Birch bark cherry (*Prunus serrula*)	C, LV, LM	glossy mahogany red
Japanese stewartia (*Stewartia pseudocamellia*)	C, LV, LM, DV	attractive, flaking
Chinese elm (*Ulmus parvifolia*)	All PNW	older trunks shed patches similarly to sycamores

UNDERSTORY TREES FOR WOODSY LANDSCAPING

Among the tall fir trees and big-leaf maples can be found the fillers that make those landscapes a friendly place of beauty. Understory plants are lovers of shade and generally are tolerant of the roots of others. Some overstory plants, such as walnut, may not allow others to grow within their root system. Here are a few that should do well for you.

Western
Hemlock

Vine maple (*Acer circinatum*)	All PNW
Serviceberry (*Amelanchier × grandiflora*)	All PNW
Madrone (*Arbutus menziesii*)	C, LV, LM, DV
Dogwood (*Cornus nutallii**)	C, LV, LM
Hazelnut (*Corylus cornuta*)	C, LV, LM
Japanese snowbell (*Styrax japonica*)	LV, LM
Western yew (*Taxus brevifolia*)	C, LV, LM, DV
Western red cedar (*Thuja plicata*)	C, LV, LM
Western hemlock (*Tsuga heterophylla*)	All PNW
Oregon myrtle (*Umbellularia californica*)	C, LV, LM

*If the fungus disease Anthracnose is found in your area, substitute resistant varieties of *Cornus Kousa* for *C. nutallii.*

TREES FOR WINDY SEASIDE GARDENS

The constant movement of air, often mild but sometimes strong enough to blow trees down, causes a problem for gardens near the ocean. These trees are selected to withstand breezes, as well as to thrive in the sea level summer heat and wintery cold.

Madrone (*Arbutus menziesii*)
Port Orford cedar (*Chamaecyparis lawsoniana*)
Hawthorn (*Crataegus* spp.)
Monterey cypress (*Cupressus macrocarpa*)
English holly (*Ilex aquifolium*)
Glossy privet (*Ligustrum lucidum*)
Norway spruce (*Picea abies*)
Sitka spruce (*Picea sitchensis*)
Shore pine (*Pinus contorta*)
Austrian pine (*Pinus nigra*)
Scotch pine (*Pinus sylvestris*)
Japanese black pine (*Pinus thunbergiana*)
Douglas fir (*Pseudotsuga menziesii*)
Pussy willow (*Salix discolor*)
Red elderberry (*Sambucus callicarpa*)
Coast redwood (*Sequoia sempervirens*)
Western red cedar (*Thuja plicata*)

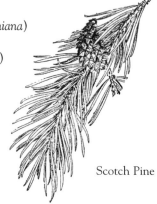

Scotch Pine

In our tree lists we have tried to avoid listing trees in zones where we know there will be problems of one kind or another. Flowering crabapples are a good example. In coastal regions, where temperature and humidity are right for several fungus diseases, we strongly urge you to use disease-resistant crabapples, or select a different kind of tree altogether, rather than dedicate all of your spare time in trying to control these problems.

FAST-GROWING TREES

The fastest may not be the best, but those of us moving into a new subdivision that has had all trees removed—and most of the good soil scraped off—could enjoy the shade from something like the empress tree while the slower growing sweetgum or beech is developing. Some will have brittle branches, and you should cross check this list with the "weak and brittle" list.

Maples (*Acer* spp.)	All PNW
Red alder (*Alnus oregona*)	C, LV, LM
White alder (*Alnus rhombifolia*)	LV, LM, HD
Monarch birch (*Betula maximowicziana*)	C, LV, LM, DV
Incense cedar (*Calocedrus decurrens*)	C, LV, LM, DV
Oregon ash (*Fraxinus latifolia*)	C, LV, LM, DV
Empress tree (*Paulownia tomentosa*)	All PNW
Poplars (*Populus* spp.)	All PNW

Japanese black pine (*Pinus thunbergiana*)	All PNW
Northern red oak (*Quercus rubra*)	All PNW
Willows (*Salix* spp.)	All PNW

How often should you fertilize a shade tree? Very seldom actually. A general rule of thumb for deciduous shade trees is that the root system will venture out from the trunk as far as the tree is tall. This means that for a twenty-five-foot tall tree, the roots go at least twenty-five feet away from the trunk. They also pick up water and fertilizer in that twenty-five-foot radius, and if they are within range of a lawn that you are feeding every eight weeks or so, they are already getting enough fertilizer. "The fact of the matter is, there are enough phosphorus and potassium reserves in most soils for the growth of all woody plants. The only thing that research has ever shown that woody plants will respond to in terms of fertilization is nitrogen. Money can be saved by buying a 21-0-0 or a 33-0-0 fertilizer rather than a 20-20-20, and the results will be fine."—George Pinyuh, Washington State University Extension Agent Emeritus, Seattle

LONG-LIVED TREES

Sitka Spruce

Old trees have character. They have been designed by nature to live forever, have strong trunks, sturdy wide-crotched branches, and tend to shrug off the winter storms and plagues of bugs that harass their weaker kin. They create giant silhouettes against the sky and provide big branches for that special swing your grandkids will always remember. They may show battle scars, but it only reflects the wisdom of their years. Each of the trees on this list can easily live fifty or more years—most can live two hundred or more years. Plant these for your grandkids!

Grand fir (*Abies grandis*)	All PNW
Red horse chestnut (*Aesculus carnea*)	All PNW
Atlas cedar (*Cedrus atlantica*)	C, LV, LM, DV
Beech (*Fagus sylvatica*)	All PNW
Maidenhair tree (*Ginkgo biloba*)	All PNW
Tulip tree (*Liriodendron tulipifera*)	All PNW
Sitka spruce (*Picea sitchensis*)	C, LV
Ponderosa pine (*Pinus ponderosa*)	LV, LM, DV, HD
Douglas fir (*Pseudotsuga menziesii*)	All PNW
Oaks (*Quercus* spp.)	C, LV, LM, DV
Weeping willow (*Salix babylonica*)	All PNW
Giant sequoia (*Sequoiadendron giganteum*)	All PNW
American elm (*Ulmus americana*)	All PNW

TREES WITH MULTIPLE TRUNKS

Trees that naturally produce many trunks can provide interest and contrast to the landscape, particularly when they have been pruned up from their base so that the trunks are visible from the base up to where the head begins. Some have bark that is colorful or interesting characteristics that draw the eye. Here are a few that might give you a beginning.

Vine maple (*Acer circinatum*)	All PNW
Amur maple (*Acer ginnala*)	All PNW
Japanese laceleaf maple (*Acer palmatum* varieties)	All PNW
Katsura tree (*Cercidiphyllum japonicum*)	All PNW
Crape myrtle (*Lagerstroemia indica*)	C, LV, LM, DV
Magnolia (*Magnolia* spp.)	Varies
Pacific wax myrtle (*Myrica californica*)	C, LV, LM
Persian parrótia (*Parrotia persica*)	C, LV, LM
Gambel oak (*Quercus gambelii*)	LM, DV, HD
Staghorn sumac (*Rhus typhina*)	All PNW
Elderberry (*Sambucus caerulea*)	All PNW
Japanese stewartia (*Stewartia pseudocamellia*)	C, LV
Oregon myrtle (*Umbellularia californica*)	C, LV, LM
Wayfaring tree (*Viburnum lantana*)	LM, HD

TREES WITH MANY SURFACE ROOTS

Some trees are particularly bad about growing many large roots near enough to the ground surface that they cause humps and bumps in the lawn or crack patio surfaces, or they compete avidly with other plants for the soil moisture and nutrients. Sometimes we bring the problem of surface rooting on ourselves by poor watering techniques. If we keep the soil surface continually moist, tree roots are naturally going to grow where they can easily obtain moisture. Sometimes it may be because we chose the wrong tree for the spot. The list below will give you some leads on what to avoid, or at least give you fair warning of shallow-rooted species and varieties.

Box elder (*Acer negundo*)	All PNW
Silver maple (*Acer saccharinum*)	All PNW
Scarlet maple (*Acer rubrum*)	All PNW
Tree of heaven (*Ailanthus altissima*)	All PNW
Ash (*Fraxinus* spp.)	All PNW
Quaking aspen (*Populus tremuloides*)	All PNW
Poplars (*Populus* spp.)	All PNW
Flowering cherry (*Prunus* spp.)	Varies
Kwanzan cherry (*Prunus serrulata* 'Kwanzan')	C, LV, LM, DV
Black locust (*Robinia pseudoacacia*)	All PNW
Willow (*Salix* spp.)	All PNW
American elm (*Ulmus americana*)	All PNW
Siberian elm (*Ulmus pumila*)	All PNW

Common sense will keep you from planting the above trees on top of a cesspool or inside a drainfield area. They grow wonderfully well, often because of the loosened soil as a result of digging and backfilling for the receiving tank and its adjacent drainfield, but given time they can also cause problems, especially plugging the drainfield lines with their roots. Plan your tree planting carefully to avoid such problems.

TREES WITH INCONVENIENT LITTER

Here are some that you might not want to place in the most public part of your landscape. While trees are always a wanted addition to the landscape, sometimes the fallout from them makes them less valuable. Some of these will keep you busy every day removing branches, leaves, flowers, or something that you did not plan for.

Horse chestnut (*Aesculus hippocastanum*)	Spiny fruits drop
Silktree (*Albizzia julibrissin*)	Leaves, spent flowers drop
Japanese angelica (*Aralia elata*)	Branches and fruit
Madrone (*Arbutus menziesii*)	Leaves and bark
European white birch (*Betula pendula*)	Twigs drop in winter
Hawthorn (*Crataegus* spp.)	Berries drop
White ash (*Fraxinus americana*)	Female trees, heavy seed crops
Honey locust (*Gleditsia triacanthos*)	Pods and leaves drop
Mulberry (*Morus alba*)	Fruit drops
Empress tree (*Paulownia tomentosa*)	Leaves, seed pods drop
Poplar (*Populus* spp.)	Brittle limbs fall
Weeping willow (*Salix babylonica*)	Twigs drop in winter
Mountain ash (*Sorbus* spp.)	Berries drop
Chinese elm (*Ulmus parvifolia*)	Seeds drop

SCRUFFY-LOOKING TREES

Look for the unusual in trees. Perhaps you need a rugged appearance, particularly if you are trying to create a landscape with a wild or rugged feeling. Some of these might be considered trees of low esteem, but they have a place when you are purposely looking for something "scruffy." Most of these trees are excellent for massing in backgrounds and for covering large manmade mistakes like exposed cut-earth banks or exposed rock. Some might provide a year-round screen.

Contorted filbert (*Corylus avellana* 'Contorta')	C, LV, LM, DV
Russian olive (*Elaeagnus angustifolia*)	DV, HD
Osage orange (*Maclura pomifera*)	DV, HD
Holly oak (*Quercus ilex*)	C, LV, LM, DV
Willow oak (*Quercus phellos*)	All PNW
Cascara (*Rhamnus purshiana*)	C, LV, LM

TREES WITH UNUSUAL FOLIAGE/COLOR

This list reflects the color of the plant during the growing season, not in the fall, when it may again turn yet another brilliant color. Use these plants as accents against a backdrop of dark green conifers or as a focal point in the landscape.

Foliage form or texture

Monkey-puzzle tree (*Araucaria araucana*)	C, LV, LM
Maidenhair tree (*Ginkgo biloba*)	All PNW
Canada red cherry (*Prunus virginiana* 'Shubert')	All PNW
Chinese umbrella pine (*Sciadoptys verticillata*)	C, LV, LM, DV
Deerhorn cedar (*Thujopsis dolabrata*)	C, LV, LM, DV
Tulip tree (*Tulipifera liriodendron*)	All PNW

Gray to blue foliage

Blue atlas cedar (*Cedrus atlantica* 'glauca')	C, LV, LM, DV
Blue weeping Alaska cedar (*Chamaecyparis nootka* 'Glauca Pendula')	C, LV, LM
Russian olive (*Elaeagnus augustifolia*)	DV, HD
Colorado blue spruce (*Picea pungens* 'glauca')	All PNW
Hoopsii Colorado spruce (*Picea pungens* 'Hoopsii')	All PNW

Red foliage

Japanese maple (*Acer palmatum* 'Bloodgood')	All PNW
Crimson King maple (*Acer platanoides* 'Crimson King')	All PNW
Schwedler maple (*Acer platanoides* 'Schwedleri')	All PNW
Royal red maple (*Acer platanoides* 'Royal Red Leaf')	All PNW
Forest Pansy redbud (*Cercis can.* 'Forest Pansy')	LM, DV, HD
Rivers European beech (*Fagus sylvatica* 'Riversii')	All PNW

Variegated foliage

Box elder (*Acer negundo*)	All PNW
Flamingo box elder (*Acer negundo* 'Flamingo')	All PNW
Drummond maple (*Acer platanoides* 'Drummondii')	All PNW
Tricolor dogwood (*Cornus florida* 'Welchii')	All PNW
Cherokee Sunset dogwood (*C. florida* 'Cherokee Sunset')	All PNW
Tri-color beech (*Fagus sylvatica* 'Tricolor')	All PNW
Variegated holly (*Ilex aquifolium* varieties)	C, LV, LM
Variegated sweetgum (*Liquidambar styraciflua* 'Variegata')	All PNW
Japanese red pine (*Pinus densiflora* 'Oculus-draconis')	C, LV, LM

TREES WITH OUTSTANDING FALL FOLIAGE COLOR

Although Jack Frost has been given most of the credit, the development of fall color in the leaves of trees depends on more than the first fall frost. The shortening of the days as winter approaches, the brilliance of late summer sunlight, and the coolness of evening and night temperatures all favor the development of certain coloring pigments in tree leaves.

"The development of leaf color in the fall is an annual signal of the autumn season for many people. This change is actually a slowing down of plant processes at the end of the growing season. Plants that develop fall color come mostly from deciduous forests of southeastern Canada, the northeastern United States, and eastern Asia. Conifer forests show little color other than green. Fall color adds another dimension of seasonal interest to home and native plants."—Dr. Ray Maleike, Washington State University Cooperative Extension Horticulturist

Vine maple (*Acer circinatum*)	All PNW
Amur maple (*Acer ginnala*)	All PNW
Japanese maples (*Acer palmatum*)	All PNW
Red maple (*Acer rubrum*)	All PNW
Sugar maple (*Acer saccharum*)	All PNW
Flowering dogwood (*Cornus florida*)	C, LV, LM, DV
Kousa dogwood (*Cornus Kousa*)	C, LV, LM, DV
Maidenhair tree (*Ginkgo biloba*)	All PNW
Larch (*Larix occidentalis*)	LM, DV, HD
Sweetgum (*Liquidambar styraciflua*)	All PNW
Sour gum (*Nyssa sylvatica*)	C, LV, LM
Sourwood (*Oxydendrum arboreum*)	C, LV, LM
Scarlet oak (*Quercus coccinea*)	All PNW
Redspire callery pear (*Pyrus calleryana* 'Redspire')	All PNW
Tall stewartia (*Stewartia monadelpha*)	C, LV, LM, DV
Japanese stewartia (*Stewartia pseudocamellia*)	C, LV, LM

Sugar Maple

TREES FOR ESPALIER

When you decide to espalier a plant, you set a work schedule for yourself that involves frequent and intimate interaction with your tree. And when you decide that an espalier would enhance your yard enough to warrant the additional work, select those plants which already exhibit lines that can be trained into your scheme. There are some outstanding evergreen trees that have been developed for their drooping habit. In fact, some of them must be supported, else they become groundcovers. Here are some to use in your selection process.

Japanese maple (*Acer palmatum* selected vars.)	All PNW
Weeping Atlantic cedar (*Cedrus atlantica* 'Pendula')	C, LV, LM, DV
Hawthorn (*Crataegus* spp.)	All PNW
Goldenchain tree (*Laburnum watereri* 'Vossii')	All PNW
Crape myrtle (*Lagerstroemia indica*)	C, LV, LM, DV
Flowering crabapple (*Malus* spp.)	All PNW
Weeping white pine (*Pinus monticola* 'Pendula')	All PNW

TREES WITH PURPLE FOLIAGE

Foliage that is different in some way, whether in color, hue, shape, or form, gives the gardener the palette to paint the landscape picture. Some will proceed through several color changes as the growing season goes from spring to summer to fall. The variations in color can cause contrasts and provide accents.

Crimson King maple (*Acer platanoides* 'Crimson King')	All PNW
Burgundy wine weeping birch (*Betula pendula* 'Purpurea')	All PNW
Eastern redbud (*Cercis canadensis* 'Forest Pansy')	LM, DV, HD
Purple hazel (*Corylus maxima* 'Purpurea')	C, LM, LV
Smoke tree (*Cotinus Coggygria* 'purpureus')	All PNW
Autumn Purple ash (*Fraxinus americana* 'Autumn Purple')	All PNW
Copper beech (*Fagus sylvatica* 'Atropunicea')	All PNW
Purple Fountain European beech (*Fagus sylvatica* 'Purple Fountain')	All PNW
Purple weeping European beech (*Fagus sylvatica* 'Purpurea Pendula')	All PNW
Purple sawtooth European beech (*Fagus sylvatica* 'Rohanii')	All PNW
Ruby Lace honeylocust (*Gleditsia triacanthos* 'Ruby Lace')	LV, LM, DV, HD
Profusion crabapple (*Malus* 'Profusion')	All PNW
Aldenham crabapple (*Malus purpurea* 'Aldenhamensis')	All PNW
Purple-leaf plum (*Prunus cerasifera* 'atropurpurea')	C, LV, LM, DV
Krauter Vesuvius cherry plum (*Prunus cerasifera* 'Krauter Vesuvius')	C, LV, LM, DV
Canada red cherry (*Prunus virginiana* 'Shubert')	All PNW

FLOWERING CRABAPPLES RESISTANT TO MILDEW AND SCAB FUNGUS DISEASES

Flowering crabapples provide a wonderful display of pastel colors to adorn the landscape in midspring. However, in the western part of the Pacific Northwest, the humidity and temperatures are ideal for two fungus diseases: powdery mildew and scab. Rather than attempt to control the fungus diseases through regular and continuing spray schedules, select a variety that has a natural resistance, or in some cases, a tolerance to the fungus problems. You will not only be money ahead, but you will have far fewer worries about these problems. Here are ten of the top crabapples recommended by Keith Warren, horticulturist, J. Frank Schmidt & Son Co.

				Resistance to:	
Variety	**Flower**	**Foliage**	**Fruit**	**Scab**	**Mildew**
Adirondack	white	green	red	excel	excel
Floribunda	pink to white	green	yellow	good	good
Golden Raindrops	white	green	yellow	excel	excel
Louisa	true pink	green	yellow	excel	good
Mary Potter	pink to white	green	red	good	fair
Prairifire	bright pink/red	red	red	excel	excel
Red Jewel	white	green	red	good	good

| | | | | Resistance to: | |
Variety	Flower	Foliage	Fruit	Scab	Mildew
Strawberry Parfait	pink/dark pink	red	yellow	excel	excel
Tschonoskii*	white	green	greenish	excel	excel
Zumi Calocarpa	pink to white	green	red	excel	good

*Unusual pyramidal shape; foliage silvery green in spring, orange/purple/scarlet in fall.

"Our line of standard-size crabapples is budded on EMLA 111, a virus-free clonal rootstock used worldwide in the apple orchard industry. It is highly adaptable to various soils, provides excellent anchorage, shows good resistance to diseases and insects. We do this to provide a solution to the crabapple's major remaining landscape problem, that of suckering."—Keith Warren, J. Frank Schmidt & Son Co., Boring, Oregon

TREES WITH ORNAMENTAL BERRIES OR SEED PODS

When selecting any plant for inclusion in the landscape, select for more than one single characteristic. An important point to know when selecting plant material is what the plant looks like during the dormant season. Does it display its fruit in clusters of red berries or does it have interesting seed pods that hang on through the winter? We will include in this list some of the evergreen types, such as holly or juniper, as well as the deciduous kinds. Use this list as a starter, and as you come upon trees that you suddenly find interesting in the dull winter, jot them down too.

Tree of heaven (*Ailanthus altissima*)	All PNW
Madrone (*Arbutus menziesii*)	All PNW
Western catalpa (*Catalpa speciosa*)	C, LV, LM, DV
Harlequin glorybower (*Clerodendrum trichotomum*)	C, LV, LM
Kousa dogwood (*Cornus Kousa*)	C, LV, LM, DV
Autumn Glory hawthorn (*Crataegus* 'Autumn Glory')	All PNW
Carriere hawthorn (*Crataegus lavallei*)	All PNW
Washington hawthorn (*Crataegus phaenopyrum*)	All PNW
Persimmon (*Diospyros kaki* vars.)	C, LV
English holly (*Ilex aquifolium*)	C, LV, LM, DV
Chinese flame tree (*Koelreuteria bipinnata*)	C, LV, LM
Goldenrain tree (*Koelreuteria paniculata*)	C, LV, LM, DV
Sweetgum (*Liquidambar styraciflua*)	All PNW
Sargent crabapple (*Malus sargentii*)	All PNW
Sourwood (*Oxydendrum arboreum*)	C, LV, LM, DV
London plane tree (*Platanus acerifolia*)	C, LV, LM, DV
Elderberry (*Sambucus* spp.)	C, LV, LM, DV
Mountain ash (*Sorbus aucuparia*)	All PNW
Japanese stewartia (*Stewartia pseudocamellia*)	C, LV, LM

Sourwood

TREES THAT FEED BUTTERFLY LARVAE

Often gardeners speak in uncomplimentary terms when they discuss the worms that feed on their ornamental plants. However, if you are to attract butterflies to your landscape, you must feed their offspring. The caterpillar, looper, or green worm that feasts on the leaves of your trees is destined to grow up to be that beautiful butterfly, or at the very least a moth that flutters about your yard. Here are some of the more likely feeding stations for these hungry little fellows. According to the Oregon Department of Fish and Wildlife, there are more than 150 species of butterflies found in Oregon, some only on the drier east side and about 20 percent found only on the west.

Maple (*Acer* spp.)	All PNW
Horse chestnut (*Aesculus* spp.)	Varies
Alder (*Alnus oregona*)	C, LV, LM, DV
Madrone (*Arbutus menziesii*)	All PNW
Birch (*Betula* spp.)	All PNW
Dogwood (*Cornus* spp.)	Varies
Hawthorn (*Crataegus* spp.)	All PNW
Apple (*Malus* spp.)	All PNW
Crabapple (*Malus* spp.)	All PNW
Pine (*Pinus* spp.)	All PNW
Sycamore (*Platanus* spp.)	LV, LM, DV, HD
Poplar (*Populus* spp.)	All PNW
Cottonwood (*Populus trichocarpa*)	All PNW
Cherry (*Prunus* spp.)	Varies
Douglas fir (*Pseudotsuga menziesii*)	All PNW
Oak (*Quercus* spp.)	LV, LM, DV, HD
Willow (*Salix* spp.)	All PNW
Elm (*Ulmus* spp.)	All PNW

TREES THAT ATTRACT HUMMINGBIRDS

Generally we think of annuals and herbaceous perennials as attractants for hummingbirds, but there are also some trees which have blossoms that attract these hummers as well. As you find other trees that seem to be friendly to hummingbirds, jot them down too.

Horse chestnut (*Aesculus* spp.)	Varies
Silk tree (*Albizia julibrissin*)	All PNW
Madrone (*Arbutus menziesii*)	All PNW
Hawthorn (*Crataegus* spp.)	All PNW
Snowdrop tree (*Halesia carolina*)	C, LV, LM, DV
Tulip tree (*Liriodendron tulipifera*)	All PNW
Flowering crabapple (*Malus* spp.)	All PNW
Idaho locust (*Robinia ambigua* 'Idahoensis')	All PNW
Willow (*Salix* spp.)	All PNW
Chaste tree (*Vitex agnus-castus*)	C, LV, LM, DV

Trees with Weak Wood or Structural Problems

Many trees are attractive in the landscape, but they may break in high winds or during the ice storms that sometimes descend on the Pacific Northwest. These are definitely not trees that you want to park your car beneath, nor that you use to arch across the house for summer coolness. The following list is divided into two groups: the trees you should avoid planting unless there simply is no better alternative for the landscape, and the ones that we feel are good species but might have problems with breaking limbs.

Use only as a last resort

Definitely do *not* depend on these trees to be the best ones you ever planted. Each has its own problems, and they are bad enough that we feel we must call your attention to them. Seriously consider these before using the trees anywhere in your landscape. Most are fast-growing, and most become problems, especially as winter storms bring ice and heavy snow.

Box elder (*Acer negundo*)	Brittle wood
Silver maple (*Acer saccharinum*)	Breaks easily
Tree of heaven (*Ailanthus altissima*)	Brittle wood
Poplar (*Populus* spp.)	Fast-growing but brittle
Black cottonwood (*Populus trichocarpa*)	Very brittle wood

Good trees but can break in severe storms

These are about as bad as the trees listed previously, but they are not entirely devoid of good qualities. Many of them are valued as flowering trees, patio trees, or as trees that can grow in severe climates. However, try to avoid planting these where they can damage structures or injure people when storms strike.

Silktree (*Albizzia julibrissin*)	Weak horizontal limbs
Goldenrain tree (*Koelreuteria paniculata*)	Denseness of tree
Honey locust (*Gleditsia triacanthos* varieties)	Brittle wood
Empress tree (*Paulownia tomentosa*)	Brittle wood
Locust (*Robinia* spp.)	Brittle wood
Willow (*Salix* spp.)	Weak wood

"When tree branches break, and this can happen to any tree, regardless of its structural soundness, if the right sort of storm happens, be prepared to give first aid. When removing limbs, cut them back to the collar at the base of the limb, rather than cutting flush with the trunk. The collar contains fast-growing cells that will quickly cover the pruning cut. Topping is a poor alternative to proper pruning. Topping upsets the crown-to-root ratio, removes buds that would produce sturdy branches, stimulates suckers or water sprouts that are not structurally sound, and makes topped trees highly vulnerable to wind and ice damage. Don't prune unless the tree really needs it. Many trees would fare better from neglect than from the butchery that is often passed off as pruning."—Van Bobbitt, Community Horticulture Coordinator, WSU Cooperative Extension, Puyallup, Washington

TREES THAT HAVE BEEN UNDERUSED

Some trees are underused simply because no one has taken the time to find out about them. Often a gardener will use old favorites because of familiarity with the plant and may not be venturesome enough to test out a new type. In the next several lists are trees that we have found—often tucked away in an arboretum or in an experiment station test block—we feel would be valuable additions to a landscape. Consider them the next time you are looking for something different in a tree, or the next time you need to replace a tree that didn't work out for you. We can't guarantee plants, for we have no control over your planting and care, but we do guarantee you will be surprised at the great variety available.

White fringetree (*Chionanthus virginicus*)	fringelike white flower petals	All PNW
Aurora Rutgers hybrid dogwood (*Cornus* 'Aurora')	disease resistant	All PNW
Celestial Rutgers hybrid dogwood (*Cornus* 'Celestial')	disease resistant	All PNW
Stellar Pink Rutgers hybrid dogwood (*Cornus* 'Stellar Pink')	disease resistant	All PNW
Pagoda dogwood (*Cornus alternifolia*)	branching pattern	All PNW
Giant dogwood (*Cornus controversa*)	size and flowers	C, LV, LM, DV
Dove tree (*Davidia involucrata*)	flowers and fruit	C, LV, LM, DV
Franklin tree (*Franklinia alatamaha*)	bark, late flowering	C, LV, LM, DV
Sourwood tree (*Oxydendrum arboreum*)	flowers, autumn foliage	C, LV, LM, DV
Flowering peach (*Prunus persica* 'Peppermint Stick')	bi-colored	C, LV, LM, DV
Birch bark cherry (*Prunus serrula*)	mahogany red bark	All PNW
Sassafras tree (*Sassafras albidum*)	aromatic bark	C, LV, LM, DV
Umbrella pine (*Sciadopitys verticillata*)	symmetry, foliage	C, LV, LM, DV
Stewartia (*Stewartia* spp.)	branching habit, flowers	C, LV, LM, DV
Fragrant snowbell (*Styrax obassia*)	flowers	C, LV, LM, DV
Sawleaf zelkova (*Zelkova serrata*)	spread of branches	C, LV, LM, DV

Underutilized attractive trees with unusual characteristics
These were selected by Paul Ries, Oregon Department of Forestry.

Paperbark maple (*Acer griseum*)	peeling bark and trunk color	All PNW
Red horse chestnut (*Aesculus* × *carnea* 'Briotti')	crimson flowers, drought resistant	All PNW
River birch (*Betula nigra*)	bronze peeling bark	All PNW
Eastern redbud (*Cercis canadensis*)	incredibly brilliant purple flowers	LM, DV, HD

Autumn Applause ash (*Fraxinus americana* 'Autumn Applause')	purple fall foliage	All PNW
Goldenrain (*Koelreuteria paniculata*)	flowers, foliage, fruits	C, LV, LM, DV
Blackgum or Tupelo (*Nyssa sylvatica*)	fall colors, branching habit	C, LV, LM, DV
Canada red cherry (*Prunus virginiana* 'Shubert')	purple leaves	All PNW
Japanese snowbell (*Styrax japonica*)	foliage and flowers, green and white tiers	C, LV, LM, DV
Lacebark elm (*Ulmus parvifolia*)	resistant to Dutch Elm Disease	C, LV

"Trees provide a myriad of economic and environmental benefits to our communities. Consider the tourism potential of big trees, shaded parks, and urban greenspaces. Or the economic drawing power trees have to attract shoppers to downtown business districts. Or the increased resale values of properties with trees compared to those without. Or the energy savings from planting a large shade tree on the south side of your home."—Paul Ries, **Oregon Department of Forestry**

10 underused trees

These were selected by Keith Warren, horticulturist, J. Frank Schmidt & Son Co. nursery. Some of these have been developed at this nursery.

Yellowwood (*Cladrastis kentukea*)	flowers	All PNW
Fernleaf beech (*Fagus sylvatica* 'Asplenifolia')	delicate foliage	All PNW
Weeping beech (*Fagus sylvatica* 'Pendula')	weeping branches	All PNW
Amur maackia (*Maackia amurensis*)	flowers	All PNW
Persian parrotia (*Parrotia persica*)	flowers, fall color	C, LV, LM, DV
Oriental photinia (*Photinia villosa*)	spring and fall foliage color	All PNW
Cascade snow cherry (*Prunus* 'Berry')	flowers	C, LV, LM, DV
Akebono flowering cherry (*Prunus yedoensis* 'Akebono')	flowers	C, LV, LM, DV
Korean mountain ash (*Sorbus alnifolia*)	flower, fruit, fall color	All PNW
Red cascade mountain ash (*Sorbus tianshanica* 'Dwarfcrown')	flower, foliage, fruit	All PNW

TREES THAT RESEED MADLY

Tree seedlings are not hard to control if you get at them in their early stages. Mowing, pulling, or the occasional use of a hoe in the flower bed beneath a maple tree will usually get rid of the young offenders. But, given time and a little neglect, you might suddenly find yourself surrounded by a forest of trees that you probably did not like in the first place. We should add a few that sprout badly too, like the flowering cherries in lawns where your mower damages the surface roots, or the honey locust suckers, or the filbert shoots that pop up.

Bigleaf maple (*Acer macrophyllum*)	All PNW
Tree of heaven (*Ailanthus altissima*)	All PNW
White ash (*Fraxinus americana*)	C, LV, LM
Empress tree (*Paulownia tomentosa*)	All PNW
Western cottonwood (*Populus fremontii*)	LV, DV, HD
Black locust (*Robinia pseudoacacia*)	All PNW

TREES LESS THAN 25-FEET TALL, FOR SMALL AREAS

Small trees can fit into many landscape situations. They can grow beneath utility wires, fit into a niche to provide interest, can be used as background that gives spring foliage and autumn color, or they can stand on their own merits, each to be admired as a small, proud tree. Sometimes it is difficult to differentiate a small tree from a large shrub, but for the most part here we are speaking of a single-trunked, branching plant with a well defined crown. Obviously a vine maple would be an example of one that could be called a small tree or a large shrub, and if you were discussing this with loggers they would probably call it a weed.

Vine maple (*Acer circinatum*)	All PNW
Amur maple (*Acer ginnala*)	All PNW
Japanese maples (*Acer palmatum* varieties)	All PNW
Siberian peashrub (*Caragana arborescens*)	All PNW
Redbud (*Cercis canadensis*)	LM, DV, HD
Hinoki cypress (*Chamaecyparis obtusa* 'Gracilis')	All PNW
Harlequin glorybower (*Clerodendrum trichotomum*)	C, LV, LM
Cornelian cherry (*Cornus mas*)	All PNW
Kousa dogwood (*Cornus Kousa*)	C, LV, LM, DV
Smoke tree (*Cotinus Coggygria*)	All PNW
Hawthorn (*Crataegus* spp.)	All PNW
Russian olive (*Elaeagnus angustifolia*)	LM, DV, HD
Leprechaun ash (*Fraxinus pennsylvanica* 'Leprechaun')	All PNW
Goldenchain tree (*Laburnum × watereri* 'Vossi')	LV, LM, DV, HD
Crape myrtle (*Lagerstroemia indica*)	C, LV, LM, DV
Flowering crabapples (*Malus* spp.)	All PNW
Blue spruce (*Picea pungens* 'Baby Blue Eyes')	All PNW
Coast pine (*Pinus contorta*)	C, LV, LM
Purple-leafed plum (*Prunus cerasifera* varieties)	All PNW
Japanese flowering cherry (*Prunus serrulata* 'Shirotae')	C, LV, LM, DV
Autumnalis cherry (*Prunus subhirtella* 'Autumnalis')	C, LV, LM, DV
Akebono cherry (*Prunus yedoensis* 'Akebono')	C, LV, LM, DV

Tall-hedge buckthorn (*Rhamnus frangula* 'Columnaris')	All PNW
Weeping-goat pussy willow (*Salix caprea* 'Pendula')	All PNW
Purple elderberry (*Sambucus nigra* 'Purpurea')	C, LV, LM, DV
Japanese snowbell (*Styrax japonicus*)	C, LV, LM
English yew (*Taxus baccata*)	All PNW
Japanese yew (*Taxus cuspidata*)	All PNW
Hicks yew (*Taxus × media* 'Hicksii')	All PNW

TREES WITH LAYERED, HORIZONTAL BRANCHING HABIT

Trees with this branching habit are best viewed with either an open background (so you can see the definitive layers) or with a background of columnar or spindle-shaped trees (so you can develop a good contrast of tree forms). This characteristic may change as the tree ages and limbs droop because of the weight of new growth, but the trees listed below should provide this character for many years in your landscape.

Noble fir (*Abies procera*)	All PNW
Monkey-puzzle tree (*Araucaria araucana*)	C, LV, LM
Deodora cedar (*Cedrus deodora*)	All PNW
Pagoda dogwood (*Cornus alternifolia*)	All PNW
Giant dogwood (*Cornus controversa*)	C, LV, LM, DV
Copper beech (*Fagus sylvatica* 'Atropunicea')	All PNW
Maidenhair tree (*Ginkgo biloba*)	All PNW
Flowering cherry (*Prunus serrulata* 'Shirofugen')	C, LV, LM, DV
Pin oak (*Quercus palustris*)	C, LV, LM, DV
Japanese snowbell (*Styrax japonicus*)	C, LV, LM

TREES IMPOSSIBLE TO GROW ANYTHING BENEATH

This is a list that you may take exception to because there are so many factors that influence plant growth. Trees may be dense enough to prevent any light from reaching the ground (thus ruling out the growth of lawn grass), may give off allelopathic materials that prevent the growth of certain plants, or may have such competitive roots that nothing else has a chance. Here are some trees that will generate enough shade or competition to complicate the growing of groundcovers, herbaceous perennials, or in some cases other woody plants. Test your plant-growing abilities with these!

English holly (*Ilex aquifolium*)	C, LV, LM
Black walnut (*Juglans nigra*)	All PNW
English walnut (*Juglans regia*)	C, LV, LM
Southern magnolia (*Magnolia grandiflora*)	C, LV, LM
Norway spruce (*Picea abies*)	All PNW
Colorado spruce (*Picea pungens*)	All PNW
Sitka spruce (*Picea sitchensis*)	C, LV
Black locust (*Robinia pseudoacacia*)	All PNW
Oregon myrtle (*Umbellularia californica*)	C, LV, LM

TREES WITH CHARACTER

The term "character," as used here, implies that this tree knows its business and will go through life being an upstanding member of its community. Character also comes from age, lumps and bumps, and disfiguration, as well as their inherent beauty.

Big-leaf maple (*Acer macrophyllum*)	All PNW
Monkey-puzzle tree (*Araucaria auracanthus*)	C, LV, LM
Madrone (*Arbutus menziesii*)	All PNW
Incense cedar (*Calocedrus decurrens*)	C, LV, LM, DV
Deodor cedar (*Cedrus deodora*)	C, LV, LM, DV
Common beech (*Fagus sylvatica*)	All PNW
Maidenhair tree (*Ginkgo biloba*)	All PNW
Tulip tree (*Liriodendron tulipifera*)	All PNW
Crabapple (*Malus* spp.)	All PNW
Ponderosa pine (*Pinus ponderosa*)	All PNW
Oak (*Quercus* spp.)	Varies
Weeping willow (*Salix babylonica*)	All PNW
Japanese umbrella pine (*Sciadopitys verticillata*)	C, LV, LM, DV
Western red cedar (*Thuja plicata*)	C, LV, LM, DV
American elm (*Ulmus americana*)	All PNW

TREES WITH FRAGRANT BLOSSOMS

Let's face it, life is the greatest when your landscape treats you to beauty and interest and then throws in fragrance as well! Here are some trees that will supply you with nice fragrances, as well as shade and interest.

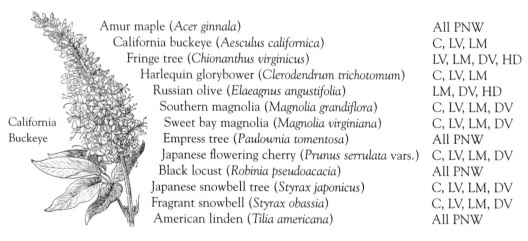

California Buckeye

Amur maple (*Acer ginnala*)	All PNW
California buckeye (*Aesculus californica*)	C, LV, LM
Fringe tree (*Chionanthus virginicus*)	LV, LM, DV, HD
Harlequin glorybower (*Clerodendrum trichotomum*)	C, LV, LM
Russian olive (*Elaeagnus angustifolia*)	LM, DV, HD
Southern magnolia (*Magnolia grandiflora*)	C, LV, LM, DV
Sweet bay magnolia (*Magnolia virginiana*)	C, LV, LM, DV
Empress tree (*Paulownia tomentosa*)	All PNW
Japanese flowering cherry (*Prunus serrulata* vars.)	C, LV, LM, DV
Black locust (*Robinia pseudoacacia*)	All PNW
Japanese snowbell tree (*Styrax japonicus*)	C, LV, LM, DV
Fragrant snowbell (*Styrax obassia*)	C, LV, LM, DV
American linden (*Tilia americana*)	All PNW

TREES THAT ARE COLD HARDY

In the western part of the Pacific Northwest the winters are generally mild enough that trees are subjected to severe winters only infrequently. In the eastern part of this region, cold and dry winters are the norm. Here are some trees selected for their ability to make it through the winters of Spokane or Boise. Add to this list as you run across elderly trees that have survived all that nature has thrown at them.

Firs (*Abies* spp.)
Maples (*Acer* spp.)
Horse chestnut (*Aesculus* spp.)
Tree of heaven (*Ailanthus altissima*)
Paper birch (*Betula papyrifera*)
Russian olive (*Elaeagnus angustifolia*)
Leprechaun ash (*Fraxinus pennsylvanica* 'Leprechaun')
White spruce (*Picea glauca*)
Quaking aspen (*Populus tremuloides*)
Black locust (*Robinia pseudoacacia*)
Idaho locust (*Robinia ambigua* 'Idahoensis')

A SAMPLER OF TREES BY THE COLOR OF THEIR FLOWER AND FLOWER SEASON

White	Season	Region
Common horse chestnut (*Aesculus hippocastanum*)	Late spring	All PNW
Western catalpa (*Catalpa speciosa*)	Late spring	All PNW
Fringe tree (*Chionanthus virginicus*)	Late spring	LV, LM, DV, HD
American yellowwood (*Cladrastis lutea*)	Late spring	All PNW
Giant dogwood (*Cornus controversa*)	Early summer	All PNW
Flowering dogwood (*Cornus florida*)	Late spring	All PNW
Kousa dogwood (*Cornus Kousa*)	Early summer	C, LV, LM, DV
Pacific dogwood (*Cornus nuttallii*)	Late spring	C, LV, LM, DV
Washington hawthorn (*Crataegus phaenopyrum*)	Early summer	All PNW
Dove tree (*Davidia involucrata*)	Spring	C, LV, LM, DV
Flowering ash (*Fraxinus ornus*)	Spring	C, LV, LM, DV
Snowdrop tree (*Halesia carolina*)	Mid spring	C, LV, LM, DV
Crape myrtles (*Lagerstroemia indica* and hybrids)	Mid summer	C, LV, LM, DV
Southern magnolia (*Magnolia grandiflora*)	Summer to fall	C, LV, LM
Kobus magnolia (*Magnolia kobus*)	Late spring	C, LV, LM, DV
Big-leaf magnolia (*Magnolia macrophylla*)	Late spring to mid summer	C, LV, LM, DV
Oyama magnolia (*Magnolia sieboldii*)	Late spring	C, LV, LM, DV
Star magnolia (*Magnolia stellata*)	Late winter/early spring	All PNW
Sweet bay magnolia (*Magnolia virginiana*)	Summer to early fall	C, LV, LM, DV
Flowering crabapples (*Malus* spp.)	Mid spring	All PNW
Sargent flowering crabapple (*Malus sargentii*)	Mid spring	All PNW
Sourwood (*Oxydendrum arboreum*)	Late summer	C, LV, LM, DV
Snow Fountain flowering cherry (*Prunus serrulata* 'Snow Fountain')	Early spring	C, LV, LM

A Sampler of Trees by the Color of Their Flower and Flower Season (*continued*)

White	Season	Region
Canada red cherry (*Prunus virginiana* 'Shubert')	Spring	C, LV, LM
Yoshino cherry (*Prunus yedoensis*)	Early spring	C, LV, LM
Bradford pear (*Pyrus calleryana*)	Mid spring	All PNW
Japanese stewartia (*Stewartia pseudocamellia*)	Mid summer	C, LV, LM
Japanese snowbell (*Styrax japonicus*)	Early summer	C, LV, LM, DV
Japanese tree lilac (*Syringa reticulata*)	Late spring	All PNW

Blue, Violet, Lavender, or Purple	Season	Region
Eastern redbud (*Cercis canadensis*)	Spring	LM, DV, HD
Purple smoke tree (*Cotinus Coggygria* 'Purpureus')	Late spring	All PNW
Crape myrtles (*Lagerstroemia indica* and hybrids)	Summer	C, LV, LM, DV
Lily magnolia (*Magnolia liliiflora* and hybrids)	Late spring	C, LV, LM, DV
Saucer magnolia (*Magnolia* × *Soulangiana*)	Early spring	All PNW
Saucer magnolia (*Magnolia* × *Soulangiana* 'Lennei')	Late spring	All PNW
Empress tree (*Paulownia tomentosa*)	Spring	All PNW
Chaste tree (*Vitex agnus-castus*)	Late summer	C, LV, LM, DV

Yellow	Season	Region
Cornelian cherry (*Cornus mas*)	Early spring	All PNW
Chinese witch hazel (*Hamamelis mollis*)	Late winter	C, LV, LM, DV
Goldenrain tree (*Koelreuteria paniculata*)	Summer	C, LV, LM, DV
Goldenchain tree (*Laburnum* × *Watereri*)	Mid spring	All PNW
Tulip tree (*Liriodendron tulipifera*)	Early summer	All PNW
Yellow cucumber tree (*Magnolia acuminata cordata*)	Late spring	All PNW
Fraser magnolia (*Magnolia fraseri*)	Late spring	C, LV, LM, DV
Japanese pagoda tree (*Sophora japonica*)	Mid to late summer	All PNW

Pink	Season	Region
Silk tree (*Albizia julibrissin*)	Mid summer	All PNW
Redbuds (*Cercis* spp.)	Early spring	LM, DV, HD
Flowering dogwood (*Cornus florida* 'Cherokee Chief')	Late spring	All PNW
Crape myrtle (*Lagerstroemia indica* and hybrids)	Mid summer	C, LV, LM, DV
Pink star magnolia (*Magnolia stellata* 'Rosea')	Early spring	All PNW
Dawn saucer magnolia (*Magnolia* × *Soulangiana* 'Dawn')	Early spring	All PNW
Flowering crabapples (*Malus hybrids*)	Mid spring	All PNW

Flowering cherries (*Prunus* spp.)	Late winter to early spring	C, LV, LM
Flowering plum (*Prunus* spp.)	Late winter to early spring	C, LV, LM, DV
Flowering peach (*Prunus persica*)	Early spring	C, LV, LM, DV
Idaho locust (*Robinia ambigua* 'Idahoensis')	Mid spring to early summer	All PNW
Salt cedars (*Tamarix* spp.)	Mid spring	C, LV, LM, DV

Red	**Season**	**Region**
Red maple (*Acer rubrum*)	Late winter	All PNW
Briotti red horse chestnut (*Aesculus carnea* 'Briotii')	Late spring	All PNW
Red buckeye (*Aesculus pavia*)	Late spring	All PNW
Crape myrtle (*Lagerstroemia indica* and hybrids)	Mid summer	C, LV, LM, DV
Red silver flowering crabapple (*Malus* 'Red Silver')	Mid spring	All PNW
Eleyi flowering crabapple (*Malus purpurea* 'Eleyi')	Mid spring	All PNW
Persian parrotia (*Parrotia persica*)	Spring	C, LV, LM

A SAMPLER OF TREES BY THEIR FALL COLOR

Color is the backbone of the autumn garden. Here are trees that will provide brilliant fall color. Remember, however, that the fall color of any given tree can vary from year to year depending on weather conditions, soil moisture, plant location, and the zone in which the tree is growing. Leaf color will not be as intense when the fall season is warm or wet, or if the tree does not receive full sun exposure. Good red color, for instance, depends on warm days followed by cool nights. Depending on genetics, some trees in the same species will widely vary in color. If the same tree is on more than one list, then that is your clue to the possibility of a color variance. It is difficult to find the "perfect" tree for any situation, but if your selection has a pleasing habit, seasonal flowers, and brilliant fall color you have a real winner!

Yellow or Gold

Vine maple (*Acer circinatum*)	All PNW
Amur maple (*Acer ginnala*)	All PNW
Norway maple (*Acer platanoides*)	All PNW
Silver maple (*Acer saccharinum*)	All PNW
European birch (*Betula* spp.)	All PNW
Katsura tree (*Cercidiphyllum japonicum*)	C, LV, LM, HD
Eastern redbud (*Cercis canadensis*)	LM, DV, HD
Kousa dogwood (*Cornus Kousa*)	C, LV, LM, DV
Golden Desert ash (*Fraxinus oxycarpa* 'Golden Desert')	All PNW
Maidenhair tree (*Ginkgo biloba*)	All PNW
Snowdrop tree (*Halesia carolina*)	C, LV, LM, DV
Mountain silver bell (*Halesia monticola*)	C, LV, LM, DV
Goldenrain tree (*Koelreuteria paniculata*)	C, LV, LM, DV
Sweetgum (*Liquidambar styraciflua*)	All PNW

Sampler of Trees by Their Fall Color (*continued*)

Yellow or Gold

Tulip tree (*Liriodendron tulipifera*)	All PNW
Flowering crabapple (*Malus* spp.)	All PNW
White mulberry (*Morus alba*)	All PNW
Poplar (*Populus* spp.)	All PNW
Flowering cherry (*Prunus* spp.)	C, LV, LM
Weeping willow (*Salix* spp.)	All PNW
American ash (*Sorbus americana*)	All PNW
Japanese stewartia (*Stewartia pseudocamellia*)	C, LV, LM

Orange

Sugar maple (*Acer saccharum*)	All PNW
Serviceberry (*Amelanchier* spp.)	All PNW
Hawthorn (*Crataegus* spp.)	All PNW
Sweetgum (*Liquidambar styraciflua*)	All PNW
Sourgum (*Nyssa sylvatica*)	C, LV, LM, DV
Sassafras (*Sassafras albidum*)	C, LV, LM, DV
Korean stewartia (*Stewartia koreana*)	C, LV, LM
Mountain stewartia (*Stewartia ovata*)	C, LV, LM

Red

Flowering dogwood (*Cornus florida*)	All PNW
Kousa dogwood (*Cornus Kousa*)	C, LV, LM, DV
Franklin tree (*Franklinia alatamaha*)	C, LV, LM, DV
Sweetgum (*Liquidambar styraciflua*)	All PNW
Sour gum (*Nyssa sylvatica*)	C, LV, LM, DV
Sourwood (*Oxydendrum arboreum*)	C, LV, LM, DV
Sargent flowering plum (*Prunus sargentii*)	All PNW
Bradford pear (*Pyrus calleryana* 'Bradford')	All PNW
Red spire callery pear (*Pyrus calleryana* 'Red Spire')	All PNW
Scarlet oak (*Quercus coccinea*)	All PNW
Pin oak (*Quercus palustris*)	All PNW
Red oak (*Quercus rubra*)	All PNW
Staghorn sumac (*Rhus typhina*)	All PNW
Tall stewartia (*Stewartia monadelpha*)	C, LV, LM, DV

Bronze

Japanese maple (*Acer palmatum* varieties)	All PNW
European beech (*Fagus sylvatica* varieties)	All PNW
Willow oak (*Quercus phellos*)	All PNW

Rust, Maroon, Burgundy, and Purple

Japanese maple (*Acer palmatum*)	All PNW
Autumn applause ash (*Fraxinus americana* 'Autumn Applause')	All PNW
Flowering ash (*Fraxinus ornus*)	C, LV, LM, DV
Sour gum (*Nyssa sylvatica*)	C, LV, LM, DV
Japanese stewartia (*Stewartia pseudocamellia*)	C, LV, LM, DV

SHRUBS

Shrubs, as discussed in this chapter, are woody perennial plants that, when selected well, make the landscape. Shrubs are used to provide background, points of interest, accents for important places, framing for a particular view, foreground, and generally to develop a picture that says, "Here is where I live." There is a bewildering array of shrubs, and they range from flowering deciduous types to evergreens, in many shapes and colors, and in many mature sizes. Some types of shrubs have so many excellent members and relatives that they deserve a chapter of their own, so we've done that for rhododendrons and azaleas, as well as roses. Some shrubs grow to such size that they become trees, and though the distinction between a tall shrub and a small tree is one of semantics, the differences are still important.

Generally, a shrub could be defined as a woody plant that may have multiple trunks and will not grow more than twenty feet high. A tree will generally have a single trunk and might attain great height. The varied sizes and shapes of the plants included in the shrub category give the gardener and landscaper a wealth of resources upon which to draw when making his or her environment more livable. You will find some small trees in this chapter in appropriate lists, as you will find some shrubs listed with the trees.

"Select your plants based on what they will do. Knowing which role the plant is to play is like knowing which piece of furniture you need for your living room. Information as to the size, shape, fabric, colors, and textures determines the final choice. The goal is a good, unified composition. Plants grow, so learn about the 'ten-year size,' their soil and exposure preferences, and their hardiness, so your choices will satisfy rather than frustrate. Plants are beguiling! If you haven't described what you need before you shop, you're likely to come home with the 'and where should I put this?' plant."—Myrna Dowsett, Landscape Designer, Portland, Oregon

SHRUBS WITH SHOWY FOLIAGE FOR SHADE

The list here is short, for most shade-preferring plants rely on their many leaves to pick up any stray rays of light, and few seem to want to sacrifice any green color for variegation. However, here are some that will fit most shade situations. Use them to lighten a dark, shady area (also check the "Attractive or Unusual Foliage" list in the chapter on rhododendrons and the "For Shady Sites" list in the chapter on herbaceous perennials).

Marlberry (*Ardisia japonica*)	C, LV
Variegated aucuba (*Aucuba japonica* vars.)	C, LV, LM
Japanese aralia (*Fatsia japonica*)	C, LV, LM
Drooping leucothoe (*Leucothoe fontanesiana* 'Rainbow')	C, LV, LM, DV
Fringe flower (*Loropetalum chinense* 'Rubrum')	C, LV
Dwarf ninebark (*Physocarpus opulifolius* 'Darts Gold')	All PNW
Variegated weigela (*Weigela florida* 'Variegata')	All PNW

SHRUBS FOR ROCK GARDENS

A rock garden provides a planting situation that combines plants and stones in a manner that gives the viewer appreciation of both. Plants must be selected carefully to fit the scale of the garden, enhance the colors and shapes of rocks and other groundcovers, and provide interest, both in growth manner and in flower or fruit. Many of the dwarf shrubs can be used in a rockery, depending on the exposure to sun, shade, and other factors that influence their growth. Here are a few to start you thinking in terms of using plants with rocks, to make your landscape interesting and inviting. Some of these may need annual pruning to keep them in bounds for a small-scale rockery setting.

Bog rosemary (*Andromeda polifolia* vars.)	C, LV, LM, DV
Irwins dwarf barberry (*Berberis stenophylla* 'Irwinii')	All PNW
Rosemary barberry (*Berberis stenophylla* 'Nana compacta')	All PNW
Crimson pygmy barberry (*Berberis thunbergii* 'Crimson Pygmy')	All PNW
Dwarf birch (*Betula nana*)	All PNW
Pyrenees cotoneaster (*Cotoneaster congestus*)	All PNW
Garland daphne (*Daphne cneorum* vars.)	C, LV, LM
Heathers (*Erica* spp.)	C, LV, LM
Dwarf forsythia (*Forsythia virdissima* 'Bronxensis')	All PNW
Salal (*Gaultheria shallon*)	C, LV, LM
Japanese holly (*Ilex crenata* vars.)	C, LV, LM, DV
Blue Chip juniper (*Juniperus horizontalis* 'Blue Chip')	All PNW
Blue Star juniper (*Juniperus squamata* 'Blue Star')	All PNW
Compact Oregon grape (*Mahonia aquifolium* 'compacta')	All PNW
Dwarf nandina (*Nandina domestica* vars.)	C, LV, LM, DV
Dwarf Japanese pieris (*Pieris japonica yakusimana*)	All PNW
Mugo pine (*Pinus mugo mugo*)	All PNW
Dwarf white pine (*Pinus strobus* 'Nana')	All PNW
Impeditum rhododendron (*Rhododendron impeditum*)	All PNW
Alpine spirea (*Spiraea japonica* 'Alpina')	All PNW
Germander (*Teucrium chamaedrys*)	All PNW
Dwarf European cranberry bush (*Viburnum opulus* 'Nanum')	All PNW

DWARF CONIFERS GOOD FOR ROCK GARDENS

What would a rock garden be without conifers, especially dwarf types that hold their form, shape, and color for such a long time without overgrowing the special garden? Here are some of the newer and more colorful additions that could be made to your landscape via the rock garden.

Dwarf Korean fir (*Abies koreana* 'Silberkugel')	All PNW
Pygmy deodor cedar (*Cedrus deodora* 'Pygmea')	C, LV, LM
Hage hinoki cypress (*Chamaecyparis obtusa* 'Hage')	All PNW
Golden Sprite false cypress (*Chamaecyparis obtusa* 'Golden Sprite')	All PNW
Tennis ball false cypress (*Chamaecyparis obtusa juniperoides* 'Gnome')	All PNW
Tsukumo false cypress (*Chamaecyparis pisifera* 'Tsukumo')	All PNW
Dwarf Little Gem spruce (*Picea abies* 'Little Gem')	All PNW
Dwarf Serbian spruce (*Picea omorika* 'Pimoko')	All PNW
Mitch's dwarf mugo (*Pinus mugo* 'Mitch's Mini')	All PNW
Dwarf Japanese white pine (*Pinus parviflora* 'Hago Rumo')	All PNW
Gregg's white pine (*Pinus strobus* 'Gregg')	All PNW
Dwarf Scots pine (*Pinus sylvestris* 'Little Brolley')	All PNW
Little Joe dwarf Canadian hemlock (*Tsuga canadensis* 'Little Joe')	All PNW

"Any time that you deal with conifers, you have a year-around situation. Conifers provide color, shape, and interest that varies through the seasons of the gardening year. Although the dwarf types listed above are noted for their compact and small size, know that they will enlarge as time passes. Know what your garden size will accept, and plant accordingly."—Don Howse, Porterhowse Nursery, Sandy, Oregon

SHRUBS THAT MAKE MOUNDS

Shrubs that grow into tidy mounds are great for the low maintenance yard, if they are properly chosen for mature size and planted to fit their space. Some plants seem to grow with indeterminate abandon, on their way upward and outward, until they reach their mature size and shape. Others, like the ones listed below, are much more careful about their looks and most always present to the viewer a picture of good behavior. Add to this list, for it will be valuable to you later in your landscape management activity as you search for the precise plant for the select place.

Heather (*Erica* spp.)	C, LV, LM
Apache plume (*Fallugia paradoxa*)	All PNW
Woadwaxen (*Genista* spp.)	All PNW
Dwarf hydrangea (*Hydrangea macrophylla* 'Pia')	C, LV, LM, DV
Dwarf Kalmia (*Kalmia latifolia* 'Elf')	C, LV, LM, DV
Lavender (*Lavandula* spp.)	All PNW
Mugo pine (*Pinus mugo mugo*)	All PNW
Dwarf white pine (*Pinus strobus* 'Nana')	All PNW
Coles Prostrate hemlock (*Tsuga canadensis* 'Coles Prostrate')	All PNW

SHRUBS FOR WET PLACES

Many of the soil types in the western part of the Pacific Northwest are of silt and clay and often overlay heavier textured clay soils. Thus, unless one chooses carefully, the plants placed with loving care may succumb to too much water and not enough oxygen during the normal nine-month wet winter. However, some plants have shallow enough roots, or may have other ways of obtaining oxygen during wet months and so will grow and thrive in those planting situations. A wet spot in the landscape will give you a chance to try some of these that we feel are good candidates for wet soils.

Brilliant red chokecherry (*Aronia arbutifolia* 'Brilliantissima')	All PNW
Spice bush (*Calycanthus occidentalis*)	C, LV, LM, DV
Red osier dogwood (*Cornus stolonifera*)	All PNW
Flowering quince (*Chaenomeles* spp.)	All PNW
Bog laurel (*Kalmia polifolia*)	C, LV, LM
Sierra laurel (*Leucothoe davisiae*)	All PNW
Drooping leucothoe (*Leucothoe fontanesiana*)	C, LV, LM, DV
Common privet (*Ligustrum vulgare*)	All PNW
Rose gold pussy willow (*Salix gracilistyla*)	All PNW
Dwarf purple osier willow (*Salix purpurea* 'Gracilis')	All PNW
Spirea (*Spiraea* spp.)	All PNW

> *If you are unsure about the drainage capability of the soils in your landscape, perform a simple percolation test and find out if plants that demand well-drained soils would survive. Dig a small hole a foot deep and fill it with water. If the water drains out within several hours, you are blessed with a soil with relatively good drainage. If the water remains in the hole for more than twenty-four hours you should select some of the plants listed above.*

SHRUBS FOR ROSEBURG, OREGON

The Master Gardener class in Roseburg was asked to list their favorites and the list below is their contribution to this book. Roseburg is in the area that we have arbitrarily called Dry Valley (DV) in our zone information. Soils are variable, often heavy with some drainage problems. The weather is generally warmer than the Willamette Valley of Oregon and somewhat drier.

Glossy abelia (*Abelia grandiflora*)
Red-twig dogwood (*Cornus stolonifera*)
Rose of Sharon (*Hibiscus syriacus*)
Japanese rose (*Kerria japonica*)
Azaleas (*Rhododendron* spp.)
Rhododendrons (*Rhododendron* spp.)
Spirea (*Spiraea* spp.)
Common snowball (*Viburnum opulus* 'Roseum')

Viburnum opulus

SHRUBS FOR ATTRACTING WILDLIFE

Plants that will attract wild things include those that can be used for nesting sites, that may provide food or shelter, that may provide any of the living needs of an animal, be it bird or four-legged critter. (Also check the naturescaping list in the chapter on trees.)

Currant

Japanese aucuba (*Aucuba japonica* vars.)	C, LV, LM, DV
Barberry (*Berberis* spp.)	All PNW
Butterfly bush (*Buddleia davidii*)	All PNW
Beautyberry (*Callicarpa* spp.)	C, LV, LM, DV
Santa Barbara ceanothus (*Ceanothus impressus*)	C, LM
Blue blossom ceanothus (*Ceanothus thyrsiflorus*)	LV, LM, DV, HD
Flowering quince (*Chaenomeles* spp.)	All PNW
Parney cotoneaster (*Cotoneaster lacteus*)	C, LV, LM, DV
Rockspray cotoneaster (*Cotoneaster microphyllus*)	C, LV, LM
February daphne (*Daphne mezereum*)	All PNW
Winged euonymus (*Euonymus alata*)	All PNW
Salal (*Gaultheria shallon*)	C, LV, LM, DV
Holly (*Ilex* spp.)	C, LV, LM, DV
Holly (*Ilex aquifolium*)	C, LV, LM
Box honeysuckle (*Lonicera nitida*)	All PNW
Oregon grape (*Mahonia aquifolium*)	All PNW
Pernettya (*Pernettya mucronata*)	C, LV, LM, DV
Mock orange (*Philadelphus lewisii*)	All PNW
Firethorn (*Pyracantha coccinea*)	All PNW
Flowering currant (*Ribes sanguineum*)	All PNW
Skimmia (*Skimmia japonica*)	C, LV, LM
Lilac (*Syringa* spp.)	All PNW
Red huckleberry (*Vaccinium parvifolium*)	C, LV, LM
Viburnum (*Viburnum* selected species)	Varies

SHRUBS FOR A NORTH-FACING DRY BANK

Problem situations exist in any landscaping job and may require a special sort of plant to fit a special sort of site. Let's say you have a north-facing slope, which means you have a lot of shade, and if it has no source of moisture you could also call it a dry-bank microclimate. Well, here are a few ideas that might help to fill that site—give them a try.

Rosemary barberry (*Berberis stenophylla*)	LV, LM, DV, HD
Blue blossom ceanothus (*Ceanothus thyrsiflorus*)	LV, LM, DV, HD
Deutzia (*Deutzia* spp.)	C, LV, LM, DV
St. Johnswort (*Hypericum* spp.)	C, LV, LM
Japanese holly (*Ilex crenata*)	All PNW
Yaupon holly (*Ilex vomitoria*)	All PNW
Salal (*Gaultheria shallon*)	C, LV, LM, DV
Oregon grape (*Mahonia aquifolium*)	All PNW
Leatherleaf viburnum (*Viburnum rhytidophyllum*)	C, LV, LM, DV
Laurustinus (*Viburnum tinus*)	C, LV, LM, DV
Periwinkle (*Vinca major, Vinca minor*)	C, LV, LM

SHRUBS FOR A SOUTH-FACING DRY HILLSIDE

Plants that can survive in this sort of locale are those that prefer full open sunlight, are tolerant to heat and possible drought during the summer. In the juniper and cotoneaster groups are many species that will fit this situation; however we list the genus for your guidance.

Rockrose (*Cistus cobariensis*)	LV, LM, DV, HD
Parney cotoneaster (*Cotoneaster parneyii*)	All PNW
Juniper (*Juniperus* spp.)	All PNW
Photinia (*Photinia fraserii*)	C, LV, LM, DV
Firethorn (*Pyracantha coccinea*)	All PNW
Rugosa rose (*Rosa rugosa*)	LV, LM, DV, HD
Yucca (*Yucca filamentosa*)	LV, LM, DV, HD

 "Because of the relatively dry nature of the West in general, we gardeners will be less frustrated over the long run if we plant less thirsty plants. All plants need watering during dry spells until they are well established—from one to three years."—Josephine County Master Gardeners, Grants Pass, Oregon

OLD-FASHIONED SHRUBS

These are the old faithfuls. Our grandmothers' gardens consisted of some of these plants that to this day remain reliable providing color, background, cuttings, accent, or flowers. Also check the list for shrubs valued for arrangements, for many of them would be included in yesterday's garden. Many are resistant to various diseases (which is why a lot of them made it to this list).

Japanese aucuba (*Aucuba japonica*)	C, LV, LM, DV
Butterfly bush (*Buddleia davidii*)	All PNW
Common boxwood (*Buxus sempervirens*)	C, LV, LM, DV
Camellia (*Camellia japonica*)	C, LV, LM, DV
Japanese flowering quince (*Chaenomeles japonica*)	All PNW
Parney cotoneaster (*Cotoneaster lacteus*)	C, LV, LM, DV
Scotch broom (*Cytisus scoparius*)	C, LV, LM, DV
Winter daphne (*Daphne odora*)	C, LV, LM, DV
Slender deutzia (*Deutzia gracilis*)	C, LV, LM, DV
Forsythia (*Forsythia* spp.)	C, LV, LM, DV
Rose of Sharon (*Hibiscus syriacus*)	All PNW
Bigleaf hydrangea (*Hydrangea macrophylla*)	C, LV, LM, DV
Peegee hydrangea (*Hydrangea paniculata* 'Grandiflora')	All PNW
Japanese kerria (*Kerria japonica*)	All PNW
Pfitzer juniper (*Juniperus chinensis* 'Pfitzerana')	All PNW
Savin juniper (*Juniperus sabina*)	All PNW
Tamarix juniper (*Juniperus sabina* 'Tamariscifolia')	All PNW
Andromeda (*Pieris japonica* and selected vars.)	All PNW
Sweet mock orange (*Philadelphus coronarius*)	All PNW
Wild mock orange (*Philadelphus lewisii*)	All PNW
Oriental arborvitae (*Platycladus orientalis*)	All PNW
Flowering almond (*Prunus triloba*)	All PNW
Western azalea (*Rhododendron occidentale*)	C, LV, LM, DV
Skimmia (*Skimmia japonica*)	C, LV, LM, DV
Bridal wreath spirea (*Spiraea prunifolia* 'Plena')	All PNW
Vanhoutte spirea (*Spiraea vanhouttei*)	All PNW
Common lilac (*Syringa vulgaris*)	All PNW
English yew (*Taxus baccata*)	C, LV, LM, DV
Oregon yew (*Taxus brevifolia*)	All PNW
American arborvitae (*Thuja occidentalis*)	C, LV, LM, DV
Weigela (*Weigela florida* vars.)	All PNW
Common snowball (*Viburnum opulus* 'Roseum')	All PNW
Laurustinus (*Viburnum tinus*)	C, LV, LM, DV

"I was raised in Nebraska. Many of the landscapes in the Midwest have the same old-fashioned shrubs that were carried to the Pacific Northwest by our pioneers. Those that have remained are those that are tolerant of our growing conditions, or are resistant to diseases and insect attacks that are common to our area. Outside of pruning for control of their growth, most were easily cultured and became a part of the Pacific Northwest landscape environment."—Master Gardener Marje Luce and her gardening cat, Igor, Ashland, Oregon

SHRUBS THAT PROVIDE FRAGRANCE TO YOUR GARDEN

Plants that supply fragrance as well as beauty and interest bring another dimension to the garden. Fragrance may be strong, as in *Daphne odora* or Korean spice viburnum, or it may be fleeting as in Mollis azalea or Genista broom. Also, sensitivity to fragrance varies from one gardener to another as will likes and dislikes for plants that provide fragrance. Myrna Dowsett, landscape designer, says this about Somerset daphne: "put this under the bedroom window for fragrance!" And you will notice at least four viburnums on this list. Use this list to investigate the plants and see if they and their fragrances will fill a need in your garden.

Glossy abelia (*Abelia grandiflora*)	C, LV, DV
Fountain butterfly bush (*Buddleia alternifolia*)	All PNW
Summer lilac (*Buddleia davidii*)	All PNW
Carolina allspice (*Calycanthus floridus*)	All PNW
Spice bush (*Calycanthus occidentalis*)	C, LV, LM, DV
Bush anemone (*Carpenteria californica*)	C
Wintersweet (*Chimonanthus praecox*)	C, LV
Mexican orange (*Choisya ternata*)	C, LV, LM
Summersweet (*Clethra alnifolia*)	C, LV, LM, DV
Winter hazel (*Corylopsis* spp.)	C, LV, LM, DV
Daphne (*Daphne* spp.)	Varies
Somerset daphne (*Daphne burkwoodii*)	C, LV, LM, DV
Spurge laurel (*Daphne laureola*)	C, LV, LM
Ebbinge's silverberry (*Elaeagnus ebbingei*)	C, LV
Fothergilla (*Fothergilla major*)	C, LV
Broom (*Genista pilosa, G. spachiana*)	C, LV, LM
Witch hazel (*Hamamelis intermedia, H. mollis*)	C, LV, LM
Pink jasmine (*Jasminum polyanthum*)	C
Lavender (*Lavandula* spp.)	C, LV, LM
Privet honeysuckle (*Lonicera pileata*)	C, LV, LM, DV
Winter honeysuckle (*Lonicera fragrantissima*)	All PNW
Chilean myrtle (*Luma apiculata*)	C
Star magnolia (*Magnolia stellata*)	All PNW
Orange jessamine (*Murraya exotica*)	C
Osmanthus (*Osmanthus* spp.)	C, LV, LM
Sweet mock orange (*Philadelphus coronarius* 'Aureus')	All PNW
Mock orange (*Philadelphus virginalis* 'Minnesota Snowflake')	All PNW
Pittosporum (*Pittosporum tobira*)	C, LV, LM
Flowering currant (*Ribes odoratum*)	All PNW
Sarcococca (*Sarcococca* spp.)	C, LV, LM, DV
Lilac (*Syringa* spp.)	All PNW
Viburnum (*Viburnum bodnantense*)	C, LV, LM
Korean spice viburnum (*Viburnum carlesii*)	All PNW
Fragrant snowball (*Viburnum carlcephalum*)	All PNW
Fragrant viburnum (*Viburnum farreri*)	C, LV, LM, DV

Winter Honeysuckle

SHRUBS THAT CAN BECOME INVASIVE

It's not highly likely, but some shrubs can seed themselves copiously enough to overrun an area, and that is the reason for this list. Some plants, particularly some of the borderline sorts, that might not be top choices in the first place, can become problems. Here are a few.

Flowering quince (*Chaenomeles* vars.)	All PNW
Sweet fern (*Comptonia asplenifolia*)	C, LV, LM, DV
Scotch broom (*Cytisus scoparius*)	C, LV, LM
English holly (*Ilex aquifolium*)	C, LV, LM
Privet honeysuckle (*Lonicera pileata*)	C, LV, LM, DV
Oregon grape (*Mahonia aquifolium*)	All PNW
Pernettya (*Pernettya mucronata*)	C, LV, LM
Japanese knotweed (*Polygonum* spp.)	All PNW
Staghorn sumac (*Rhus typhina*)	All PNW
Red flowering currant (*Ribes sanguineum*)	C, LV, LM
Box blueberry (*Vaccinium ovatum*)	C

SHRUBS NARROW AND UPRIGHT FOR TIGHT PLACES

There invariably is a place in the landscape that is just too narrow for a "normal-sized" shrub to fit, but where you would dearly love to see some sort of plant accentuate the landscape. Alongside a wall or between a driveway and a sidewalk are givens, but these sorts of places can also include an inside corner where walls meet, or a place in the landscape where you need to tell people that something happens there. Anyway, here are a few slender-shaped plants that might just fill the bill.

Graham Blandy boxwood (*Buxus sempervirens* 'Graham Blandy')	C, LV, LM, DV
Sekkan-sugi Japanese cedar (*Cryptomeria japonica* 'Sekkan-sugi')	C, LV, LM
Redvein enkianthus (*Enkianthus* spp.)	C, LV, LM
Hetzi columnar juniper (*Juniperus chinensis* 'Hetzi Columnaris')	All PNW
Spearmint juniper (*J. chinensis* 'Spearmint')	C, LV, LM, DV
Irish juniper (*J. chinensis* 'Stricta')	All PNW
Wintergreen juniper (*J. chinensis* 'Wintergreen')	C, LV, LM, DV
Blue haven juniper (*Juniperus scopulorum* 'Blue Haven')	All PNW
Skyrocket red cedar (*Juniperus virginiana* 'Skyrocket')	All PNW
Oregon grape (*Mahonia aquifolium*)	All PNW
Leatherleaf mahonia (*Mahonia bealei*)	C, LV, LM, DV
Heavenly bamboo (*Nandina domestica*)	C, LV, LM, DV
Dwarf Alberta spruce (*Picea glauca* 'Conica')	All PNW
Colorado spruce (*Picea pungens* 'Iseli fastigiate')	All PNW
Indian hawthorn (*Raphiolepis indica*)	C, LV, LM
Irish yew (*Taxus baccata* 'Fastigiata')	C, LV, LM
Gold Irish yew (*Taxus baccata* 'Fastigiata Aurea')	C, LV, LM
DeGroot's Spire Am. arborvitae (*Thuja occidentalis* 'DeGroot's Spire')	All PNW
Pyramidal arborvitae (*Thuja occidentalis* 'Pyramidalis')	All PNW
Emerald green arborvitae (*Thuja occidentalis* 'Smaragd')	All PNW

SHRUBS THAT CAN BLOOM IN SHADY LANDSCAPES

All plants need sunlight to grow and to bloom. However, there are some that either prefer less than full sunlight or will tolerate some shade and may look even better when grown in shaded locations. The plants listed below will do well in the summer shade of big-leaf maples or scattered in the dense shade of Douglas firs. Don't forget to water them a little extra in those locations, as the trees that are giving the shade will also take most of the water and minerals.

February
Daphne

Barberry (*Berberis thunbergii* 'Aurea')	All PNW
Carolina allspice (*Calycanthus floridus*)	All PNW
Camellia (*Camellia* spp.)	C, LV, LM
Summersweet (*Clethra alnifolia*)	C, LV, LM, DV
Cleyera (*Cleyera japonica*)	C, LV, LM
Winter hazel (*Corylopsis* spp.)	C, LV, LM, DV
February daphne (*Daphne mezereum*)	All PNW
Spurge laurel (*Daphne laureola*)	C, LV, LM
Winter daphne (*Daphne odora* 'Marginata')	C, LV, LM, DV
Redvein enkianthus (*Enkianthus* spp.)	C, LV, LM, DV
Dwarf fothergilla (*Fothergilla gardenii*)	C, LV, LM
Fuchsia (*Fuchsia hybrida*)	C, LV, LM
Bigleaf hydrangea (*Hydrangea macrophylla*)	C ,LV, LM, DV
Mountain laurel (*Kalmia latifolia* vars.)	All PNW
Japanese rose (*Kerria japonica*)	All PNW
Drooping leucothoe (*Leucothoe fontanesiana*)	C, LV, LM, DV
Oregon grape (*Mahonia aquifolium*)	All PNW
Leatherleaf mahonia (*Mahonia bealei*)	All PNW
Burmese mahonia (*Mahonia lomariifolia*)	C, LV, LM
Osmanthus (*Osmanthus* spp.)	C, LV, LM
Lily-of-the-valley shrub (*Pieris japonica* vars.)	All PNW
Pittosporum (*Pittosporum tobira*)	C, LV
Sarcococca (*Sarcococca* spp.)	C, LV, LM
Red huckleberry (*Vaccinium parvifolium*)	C, LV, LM
Korean spice viburnum (*Viburnum carlesii*)	All PNW
Nannyberry (*Viburnum lentago*)	All PNW

SHRUBS THAT WILL GROW IN HEAVY SHADE

This is a list you should carry forever in your gardening apron! Shade is a valued item in landscapes in the eastern part of the PNW region. In the western half of the region shade is a given, for once the trees are established, they proceed to do what they were designed to do—give shade. In both areas it is nice when we have other plants that will survive, and perhaps even thrive, in the shade. Here are some of the better types of shrubs that we think will fill the bill in the shade, so give them a try.

Japanese aucuba (*Aucuba japonica* vars.)	C, LV, LM, DV
Common boxwood (*Buxus sempervirens*)	C, LV, LM, DV
Camellia (*Camellia* spp.)	C, LV, LM
Gilt Edge silverberry (*Elaeagnus ebbengei* 'Gilt Edge')	C, LV, LM

Euonymus (*Euonymus fortunei radicans*)	All PNW
Japanese aralia (*Fatsia japonica*)	C, LV, LM
Drooping leucothoe (*Leucothoe fontanesiana*)	C, LV, LM, DV
Oregon grape (*Mahonia aquifolium*)	All PNW
Burmese mahonia (*Mahonia lomariifolia*)	C, LV, LM
Longleaf mahonia (*Mahonia nervosa*)	C, LV, LM
Holly leaf osmanthus (*Osmanthus heterophyllus* vars.)	C, LV, LM
Japanese knotweed (*Polygonum cuspidatum*)	All PNW
English laurel (*Prunus laurocerasus* 'Mount Vernon')	C, LV, LM
Red flowering currant (*Ribes sanguineum*)	All PNW
Japanese skimmia (*Skimmia japonica*)	C, LV, LM
Common snowberry (*Symphoricarpos albus, S. chenaultii*)	All PNW
Evergreen huckleberry (*Vaccinium ovatum*)	C, LV, LM
Nannyberry (*Viburnum lentago*)	All PNW

"Although it may be frustrating to see all the plants you can't grow in the shade, there are many beautiful ones that can...and on a hot summer's day there's nothing like a cool shady garden! Be careful to notice the degree of shade in various parts of your garden (and the possibility of this changing as trees in the area grow)."—Ray and Peg Prag, Forest Farm, Williams, Oregon

SHRUBS WITH BRILLIANTLY COLORED NEW FOLIAGE

Some of the newer hybrid woody ornamental shrubs appearing at retail garden centers have as one of their attributes foliage that is brightly colored when it first appears. Shades of red, pink, and gold are now seen in spring gardens where some of the following shrubs are being used. Let them help you brighten an otherwise less-than-exciting place in your landscape.

Prostrate white abelia (*Abelia grandiflora* 'Prostrata')	C, LV, DV
Japanese maple (*Acer palmatum* vars.)	All PNW
Dwarf box-leafed barberry (*Berberis buxifolia* 'Nana')	All PNW
Golden Japanese barberry (*Berberis thunbergii* 'Aurea')	All PNW
Beautyberry (*Callicarpa bodinieri* 'Profusion')	C, LV, LM, DV
Scotch heather (*Calluna vulgaris* vars.)	C, LV, LM
Heavenly bamboo (*Nandina domestica* vars.)	C, LV, LM, DV
Fraser's red-tip photinia (*Photinia fraseri*)	C, LV, LM
Japanese photinia (*Photinia glabra*)	C, LV, LM
Forest Flame pieris (*Pieris* hybrid 'Forest Flame')	All PNW
Mountain Fire pieris (*Pieris japonica* 'Mountain Fire')	All PNW
Valley Rose pieris (*Pieris japonica* 'Valley Rose')	All PNW
Valley Valentine pieris (*Pieris japonica* 'Valley Valentine')	All PNW
Froebel spirea (*Spiraea bumalda* 'Froebelii')	All PNW
Goldflame spirea (*Spiraea bumalda* 'Goldflame')	All PNW
Goldmound spirea (*Spiraea bumalda* 'Goldmound')	All PNW
Limemound spirea (*Spiraea bumalda* 'Limemound')	All PNW

SHRUBS FOR DRY SITES

Particularly in the eastern part of the Pacific Northwest, gardeners must either plan to water regularly and frequently, or use plants that will withstand dry conditions. However, even in the wetter part of the Pacific Northwest, when the rain ceases in late spring, gardeners must plan for a dry summer growing season. With the climate in mind, you plan accordingly. You will often find that after the first couple of growing summers, the more mature a plant becomes, the better it is able to withstand drought conditions, at least for a moderate period of time. However, even if you live in a fairly damp area, your landscape or yard may have dry "islands." It is for those places that this list was developed.

Strawberry tree (*Arbutus unedo*)	C, LV, LM, DV
Manzanita (*Arctostaphylos* spp. and vars.)	C, LV, LM, DV
Barberry (*Berberis* spp.)	All PNW
Butterfly bush (*Buddleia davidii*)	All PNW
Bush anemone (*Carpenteria californica*)	C, LV, LM, DV
Concha wild lilac (*Ceanothus* 'Concha')	C, LV, LM
Frosty Blue wild lilac (*Ceanothus* 'Frosty Blue')	C, LV, LM
Flowering quince (*Chaenomeles japonica*)	All PNW
Rockrose (*Cistus* spp.)	LM, DV
Warminster broom (*Cytisus praecox*)	C, LV, LM, DV
Silverberry (*Elaeagnus pungens* vars.)	C, LV, LM, DV
Golden silverberry (*Elaeagnus pungens* 'Maculata')	C, LV, LM, DV
Broom (*Genista* spp.)	C, LV, LM, DV
Rose of Sharon (*Hibiscus syriacus*)	All PNW
Juniper (*Juniperus* spp. and vars.)	All PNW
Heavenly bamboo (*Nandina domestica* vars.)	C, LV, LM, DV
Photinia (*Photinia* spp.)	C, LV, LM
Cinquefoil (*Potentilla fruticosa* vars.)	All PNW
Firethorn (*Pyracantha coccinea* vars.)	All PNW
Fragrant sumac (*Rhus aromatica*)	DV, HD
Smooth sumac (*Rhus glabra*)	All PNW
Staghorn sumac (*Rhus typhina*)	All PNW
Rosemary (*Rosmarinus officinalis*)	C, LV, LM, DV
Yucca (*Yucca* spp.)	All PNW

"Cistus thrives in light, well-drained soil, full sun, and is drought tolerant when established. The name "rockrose" comes from the highly visible one- to five-inch crepelike flowers with yellow/gold stamens that recur throughout the summer and into early autumn."—Maurice Horn, partner-owner, Joy Creek Nursery, Scappoose, Oregon

SHRUBS WITH BOLD, COARSE-TEXTURED FOLIAGE

Shrubs with large, attractive leaves or odd branching habits are an immediate attraction. They can work as accent plants, or to draw a person into the landscape. The same effect can be achieved by using shade trees with interesting bark or trunk character, so check that list in the shade tree chapter.

Japanese aucuba (*Aucuba japonica*)	C, LV, LM, DV
Mr. Goldstrike aucuba (*Aucuba japonica* 'Mr. Goldstrike')	C, LV, LM, DV
Picturata Japanese aucuba (*Aucuba japonica* 'Picturata')	C, LV, LM
Camellia (*Camellia japonica* spp.)	C, LV, LM, DV
Gilt Edge silverberry (*Elaeagnus ebbengei* 'Gilt Edge')	C, LV
Fatshedera (*Fatshedera lizei*)	C, LV, LM, DV
Japanese aralia (*Fatsia japonica*)	C, LV, LM, DV
Bigleaf hydrangea (*Hydrangea macrophylla*)	C, LV, LM, DV
Alice oakleaf hydrangea (*Hydrangea quercifolia* 'Alice')	All PNW
Snowflake oakleaf hydrangea (*Hydrangea quercifolia* 'Snowflake')	All PNW
Burmese mahonia (*Mahonia lomariifolia*)	C, LV, LM
English laurel (*Prunus laurocerasus*)	C, LV, LM, DV
Deerhorn cedar (*Thujopsis dolabrata*)	C, LV, LM, DV
Leatherleaf viburnum (*Viburnum rhytidophyllum*)	C, LV, LM, DV
Gold sword yucca (*Yucca filamentosa* 'Gold Sword')	All PNW
Ivory tower yucca (*Yucca filamentosa* 'Ivory Tower')	All PNW

SHRUBS THAT BLOOM FOUR WEEKS OR LONGER

Shrubs with long-lasting flower color are like beacons in the landscape. The length of time that blooms remain on a plant will depend greatly on the local weather. In spring seasons that remain humid and cool for three or more months, many of the spring bloomers will hold their blossoms and continue to give their beauty to the landscape. Also, check the rhododendron chapter and the rose chapter for other bloomers that last for long periods. There are not very many that fit the general category (that will remain for a month or so in spite of the weather), but here are a few that will give you a start on your list.

Glossy abelia (*Abelia grandiflora* vars.)	C, LV, DV
Butterfly bush (*Buddleia davidii* vars.)	All PNW
Sasanqua camellia (*Camellia sasanqua*)	C, LV, LM
Japanese flowering quince (*Chaenomeles japonica*)	All PNW
Rockrose (*Cistus* spp.)	C, LV, LM, DV
Daphne (*Daphne odora*)	C, LV, LM
Hardy fuchsia (*Fuchsia magellanica*)	C, LV, LM
Rose of Sharon (*Hibiscus syriacus*)	All PNW
Hydrangea (*Hydrangea* spp.)	All PNW
Showy jasmine (*Jasminium floridum*)	C, LV, LM
Mountain laurel (*Kalmia latifolia*)	All PNW
Japanese rose (*Kerria japonica*)	All PNW
Crape myrtle (*Lagerstroemia indica* vars.)	C, LV, LM
Lavender (*Lavandula* spp.)	All PNW
Sweet olive (*Osmanthus fragrans*)	C, LV, LM
Lily-of-the-valley shrub (*Pieris* spp.)	C, LV, LM, DV
Cinquefoil (*Potentilla fruticosa* vars.)	All PNW
Indian hawthorn (*Raphiolepis indica*)	C, LV, LM
Laurustinus (*Viburnum tinus* vars.)	C, LV, LM, DV
Weigela (*Wiegela florida* vars.)	All PNW

SHRUBS FOR MINIATURE HEDGES

Landscapes designed with a formal scheme may require some very low-growing, neatly trimmed hedges. For this you must select the plants that will withstand the constant trimming and also those that grow slowly enough that trimming is not a chore. Some of the neatest low hedges can be found at the Japanese Garden in Portland, where one of the finest is a hedge of low-growing evergreen azaleas.

Crimson pygmy barberry (*Berberis thunbergii* 'Crimson Pygmy')*	All PNW
Little leaf box (*Buxus microphylla* 'Morris Midget')	C, LV, LM, DV
Dwarf Korean box (*Buxus sinica* var. *insularis*)	All PNW
Chinese holly (*Ilex cornuta* 'Dwarf Burford')	C, LV, LM, DV
Dwarf Chinese holly (*Ilex cornuta* 'Rotunda')	C, LV, LM, DV
Japanese holly (*Ilex crenata* 'Helleri')	All PNW
English lavender (*Lavandula angustifolia* 'Hidcote')	C, LV, LM, DV
Oregon boxwood (*Paxistima canbyi*)	All PNW
Kurume azaleas (*Rhododendron kurume* 'Hinodegiri')	C, LV, LM
Roses (miniatures, see chapter on roses)	
Lavender cotton (*Santolina chamaecyparissus*)	All PNW
Germander (*Teucrium chamaedrys*)	All PNW
American arborvitae (*Thuja occidentalis* 'Nana')	All PNW

*deciduous

Berberis darwinii

EVERGREEN SHRUBS THAT PROVIDE WINTER INTEREST

Winters are varied in the Pacific Northwest, being generally bright and sunny in the eastern part and generally dull and gray in the West. In either part of the region, the use of evergreens to supply year-round interest is a good plan. Some evergreens change color in winter, some change forms, and others are reliably "their own self" from season to season. As you pursue more information about these plants, look for those that will fit your own landscape the best.

Japanese aucuba (*Aucuba japonica* variegated forms)	foliage	C, LV, LM
Darwin barberry (*Berberis darwinii*)	foliage, berries	C, LV, LM, DV
Warty barberry (*Berberis verruculosa*)	foliage	C, LV, LM, DV
Sasanqua camellia (*Camellia sasanqua*)	blooms	C, LV, LM
Bearberry cotoneaster (*Cotoneaster dammeri*)	berries	All PNW
Rock cotoneaster (*Cotoneaster horizontalis*)	form	All PNW
Japanese cryptomeria (*Cryptomeria japonica* 'Tansu')	foliage	All PNW
Euonymus (*Euonymus fortunei* variegated forms)	foliage	C, LV, LM, DV
English holly (*Ilex aquifolium* vars.)	berries, foliage	C, LV, LM
Chinese holly (*Ilex cornuta* vars.)	berries, foliage	C, LV, LM
Japanese holly (*Ilex crenata* vars.)	foliage	C, LV, LM, DV
Southern magnolia (*Magnolia grandiflora*)	foliage	C, LV, LM, DV

Sweet bay (*Magnolia virginiana*)	foliage	C, LV, LM, DV
Oregon grape (*Mahonia aquifolium*)	foliage	All PNW
Nandina (*Nandina domestica*)	foliage	C, LV, LM, DV
Firethorn (*Pyracantha coccinea*)	berries	All PNW
Indian hawthorn (*Raphiolepis* spp.)	foliage	C, LV
Spreading English yew (*Taxus baccata* 'Repandens')	foliage	C, LV, LM, DV
Emerald arborvitae (*Thuja occidentalis* 'Emerald')	foliage	All PNW

SHRUBS FOR ALKALINE SOILS

The soils in the eastern portion of this region are generally neutral to alkaline in reaction. Some gardeners spend a lot of time and money adapting the microclimate of their soils to accept more acid-loving plants, such as rhododendrons and heather, but to live with nature it's best to accept what it gives. Many plants will thrive in alkaline soils if other factors are acceptable—general climate, sun, and the ever-present wind. Here are some plants that we believe should be considered for their tolerance to alkaline soils.

Strawberry tree (*Arbutus unedo*)	All PNW
Common wormwood (*Artemesia absinthium*)	All PNW
Silver king artemesia (*Artemesia ludoviciana albula*)	All PNW
Butterfly bush (*Buddleia davidii*)	All PNW
Western redbud (*Cercis occidentalis*)	C, LV, LM, DV
Curl-leaf mountain mahogany (*Cercocarpus ledifolius*)	All PNW
Rockrose (*Cistus* spp.)	LM, DV
Cranberry cotoneaster (*Cotoneaster apiculatus*)	All PNW
Rock daphne (*Daphne cneorum*)	LM, DV, HD
Silverberry (*Elaeagnus commutata, E. pungens*)	All PNW
Junipers (*Juniperus* spp.)	All PNW
Cinquefoil (*Potentilla fruticosa*)	All PNW
Flowering almond (*Prunus triloba*)	All PNW
Pyracantha (*Pyracantha coccinea*)	All PNW
Alpine currant (*Ribes alpinum*)	DV, HD
Golden currant (*Ribes aureum*)	All PNW
Black currant (*Ribes nigrum* 'Consort')	LM, DV, HD
Lilac (*Syringa vulgaris* vars.)	All PNW
Tamarix (*Tamarix* spp.)	LM, DV, HD
Chaste tree (*Vitex agnus-castus*)	
	LM, DV, HD

"The soil around your newly planted shrub should be kept evenly moist for its first two years in the ground. Trees and shrubs will not benefit from lawn watering. They need less frequent, but deeper watering. The minimum amount of water that plants need for survival is three to four heavy, deep irrigations per year. To thrive, they will need six to eight deep irrigations per year."—Michael Bauer, Oregon State University Extension Agent, Central Oregon

SHRUBS FOR GOOD GROUNDCOVERS

Many of us look for groundcovers that could be substitutes for grass—and quickly find that there is not a substitute for grass. Seldom do you find a groundcover plant that can be walked upon, driven across, or that you can drive your tent stakes through. Groundcover plants as defined here are those that you would use to replace a lawn only from the standpoint that you no longer care to mow it! There are many plants that can fit the requirements of a groundcover, but let's consider those that only grow to a foot or so tall and sprawl across territory more than they grow upwards. For more groundcovering plants, consult the groundcover chapter. Here are a few of the shrub types that will fit that category.

Prostrate glossy abelia (*Abelia grandiflora* 'Prostrata')	C, LV, DV
Gold Ring red barberry (*Berberis thunbergii*, var. *atro* 'Golden Ring')	All PNW
Kobold Japanese barberry (*Berberis thunbergii* 'Kobold')	All PNW
Point Reyes ceanothus (*Ceanothus gloriosus*)	C, LV, LM
Rockrose (*Cistus* spp.)	LM, DV
Eichholz cotoneaster (*Cotoneaster dammeri* 'Eichholz')	C, LV, LM, DV
Bearberry cotoneaster (*Cotoneaster dammeri* 'Lowfast')	C, LV, LM, DV
Ground cotoneaster (*Cotoneaster horizontalis perpusillus*)	All PNW
Garland daphne (*Daphne cneorum* 'Ruby Glow')	C, LV, LM, DV
Heather (*Erica*), all species	C, LV, LM
Euonymus (*Euonymus fortunei* vars.)	C, LV, LM, DV
Salal (*Gautheria shallon*)	C, LV, LM
Broom (*Genista pilosa*)	C, LV, LM
Dwarf yaupon holly (*Ilex vomitoria* 'Nana')	C, LV, LM
Juniper (*Juniperus* spp.)	All PNW
Coast leucothoe (*Leucothoe axillaris*)	C, LV, LM
Pheasant berry (*Leycesteria formosa*)	C, LV, LM
Compact Oregon grapeholly (*Mahonia aquifolium* 'Compacta')	C, LV, LM
Creeping mahonia (*Mahonia repens*)	All PNW
Dwarf Little Gem spruce (*Picea abies* 'Little Gem')	All PNW
Prostrate Colorado spruce (*Picea pungens* 'Prostata')	All PNW
Lowboy scarlet firethorn (*Pyracantha coccinea* 'Lowboy')	C, LV, LM, DV
Spirea (*Spiraea × bumalda* vars.)	C, LV, LM, DV
Alpine Japanese spirea (*Spiraea japonica* 'Alpina')	All PNW
Little Princess Japanese spirea (*Spiraea japonica* 'Little Princess')	All PNW
Repandens English yew (*Taxus baccata* 'Repandens')	C, LV, LM
Cole's Prostrate Canadian hemlock (*Tsuga can.* 'Cole's Prostrate')	All PNW
Creeping blueberry (*Vaccinium crassifolium*)	C, LV, LM, DV
David viburnum (*Viburnum davidii*)	C, LV, LM

"Ecologically, salal is an important shrub. Common in a variety of habitats, from bogs to dry, well-drained slopes. Most abundant in evergreen forests. Makes an excellent groundcover. Fruit edible. Low-growing in dry, sunny conditions, much taller in moist, shady conditions."—Linda Robinson, Naturescaping for Clean Rivers

SHRUBS FOR EITHER SUN OR PARTIAL SHADE

This is a good list to have at hand as the landscape matures from a new planting to one that has large shrubs and trees that have blocked out part, if not all of the light. Some shrubs are not particularly choosey about their exposure to sunlight or their livability in shade. This characteristic allows you to repeat textures or plants throughout a landscape design, and gives the landscape a longevity that is often shortened when you use shrubs only adapted to sunlight. Here are a few to try.

Skimmia

Glossy abelia	C, LV, DV
(*Abelia grandiflora* 'Edward Goucher')	
Japanese maple	All PNW
(*Acer palmatum* 'Butterfly')	
Japanese aucuba (*Acuba japonica*)	C, LV, LM
Barberry (*Berberis thunbergii* vars.)	All PNW
Wintergreen barberry (*Berberis julianae*)	All PNW
Butterfly bush (*Buddleia davidii*)	All PNW
Boxwood (*Buxus sempervirens*)	C, LV, LM, DV
Beautyberry (*Callicarpa bodinieri* 'Profusion')	C, LV, LM, DV
Sasanqua camellia (*Camellia sasanqua* vars.)	C, LV, LM, DV
Winter hazel (*Corylopsis* spp.)	C, LV, LM, DV
Irish heath (*Daboecia cantabrica* vars.)	C, LV, LM, DV
Winter daphne (*Daphne odora*)	C, LV, LM
Slender deutzia (*Deutzia gracilis*)	All PNW
Red-veined enkianthus (*Enkianthus campanulatus*)	C, LV, LM, DV
Escallonia (*Escallonia* spp.)	C, LV, LM
Dwarf fothergilla (*Fothergilla gardenii*)	C, LV, LM
Coast silktassel (*Garrya eliptica*)	C, LV
Salal (*Gaultheria shallon*)	C, LV, LM
Hydrangea (*Hydrangea* spp.)	All PNW
Mountain laurel (*Kalmia latifolia* vars.)	All PNW
Japanese rose (*Kerria japonica*)	All PNW
Beautybush (*Kolkwitzia amabilis*)	All PNW
Leucothoe (*Leucothoe* spp.)	C, LV, LM
Mahonia (*Mahonia* spp.)	Varies
Nandina (*Nandina domestica* vars.)	C, LV, LM, DV
Osmanthus (*Osmanthus* spp.)	C, LV, LM
Sweet mock orange (*Philadelphus coronarius*)	All PNW
Japanese pieris (*Pieris* spp. and vars.)	All PNW
Indian hawthorn (*Raphiolepis indica* vars.)	C, LV, LM
Sarcococca (*Sarcococca* spp.)	C, LV, LM
Skimmia (*Skimmia japonica*)	C, LV, LM
Spirea (*Spiraea* spp.)	All PNW
Vaccinium (*Vaccinium* spp.)	C, LV, LM

EVERGREEN SHRUBS FOR BACKGROUND AND SCREENS

Background plants are indispensable in the landscape to help set off or emphasize the beauty, color, interest or form of others. To be effective, the background planting should be tall enough to contrast with the plants you are using in the foreground. Often these plants become a screen that either blocks an undesirable view or somehow changes the microclimate for a part of the garden. Background plants also can provide interest through flowers, fruits, fall color, new color, and so forth. Background screens can also be used to divide garden rooms.

English Holly

Barberry (*Berberis* spp.)	All PNW
Camellia (*Camellia japonica* vars.)	C, LV, LM, DV
Slender hinoki false cypress (*Chamaecyparis obtusa* 'Gracilis')	All PNW
English holly (*Ilex aquifolium*)	C, LV, LM
Hetzi columnar juniper (*Juniperus chinensis* 'Hetzii columnaris')	All PNW
Spartan juniper (*J. chinensis* 'Spartan')	All PNW
Spearmint juniper (*J. chinensis* 'Spearmint')	C, LV, LM, DV
Wintergreen juniper (*J. chinensis* 'Wintergreen')	All PNW
Gray Gleam juniper (*J. scopulorum* 'Gray Gleam')	All PNW
Wichita Blue juniper (*J. scopulorum* 'Wichita Blue')	All PNW
Skyrocket red cedar (*J. virginiana* 'Skyrocket')	All PNW
Japanese privet (*Ligustrum japonicum*)	C, LV, LM, DV
Texan Japanese privet (*Ligustrum japonicum* 'Texanum')	C, LV, LM, DV
Holly leaf osmanthus (*Osmanthus heterophyllus* vars.)	C, LV, LM, DV
Burkwood osmarea (*Osmarea burkwoodi*)	C, LV, LM, DV
English laurel (*Prunus laurocerasus*)	C, LV, LM, DV
Portugal laurel (*Prunus lusitanica*)	C, LV, LM, DV
Photinia (*Photinia fraserii, P. glabra*)	C, LV, LM
Yew (*Taxus* spp.)	C, LV, LM, DV
Irish yew (*Taxus baccata* 'Stricta')	C, LV, LM, DV
Hatfield yew (*Taxus media* 'Hatfieldii')	C, LV, LM, DV
American arborvitae (*Thuja* spp. and vars.)	All PNW
Pyramidal arborvitae (*Thuja occidentalis* 'Fastigiata')	All PNW
Emerald arborvitae (*Thuja occidentalis* 'Emerald')	All PNW
Laurustinus (*Viburnum tinus*)	C, LV, LM, DV
American cranberry bush (*Viburnum trilobum*)	All PNW

 Planting methods have changed during the past few years. For years we have added organic matter like peat moss, compost, or animal manure to the planting hole to enrich the soil and supposedly to improve plant growth. Research, however, shows no benefit from amending the backfill soil. In fact, organic matter added to individual planting holes in clay soil may hold excess moisture around plant roots after irrigation or rainfall. Even in well-drained soils, amendments to the planting hole may cause roots to grow within the hole rather than to the outside soil where it would properly anchor the plant. Now the proper method is to backfill with the same soil that came out of the planting hole.

SHRUBS PRIZED FOR FLOWER AND FOLIAGE ARRANGEMENTS

Here is a list of shrubs that provide interest and beauty in their foliage, flowers, or a combination of both. If you like to create arrangements, you should have some of these in your landscape for your supply. As you become familiar with plants on this list, you will find that those with waxy, tough leaves, Oregon grape for example, will hold up for weeks, while new growth of photinia or flowers of red currant may only last several days. Spring bloomers can best be used in late winter and early spring, just before they open their flowers. Bring branches indoors and let the flowers open in a warm room, then keep the arrangement in fresh water and placed in a cool site for long life of the flowers. One further suggestion: Learn to cut foliage in such a way that the plant still looks good after you have taken an armful of branches. Cut just above a side shoot or healthy bud that will continue the growth after you have taken the your arrangement materials. Don't shear the plants, as that only produces lots of small, stemmy shoots.

Hairy manzanita (*Arctostaphylos columbiana*)	C, LV, LM, DV
Common manzanita (*A. manzanita*)	C, LV, LM, DV
Camellia (*Camellia japonica* vars.)	C, LV, LM, DV
Sasanqua camellia (*C. sasanqua* vars.)	C, LV, LM, DV
Japanese flowering quince (*Chaenomeles japonica* vars.)	All PNW
Wintersweet (*Chimonanthus praecox*)	C, LV
Winter hazel (*Corylopsis* spp.)	All PNW
Winter daphne (*Daphne odora* 'Aureo-marginata')	C, LV, LM
Gilt Edge silverberry (*Elaeagnus ebbingei* 'Gilt Edge')	C, LV, LM
Winged euonymus (*Euonymus alata*)	All PNW
Forsythia (*Forsythia intermedia*)	C, LV, LM, DV
Chinese witch hazel (*Hamamelis mollis*)	C, LV, LM, DV
Double Japanese kerria (*Kerria japonica* 'Pleniflora')	All PNW
Oregon grape (*Mahonia aquifolium*)	All PNW
Heavenly bamboo (*Nandina domestica*)	C, LV, LM, DV
Fraser photinia (*Photinia fraseri*)	C, LV, LM, DV
Lily-of-the-valley shrub [Andromeda] (*Pieris japonica* 'Crispa')	All PNW
Variegated pittosporum (*Pittosporum tobira* 'Variegata')	C, LV, LM
Firethorn (*Pyracantha* spp.)	All PNW
Indian hawthorn (*Raphiolepis indica* vars.)	C, LV, LM
Red-flowering currant (*Ribes sanguineum*)	C, LV, LM, DV
Double bridal wreath spirea (*Spiraea reevesiana*)	C, LV, LM, DV
Lilac (*Syringa vulgaris*)	All PNW
Korean spice viburnum (*Viburnum carlesii*)	All PNW
European cranberry bush viburnum (*Viburnum opulus*)	All PNW
Spring bouquet laurustinus (*Viburnum tinus* 'Spring Bouquet')	C, LV, LM, DV
Weigela (*Weigela florida* vars.)	All PNW

SHRUBS THAT DESERVE WIDER USE

Every year new and different plant materials are introduced to the landscape trade and then to the gardening public. Many of the newer types are hybrids that incorporate some of the best qualities of their parents, and in many cases may have qualities of disease resistance, tolerance to particular growing conditions, unique growth habits, fall or spring foliage color, or surprises in the color of new growth. Here are some that we feel you should look into as you relandscape or develop your new landscape. Some are old standbys that have been forgotten. Others are new.

Blue mist (*Caryopteris clandonensis* 'Dark Knight')	All PNW
Japanese flowering quince (*Chaenomeles japonica* vars.)	All PNW
Redvein enkianthus (*Enkianthus campanulatus*)	C, LV, LM
Escallonia (*Escallonia* spp.)	C, LV, LM
Lace cap hydrangea (*Hydrangea macrophylla* 'Mariesii')	C, LV, LM
English holly (*Ilex aquifolium* dwarf vars.)	C, LV, LM
Mountain laurel (*Kalmia latifolia* vars.)	All PNW
Rainbow drooping leucothoe (*Leucothoe fontanesiana* 'Rainbow')	C, LV, LM, DV
Pheasant berry (*Leycesteria formosa*)	C, LV, LM
Gold and silver flower (*Lonicera japonica* 'Aureo-reticula')	C, LV, LM
Galaxy lily magnolia (*Magnolia liliiflora* 'Galaxy')	C, LV, LM, DV
Burmese mahonia (*Mahonia lomariifolia*)	C, LV, LM
Holly-leaf osmanthus (*Osmanthus heterophyllus* vars.)	C, LV, LM, DV
Dwarf mucronata spruce (*Picea abies* 'Mucronata')	All PNW
Forest Flame Japanese pieris (*Pieris* hybrid 'Forest Flame')	All PNW
Mountain Fire Japanese pieris (*Pieris japonica* 'Mountain Fire')	All PNW
Valley Rose Japanese pieris (*Pieris japonica* 'Valley Rose')	All PNW
Valley Valentine Japanese pieris (*Pieris japonica* 'Valley Valentine')	All PNW
Dwarf white pine (*Pinus strobus* 'Nana')	All PNW
Fragrant sarcococca (*Sarcococca ruscifolia*)	C, LV, LM
Goldflame spirea (*Spiraea bumalda* 'Goldflame')	All PNW
Viburnum (*Viburnum* spp.)	All PNW
Weigela (*Weigela florida* vars.)	All PNW

SHRUBS WITH ORNAMENTAL FRUIT OR BERRIES

A plant that grows ornamental fruits, usually in the form of berries, and that hangs onto them through the summer and fall, gives added interest to the landscape. Especially valued are those that are held through the entire winter. Many of these are also attractive to birds, for an obvious reason, and in fact may be picked free of fruit as our hungry feathered friends spot your berry supply. Some of the fruiting types require a pollinator nearby to assure a berry set; *Viburnum davidii* and *Skimmia* are two that need pollinators somewhere near. The fall is a good time to shop for fruiting types of shrubs because you can see the actual thing.

Strawberry tree (*Arbutus unedo*)	C, LV, LM, DV
Dwarf magallen barberry (*Berberis buxifolia* 'Nana')	All PNW
Mentor barberry (*Berberis mentorensis*)	All PNW

Sparkle Japanese barberry (*Berberis thunbergii* 'Sparkle')	All PNW
Warty barberry (*Berberis verruculosa*)	C, LV, LM, DV
Profusion beautyberry (*Callicarpa bodinieri* 'Profusion')	C, LV, LM, DV
Cornelian cherry (*Cornus mas*)	All PNW
Rockspray cotoneaster (*Cotoneaster horizontalis*)	All PNW
Silverberry (*Elaeagnus pungens*)	C, LV, LM, DV
Winged euonymus (*Euonymus alata*)	All PNW
Greenlane euonymus (*Euonymus fortunei* 'Greenlane')	All PNW
Pineapple guava (*Feijoa sellowiana*)	C, LV
Holly (*Ilex* spp. and vars.)	C, LV, LM
Beautybush (*Kolkwitzia amabilis*)	All PNW
Pheasant berry (*Leycesteria formosa*)	C, LV, LM
Twinberry (*Lonicera involucrata*)	C, LV, LM, DV
Berries Jubilee woodbine (*Lonicera periclymenum* 'Berries Jubilee')	All PNW
Privet honeysuckle (*Lonicera pileata*)	C, LV, LM, DV
Oregon grape (*Mahonia aquifolium*)	All PNW
Nandina (*Nandina domestica*)	C, LV, LM, DV
Pernettya (*Pernettya mucronata*)	C, LV, LM, DV
Firethorn (*Pyracantha* spp. and vars.)	All PNW
Sarcococca (*Sarcococca* spp.)	C, LV, LM
Skimmia (*Skimmia japonica*)	C, LV, LM
Stranvaesia (*Stranvaesia davidiana*)	C, LV, LM, DV
Common snowberry (*Symphoricarpos albus*)	All PNW
Snowberry (*Symphoricarpos chenaultii* vars.)	All PNW
Coralberry (*Symphoricarpos orbiculatus*)	All PNW
Creeping blueberry (*Vaccinium crassifolium*)	C, LV, LM
Laurustinus (*Viburnum tinus*)	C, LV, LM, DV
David viburnum (*Viburnum davidii*)	C, LV, LM

EVERGREEN SHRUBS FOR CLIPPED HEDGE

A better-looking clipped hedge will be the result of carefully selecting the right type of evergreen. Large-leafed plants usually end up with some leaves cut in half, or with a part of the leaf remaining that soon turns brown on the cut edge. One of the main large-leafed types is English laurel (*Prunus laurocerasus*), and it commonly shows cut edges where it is pruned to hedge form. Select smaller-leafed forms for a more "perfect" hedge (and you will find that small-leafed forms do not grow back as quickly as the more robust large-leafed types). When pruning hedges, always prune so the top is narrower than the base. This is to insure that all leaves receive sunlight, and therefore remain healthy and alive. Otherwise, the bottom becomes leggy and bare.

Glossy abelia (*Abelia grandiflora*)	C, LV, DV
Boxwood (*Buxus* spp.)	C, LV, LM, DV
False cypress (*Chamaecyparis lawsonianca* vars.)	C, LV, LM, DV
Escallonia (*Escallonia* spp.)	C, LV, LM, DV
Euonymus (*Euonymus japonica* vars.)	C, LV, LM, DV
Chinese holly (*Ilex cornuta* vars.)	C, LV, LM

Evergreen Shrubs for Clipped Hedge (continued)

Japanese holly (*Ilex crenata* vars.)	All PNW
Yaupon holly (*Ilex vomitoria* vars.)	C, LV, LM, DV
Hetzi columnar juniper (*Juniperus chinensis* 'Hetzii Columnaris')	All PNW
Spearmint juniper (*Juniperus chinensis* 'Spearmint')	C, LV, LM, DV
Gray Gleam juniper (*Juniperus scopulorum* 'Gray Gleam')	All PNW
Skyrocket juniper (*Juniperus virginiana* 'Skyrocket')	All PNW
Japanese privet (*Ligustrum japonicum* vars.)	C, LV, LM, DV
Wax-leaf privet (*Ligustrum texanum*)	C, LV, LM
Delavay osmanthus (*Osmanthus delavayi*)	C, LV, LM, DV
Holly-leaf osmanthus (*Osmanthus heterophyllus*)	C, LV, LM, DV
Japanese yew (*Taxus cuspidata* 'Capitata')	All PNW
Hatfield pyramidal yew (*Taxus media* 'Hatfieldii')	All PNW
Hicks intermediate yew (*Taxus media* 'Hicksii')	All PNW
Arborvitae (*Thuja occidentalis* vars.)	All PNW
Canadian hemlock (*Tsuga canadensis*)	All PNW
Western hemlock (*Tsuga heterophylla*)	C, LV, LM, DV
Mountain hemlock (*Tsuga mertensiana*)	All PNW

SHRUBS FOR TRAINING INTO SMALL TREES

Some shrubs have the ability to reach fifteen or twenty feet in height, and often with a similar spread. And if they have been badly selected or sited, they become a constant pruning problem as you attempt to subdue them. Why not train them into small trees? The shrubs in this list are those we suggest selecting for use in the landscape where a small tree would work. Also, check the small tree list in the tree chapter for more ideas.

Strawberry tree (*Arbutus unedo*)	C, LV, LM, DV
Camellia (*Camellia* spp.)	C, LV, LM
Franchet cotoneaster (*Cotoneaster franchetii*)	All PNW
Red escallonia (*Escallonia rubra*)	C, LV
Coast silktassel (*Garrya elliptica*)	C, LV, LM, DV
English holly (*Ilex aquifolium*)	C, LV, LM, DV
Blue Prince hybrid holly (*Ilex meserveae* 'Blue Prince')	All PNW
Blue Princess hybrid holly (*I. meserveae* 'Blue Princess')	All PNW
Nellie Stevens holly (*I.* 'Nellie R. Stevens')	C, LV
Sweet bay (*Laurus nobilis*)	C, LV
Wax leaf privet (*Ligustrum japonicum*)	C, LV, LM, DV
Dark pink hybrid magnolia (*Magnolia stellata* 'Dark Pink')	All PNW
Sweet olive (*Osmanthus fragrans*)	C, LV
Photinia (*Photinia* spp.)	C, LV, LM, DV
English laurel (*Prunus laurocerasus*)	C, LV, LM, DV
Portugal laurel (*Prunus lusitanica*)	C, LV, LM, DV
Majestic Beauty Indian hawthorn (*Raphiolepis* 'Majestic Beauty')	C, LV, LM
Staghorn sumac (*Rhus typhina*)	All PNW
Cutleaf staghorn sumac (*Rhus typhina* 'Laciniata')	All PNW
Common snowball (*Viburnum opulus* 'Sterile')	All PNW

"Often, when a landscape is nearing maturity, a major problem involves deciding how to handle overgrown and crowded shrubbery. Sometimes it is best to take a chain saw and remove the mass of trunks, twigs, and branches. However, with a little patience and planning, many can be rejuvenated. Spring or early summer are the best times for rejuvenation. Start by removing dead branches, thin those remaining, head back long limbs to force dormant buds to grow. As growth develops during the summer and the following year, train the new growth into the form desired."—Jorge Garcia, Latin Landscapes, Portland

SHRUBS FOR ESPALIER

The art of espalier is one of pruning and training to create a particular effect with plant material. For this to work, you must have a picture in mind of what you want to create and the right plant material. Common examples are apple trees on dwarf rootstocks which can give you fruit production along a fence, or firethorn espaliered against a garage wall to give you cordons of beautiful red berries along the horizontal limbs. Many different sorts of woody plants can be espaliered; all it takes is a little extra effort.

Basically, espaliers are formed by pruning and training the trunks and limbs and fastening them to a support. Nails, wire, hooks, and fishing line are often the holders of plant materials, so use whatever you need to get the form you want. Espaliers can be formal, say to look like a candelabra, or informal, where the natural form of the plant is used to define the shape and twigs and limbs are removed as needed to maintain that form. If you are planning to include espalier as a part of your landscape, we suggest you find a book that outlines the procedures and gives instructions. Some of the plants listed include trees, such as cedars, but as espaliers they can be kept low and become more shrublike in their growth.

Sasanqua camellia (*Camellia sasanqua*)	C, LV, LM, DV
Weeping blue atlas cedar (*Cedrus atlantica* 'Glauca Pendula')	C, LV, LM, DV
Weeping deodar cedar (*Cedrus deodara* 'Pendula')	C, LV, LM
Flowering quince (*Chaenomeles* vars.)	All PNW
Peking cotoneaster (*Cotoneaster acutifolius*)	All PNW
Cotoneaster (*Cotoneaster lacteus, C. parneyi*)	C, LV, LM, DV
Escallonia (*Escallonia* spp. and vars.)	C, LV, LM
Burning bush euonymus (*Euonymus alata*)	All PNW
Euonymus (*Euonymus fortunei* vars.)	All PNW
Pineapple guava (*Feijoa sellowiana*)	C, LV
Forsythia (*Forsythia intermedia*)	C, LV, LM, DV
Privet honeysuckle (*Lonicera pileata*)	C, LV, LM, DV
African fern pine (*Podocarpus gracilior*)	C, LV, LM
Southern yew pine (*Podocarpus macrophyllus*)	C, LV, LM
Flowering pomegranate (*Punica granatum* 'Double Red')	All PNW
Firethorn (*Pyracantha coccinea, P. fortuneana*)	All PNW
Narrow-leaf firethorn (*Pyracantha angustifolia*)	All PNW
Sarcococca (*Sarcococca ruscifolia*)	C, LV, LM, DV
Doublefile viburnum (*Viburnum plicatum tomentosum*)	All PNW

SHRUBS FOR CONTAINERS

Container gardening is a very popular method for creating portable landscapes. There is no reason that the small-space gardener should miss out on the special features that some shrubs can offer. Larger garden areas can use groups of containerized shrubs to create backdrops for annuals and perennials or develop the illusion of small garden rooms. The following shrubs can be used as specimens, accents for texture, or basic garden room dividers. Most could be planted alone in a large whiskey-barrel-size container. Groundcovers can be added at the base of many for contrast. Containers require extra care and watering during warm summer months and may need winter protection, depending on your climate zone.

Glossy abelia (*Abelia grandiflora*)	C, LV, DV
Edward Goucher abelia (*Abelia grandiflora* 'Edward Goucher')	C, LV, DV
Japanese aucuba (*Aucuba japonica* vars.)	C, LV, LM
Azaleas (*Azaleas* var.)	C, LV, LM
Japanese barberry (*Berberis thunbergii*)	All PNW
Common boxwood (*Buxus sempervirens*)	C, LV, LM, DV
Flowering quince (*Chaenomeles* spp.)	All PNW
Parney cotoneaster (*Cotoneaster lacteus*)	C, LV, LM, DV
Silverberry (*Elaeagnus pungens*)	C, LV, LM
Hardy fuchsia (*Fuchsia magellanica*)	C, LV, LM, DV
Rose of Sharon (*Hibiscus* var.)	All PNW
Big-leaf hydrangea (*Hydrangea macrophylla*)	C, LV LM, DV
Dwarf English holly (*Ilex* spp.)	C, LV, LM, DV
Junipers (*Juniperus* spp.)	All PNW
Oregon grape (*Mahonia* spp.)	All PNW
Dwarf mugo pine (*Pinus mugo mugo*)	All PNW
Potentilla (*Potentilla fruiticosa* var.)	All PNW
Dwarf rhododendrons (*Rhododendrons* var.)	All PNW
Spireas (*Spiraea* spp.)	All PNW
Spring Bouquet viburnum (*Viburnum tinus* 'Spring Bouquet')	C, LV, LM, DV

 Smaller shrubs, particularly the evergreen sorts, have a special place in container gardens. In large planters or in groupings of containers, woody plants can impart a feeling of permanence and solidarity that is not achievable with herbaceous and/or annual plants. The often dramatic effects that they can provide make them well worth the extra care needed to give winter protection to roots and tops.

LOW SHRUBS THAT WON'T HIDE PICTURE WINDOWS

The problem with old landscapes is that often you can no longer see the house, usually because some poor selections were made when the landscape was first planted. A popular educational program that Master Gardeners in Oregon deliver is called "Landscaping for Home Security." A major emphasis of this program is that of selecting the right plants, or finding a way to trim the plant so you can see windows and doors without sacrificing the beauty or utility of the plant. This list will be useful to you as you are either beginning your landscape, or rebuilding it when you yank out those overgrown plants that keep you from seeing out. This list was built on the premise that the picture window is the most likely to be overgrown, thus the plants in this list mature at eighteen to thirty-six inches. Also, we have listed only selected plants from many that are available and effective, so be prepared to search out the types listed and see what their cousins look like. You might like them better than we did.

Scotch heather (*Calluna vulgaris* selected vars.)	C, LV, LM, DV
Compact bronze hinoki cypress (*Chamaecyparis obtusa* 'Pygmaea Aurescens')	All PNW
Rockrose (*Cistus corbariensis*)	LM, DV
Coral beauty cotoneaster (*Cotoneaster dammeri* 'Coral Beauty')	All PNW
Garland daphne (*Daphne cneorum*)	C, LV, LM, DV
Slender deutzia (*Deutzia gracilis*)	All PNW
Heather (*Erica* selected spp. and vars.)	C, LV, LM, DV
Ivory Jade euonymus (*Euonymus fortunei* 'Ivory Jade')	All PNW
Woadwaxen (*Genista* spp.)	C, LV, LM, DV
Pink Elf hydrangea (*Hydrangea macrophylla* 'Pink Elf')	C, LV, LM, DV
Japanese holly (*Ilex crenata* vars.)	C, LV, LM, DV
Blue Pacific shore juniper (*Juniperus conferta* 'Blue Pacific')	All PNW
Junipers (selected *Juniperus sabina* vars.)	All PNW
Blue Star juniper (*Juniperus squamata* 'Blue Star')	All PNW
Drooping leucothoe (*Leucothoe fontanesiana* 'Rainbow')	C, LV, LM, DV
Longleaf mahonia (*Mahonia nervosa*)	C, LV, LM, DV
Dwarf heavenly bamboo (*Nandina domestica*, dwarf vars.)	C, LV, LM, DV
Pernettya (*Pernettya mucronata*)	C, LV, LM, DV
Little Gem spruce (*Picea abies* 'Little Gem')	All PNW
Nest spruce (*Picea abies* 'Nidiformis')	All PNW
Blue nest spruce (*Picea mariana* 'Nana')	All PNW
Dwarf globe blue spruce (*Picea pungens* 'Globosa')	All PNW
Cinquefoil (*Potentilla fruticosa* 'Klondike')	All PNW
Red ace cinquefoil (*P. fruticosa* 'Red Ace')	All PNW
Sutter's gold cinquefoil (*P. fruticosa* 'Sutter's Gold')	All PNW
Sweet box (*Sarcococca hookerana humilis*)	C, LV, LM, DV
Spirea (*Spiraea bumalda*, selected vars.)	All PNW
Davids viburnum (*Viburnum davidii*)	C, LV, LM, DV
Dwarf European cranberry bush (*Viburnum opulus* 'Nanum')	All PNW

Deutzia

DECIDUOUS SHRUBS WITH GOOD FALL COLOR

Evergreen shrubs are the mainstays of most yards, but they do not generally give much seasonal color, other than varying shades of green. Some deciduous shrubs become the beacons of the plant world when the autumn season approaches. Fall coloration will vary with the climatic factors that you experience in your particular location. Some of the best colors come when we have dry summers with little rain. Here are a few of the more reliable deciduous shrubs for fall color.

Staghorn
Sumac

Deciduous Shrubs with Good Fall Color (continued)
Red to purple or maroon

Red chokecherry (*Aronia arbutifolia*)	LV, LM, DV, HD
Disanthus (*Disanthus cercidifolius*)	C, LV, LM, DV
Winged euonymus (*Euonymus alata*)	All PNW
Doublefile viburnum (*Viburnum plicatum tomentosum*)	C, LV, LM
Zenobia (*Zenobia pulverulenta*)	C, LV, LM, DV

Red to Orange

Serviceberry (*Amelanchier* × *grandiflora*)	LV, LM, DV, HD
Red vein enkianthus (*Enkianthus campanulatus*)	C, LV, LM
Fothergilla (*Fothergilla gardenii, F. major*)	C, LV, LM
Witch hazel (*Hamamelis* spp.)	C, LV, LM, DV
Fragrant sumac (*Rhus aromatica*)	All PNW
Flameleaf sumac (*Rhus copallina*)	All PNW
Smooth sumac (*Rhus glabra*)	All PNW
Staghorn sumac (*Rhus typhina*)	All PNW
Linden viburnum (*Viburnum dilatatum*)	C, LV, LM, DV
European cranberry bush (*Viburnum opulus* 'Nanum')	All PNW
Common snowball (*Viburnum opulus* 'Roseum')	All PNW

Yellow

Rosa rugosa	LV, LM, DV, HD
Virginia rose (*Rosa virginiana*)	LV, LM, DV, HD
Blueberry (*Vaccinium corymbosum*)	C, LV, LM

"The witch hazel 'Sandra,' has tiny flowers, but excellent orange blossom fragrance, and a fall color more red than other witch hazels."—Steve Carruthers, landscape designer, Portland, Oregon

A Sampler of Shrubs for Interest in Each Season

Seasonal considerations are critical to making your landscape interesting. The following list of shrubs are grouped by season. Some plants have showy flowers, some have beautiful fall color or berries that persist into winter, some offer surprises of interesting silhouettes or bark color. Your landscape design should reflect the best that each season has to offer. A helpful hint for fall and winter interest is to go inside and look out. Place plants so that you can see them from inside when the weather is cold or rainy and place fragrant plants where you will be near enough to enjoy them.

Spring to Early Summer	Interesting Feature	Region
Japanese camellia (*Camellia japonica*)	Flowers	C, LV, LM
Flowering quince (*Chaenomeles* spp.)	Flowers	All PNW
Rockrose (*Cistus* spp.)	Flowers	LM, DV
Warminster broom (*Cytisus praecox*)	Flowers	C, LV, LM, DV
Garland daphne (*Daphne cneorum*)	Flowers, Fragrance	C, LV, LM, DV
Red-veined enkianthus (*Enkianthus campanulatus*)	Flowers	C, LV, LM, DV
Heather (*Erica* spp.)	Flowers	C, LV, LM, DV

Forsythia (*Forsythia* spp.)	Flowers	All PNW
Lydia broom (*Genista lydia*)	Flowers	C, LV, LM, DV
Mountain laurel (*Kalmia latifolia*)	Flowers	All PNW
Japanese kerria (*Kerria japonica*)	Flowers	All PNW
Mock orange (*Philadelphus coronarius*)	Flowers, Fragrance	All PNW
Photinia (*Photinia fraseri*)	New leaves	C, LV, LM, DV
Indian hawthorn (*Raphiolepis indica* vars.)	Flowers	C, LV, LM
Rhododendrons and azaleas	Flowers, Foliage	All PNW
Flowering currant (*Ribes odoratum*)	Flowers, Fragrance	All PNW
Red flowering currant (*Ribes sanguineum*)	Flowers	C, LV, LM, DV
Sarcococca (*Sarcococca ruscifolia*)	Fragrance	C, LV, LM, DV
Goldflame spirea (*Spiraea bumalda* 'Goldflame')	Foliage	All PNW
Bridal wreath spirea (*Spiraea prunifolia*)	Flowers	All PNW
Common lilac (*Syringa vulgaris*)	Flowers	All PNW
Viburnums (*Viburnum* spp.)	Flowers	C, LV, LM, DV

Summer to Early Fall	**Interesting Feature**	**Region**
Glossy abelia (*Abelia grandiflora* 'Edward Goucher')	Flowers	C, LV, DV
Strawberry tree (*Arbutus unedo* 'Compacta')	Fruit	C, LV, LM, DV
Golden Japanese barberry (*Berberis thunbergii* 'Aurea')	Foliage	All PNW
Crimson red barberry (*Berberis thunbergii* 'Crimson Pygmy')	Foliage	All PNW
Butterfly bush (*Buddleia davidii*)	Flowers	All PNW
Scotch heather (*Calluna* spp.)	Flowers	C, LV, LM, DV
Carolina allspice (*Calycanthus floridus*)	Fragrance	All PNW
Blue mist (*Caryopteris clandonensis* 'Dark Knight')	Flowers	All PNW
Sweet pepperbush (*Clethra alnifolia*)	Fragrance	C, LV, LM, DV
Irish heath (*Daboecia cantabrica*)	Flowers	C, LV, LM, DV
Heather (*Erica* spp.)	Flowers	C, LV, LM, DV
Escallonia (*Escallonia* spp.)	Flowers	C, LV, LM, DV
Autumn Glory veronica (*Hebe* 'Autumn Glory')	Flowers	C, LV, LM
Garden hydrangea (*Hydrangea macrophylla*)	Flowers	C, LV, LM, DV
Peegee hydrangea (*Hydrangea paniculata*)	Flowers	All PNW
Oakleaf hydrangea (*Hydrangea quercifolia*)	Flowers	All PNW
Osmanthus (*Osmanthus heterophyllus*)	Fragrance	C, LV, LM, DV
Bush cinquefoil (*Potentilla fruiticosa* var.)	Flowers	All PNW
Weigelia (*Weigelia* spp.)	Flowers	All PNW
Yucca (*Yucca* spp.)	Flowers	All PNW

Fall	**Interesting Feature**	**Region**
Glossy abelia (*Abelia grandiflora* vars.)	Flowers	C, LV, DV

Japanese barberry (*Berberis* spp.)	Foliage	All PNW
Profusion beautyberry (*Callicarpa bodinieri* 'Profusion')	Berries	C, LV, LM, DV
Scotch heather (*Calluna* spp.)	Flowers	C, LV, LM, DV
Cotoneaster (*Cotoneaster* spp.)	Berries	C, LV, LM, DV
Disanthus (*Disanthus cercidifolius*)	Foliage	C, LV, LM, DV
Enkianthus (*Enkianthus campanulatus*)	Foliage	C, LV, LM, DV
Winged euonymus (*Euonymus alata*)	Foliage	All PNW
Big-leaf hydrangea (*Hydrangea macrophylla*)	Flowers	C, LV, LM, DV
Peegee hydrangea (*Hydrangea paniculata*)	Foliage	All PNW
Heavenly bamboo (*Nandina domestica*)	Berries	C, LV, LM, DV
Pernettya (*Pernettya mucronata*)	Berries	C, LV, LM, DV
Firethorn (*Pyracantha* spp.)	Berries	All PNW
Sarcococca (*Sarcococca hookerana humilis*)	Berries	C, LV, LM, DV
Japanese skimmia (*Skimmia japonica*)	Berries (female)	C, LV, LM
Stranvaesia (*Stranvaesia davidiana*)	Berries, Foliage	C, LV, LM, DV
Pink Dawn viburnum (*Viburnum bodnantense* 'Pink Dawn')	Flowers, Fragrance	C, LV, LM, DV
European cranberry bush (*Viburnum opulus*)	Foliage, Berries	All PNW
Common snowball (*Viburnum opulus* 'Roseum')	Berries	All PNW

Winter to Early Spring	**Interesting Feature**	**Region**
Sasanqua camellia (*Camellia sasanqua* vars.)	Flowers	C, LV, LM, DV
Wintersweet (*Chimonanthus praecox*)	Fragrance	C, LV, LM, DV
Red osier dogwood (*Cornus stolonifera*)	Twigs	All PNW
Cotoneaster (*Cotoneaster* spp.)	Berries	C, LV, LM, DV
February daphne (*Daphne mezereum*)	Flowers, Fragrance	All PNW
Winter daphne (*Daphne odora*)	Flowers, Fragrance	C, LV, LM, DV
Chinese witch hazel (*Hamamelis mollis*)	Flowers	C, LV, LM, DV
Common witch hazel (*Hamamelis virginiana*)	Flowers	All PNW
English holly (*Ilex aquifolium*)	Berries	C, LV, LM, DV
Winter jasmine (*Jasminum nudiflorum*)	Flowers	C, LV, LM, DV
Leucothoe (*Leucothoe* 'Girard's Rainbow')	Foliage	C, LV, LM
Star magnolia (*Magnolia stellata*)	Flowers	All PNW
Burmese mahonia (*Mahonia lomariifolia*)	Flowers	C, LV, LM
Dwarf nandina (*Nandina domestica* vars.)	Foliage	C, LV, LM, DV
Dwarf purple osier willow (*Salix purpurea* 'Gracilis')	Twigs	All PNW
Snowberry (*Symphoricarpos albus*)	Berries	All PNW
Coral berry (*Symphoricarpos orbiculatus*)	Berries	All PNW
David viburnum (*Viburnum davidii*)	Berries	C, LV, LM, DV

RHODODENDRONS
AND AZALEAS

There are entire books written about the hundreds of varieties of rhododendrons and azaleas available. The lists you will find here are simply to give you some ideas and to get you started. Rhododendrons have an amazing range of hardiness, whereas the azaleas are often lost when exposed to several days of 20 degree F temperatures. Check with your local nurseries for variety availability and for hardiness of whatever plant you are considering.

When using rhododendrons and azaleas in the landscape, keep in mind that they are shallow-rooted plants, much more so than most other woody plants. They need well-drained soils, and will do best in soils that are fertile and amended with lots of well-rotted organic material. Mulches also help these plants to establish themselves, serving to minimize soil temperature extremes and helping to keep soil moisture intact. Most varieties of these plants do well in partial shade. Few do well in full, hot, afternoon sun, or in areas where they receive reflected heat from walls or other structures. Place them where they will be protected from winter winds, which can cause leaf "burning" by dehydrating the foliage during periods of dry cold.

While the tendency is to select a rhododendron or azalea when it is in bloom, take the time to study the plant to see what other characteristics it has to make it interesting the rest of the year. These plants generally bloom for a month or so in mid to late spring. Then, for the next eleven months you have the rest of the plant to look at. Consider its form, shape, interesting leaves, and other characteristics to make sure the plant will be a valuable addition to the year-long garden.

The root weevil list is one designed to guide you in selecting plants that have some resistance to, or tolerance of, the leading insect pests of rhododendrons and azaleas. When selecting any plant for the garden, consider what sort of problems to expect, and also search for those plants that have some natural resistance to the pests that are a constant worry.

RHODODENDRONS AND AZALEAS FOR GROUNDCOVER

Some of the low-growing and spreading types of evergreen azaleas (a) and rhododendrons (r) can be used in the landscape as groundcovers. They bloom vividly from midspring until early summer, depending on your choice of types and varieties. When planning your landscape to use these plants, keep in mind that they are very shallowly rooted and should be mulched to keep the roots damp during the dry summer.

Coral Bells
Azalea

Bow Bells (r)
Cilpinense (r)
Ernie Dee (r)
Gumpo Pink (a)
Hini Crimson (a)
Mother Greer (r)
Purple Gem (r)
Small Gem (r)

Carmen (r)
Coral Bells (a)
Flame Creeper (a)
Gumpo White (a)
Impeditum (r)
Ptarmigan (r)
R. keiskei (r)
Snow Lady (r)

RHODODENDRONS AND AZALEAS THAT ARE TALL

Some rhododendrons and azaleas mature at heights of more than six feet. Do not plant these in front of your picture window, unless you plan to peek through the trunks or to hide the window permanently. These plants need to be used in background plantings, to accent a particular place in the garden, or be planted to provide a barrier of flowers (in late spring) and foliage. Pruning is not the answer to a badly placed plant. Plan ahead and make sure you know how tall and wide the plant will become in a reasonable length of time, and site it so you don't have to worry about keeping it in bounds that are less than the normal growth parameters.

Aladdin (r)
Antoon Van Welie (r)
Cannon's Double (a)
Fastuosum Plenum (r)
Lem's Monarch (r)
Loderi King George (r)
President Lincoln (r)
R. occidentale (a)
Sappho (r)
Sunset Pink (a)
White Grandeur (a)

Anna Rose Whitney (r)
Autumn Gold (r)
Cynthia (r)
Golden Lights (a)
Loderi hybrids (r)
Mrs. G. W. Leak (r)
R. catawbiense 'Album' (r)
R. Schlippenbachii (a)
Stewartsonian (a)
Taurus (r)

Take the time to visit local garden stores, herbariums, parks, and other places where lots of rhododendrons and azaleas are used in the landscape, and make a selection after observing many plants. These will be long-lived members of your landscape if you select wisely, short term vagabonds if you don't.

RHODODENDRONS THAT SHOW RESISTANCE TO ROOT WEEVIL DAMAGE

People who try to grow rhodys in the Pacific Northwest know that the major problem, once they have overcome the climatic concerns and corrected the soil to an acid pH, are root weevils. The adult weevil notches the outer margins of leaves, usually beginning in late spring, then the larvae form girdles the trunk and upper root system during the winter. Between the two stages of this pest's cycle, a susceptible rhododendron will look tattered and torn or die. If your garden seems to be a haven for this insect pest, try some of these varieties that have been found through careful research to not be as tasty to the weevil.

Hybrid	Bloom color	Rating*
PJM	Pink	100
Jock	Pink	92
Sapphire	Blue	90
Rose Elf	White, blushed violet/pink	89
Cilipinense	White	88
Lucky Strike	Salmon pink	83
Exbury Naomi	Lilac with yellow tinge	81
Virginia Richards	Yellow, crimson blotch	81
Cowslip	Cream, pink	80
Luscombei	Rose pink	80
Vanessa	Pink	80
Oceanlake	Violet blue	80
Dora Amateis	White, lightly spotted green	79
Crest	Yellow	79
Rainbow	Carmine-pink	76
Point Defiance	Pink	76
Naomi	Pink	76
Pilgrim	Rich pink	76
Letty Edwards	Yellow	76
Odee Wright	Yellow	76
Moonstone	Yellow	73
Lady Clementine Mitford	Pink	72
Candi	Bright rose	72
Graf Zeppelin	Bright pink	71
Snow Lady	Pure white	71
Loderi Pink Diamond	Delicate pink	71
Faggatter's favorite	Cream with pink	70

*The higher the number the less feeding damage is expected. A rating of 100 indicates complete resistance.

 Control of the root weevil consists of several approaches, none of which seem to be entirely effective. That is why we have listed those above whose inherent flavors repel the pest. For those of you who already have weevil-ridden plants, spray in mid to late spring with acephate or other recommended pesticides. This is to try to get rid of the adults, which chew notches in the edges of leaves. Then, in early fall, apply a parasitic nematode (available at most garden stores and sold under several brand names) to the soil where you suspect the weevil larvae will be hatching. Then, in late winter reapply nematodes or apply an insecticide drench to the root area of your susceptible rhododendrons and azaleas. Good luck!

RHODODENDRONS AND AZALEAS FOR COLDEST REGIONS

Both of these plants have members that are completely hardy to some of the coldest winters in the United States. Called "H-1 Varieties" in most nursery catalogues, there are more than forty varieties that can live through winters where the temperatures drop as low as -25 degrees F. Treat these with respect and plant them in a spot that will protect them from freezing winds, which are so destructive to their foliage, and in soils that are slightly on the acid side of the pH scale. If you do that for them, you will enjoy them forever.

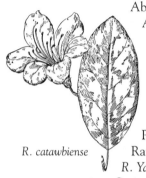

R. catawbiense

Abraham Lincoln (r)
Apricot Surprise (a)
Casanova (r)
Chesapeake (r)
Exbury hybrids (a)
Henry's Red (r)
Lodestar White (r)
Orchid Lights (a)
PJM (r)
Ramapo (r)
R. Yakushimanum (r)
Spring Dawn (r)

America (r)
April Rose (r)
Catawbiense Grandiflorum (r)
English Roseum (r)
Ghent hybrids (a)
Mollis hybrids (a)
Nova Zembla (r)
Pioneer (r)
Purple Gem (r)
R. catawbiense 'Album' (r)
Rosy Lights (a)
White Lights (a)

"I would like to convince many of you who may feel left out that you can grow rhododendrons in your climate. With careful moisture control, sufficient light, mulching, and proper protection, some species and various new hybrids can be grown in rather rugged parts of the country. An oasis of climate can be created artificially, making possible the use of rhododendrons. You can join the increasing number of rhododendron enthusiasts."—Ted Van Veen, Van Veen Nursery, Portland

RHODODENDRONS AND AZALEAS WITH FRAGRANT BLOOMS

Not many of the rhododendrons or azaleas are fragrant; however, we have pulled together a list from the nurserymen who grow these lovely plants, and we think you will find some varieties that fit nicely into your planned landscape. Plant them where you can enjoy their fragrance as you walk by or as you pause to admire their blossoms.

Beaufort (r)
Countess of Haddington (r)
Exbury hybrids (some)(a)
Fragrantissimum (r)
Ignatius Sargent (r)
Loderi King George (r)
Martha Issacson (r)
Mother of Pearl (r)
Naomi (r)

Cadis (r)
Dora Amateis (r)
Exbury Parade (a)
Gold Western Azalea (a)
Lodauric (r)
Loder's White (r)
Mission Bells (r)
Mrs. A. T. de LaMare (r)
Pink and Sweet (a)

Poukhanense (a)

R. *Fortunei* (r)

R. *occidentale* (a)

Snow Lady (r)

R. *Calophytum* (r)

R. *luteum* (a)

Sapphire (r)

Viscosum hybrids (a)

"Even though many varieties of rhododendrons and azaleas are extremely hardy and can be planted in the higher and colder gardening areas of this region, they do not tolerate alkaline soils. If your soil is neutral in reaction (pH 7) or on the alkaline side, incorporate copious amounts of peat moss and other acid-producing organic material into the planting area and follow with an annual application of garden sulfur to maintain the desired, slightly acidic, soil reaction."—Gray Thompson, Extension Agent Emeritus, Milwaukie, Oregon

TED VAN VEEN'S SELECTED LIST

Ted Van Veen, noted author of rhododendron books, speaker, and owner-operator of Van Veen Nursery, provided this list. He calls it "a collection of twenty-five rhododendrons suitable for the milder climates of Pacific Northwest gardens, selected for variety of color and growth habit, and some with unique plant character."

Anah Kruschke	Lavender blue	Heat and sun tolerant
Anna Rose Whitney	Rose pink	Heat tolerant
Autumn Gold	Salmon pink, orange center	Light shade
Crater Lake	Sapphire blue	Small leaves
Cynthia	Rosy red	Heat and sun tolerant
Daphnoides	Light purple	Unusual foliage
Dora Amateis	White	Aromatic foliage
Jean Marie de Montague	Scarlet red	Most popular red
Jingle Bells	Orange/yellow, red throat	Low spreading
Lem's Monarch	Pink	Large leaves
Loder's White	White	Heavy flowering
Mardi Gras	Soft pink to blush white	Heat tolerant
Mist Maiden	White	Under leaf velvety
Mrs. Furnivall	Pink	Highly prized for bloom
Noyo Brave	Bright pink	Handsome foliage
Odee Wright	Bright yellow	Waxy dark green leaves
PJM	Lavender pink	Aromatic leaves
Polynesian Sunset	Orange to salmon	Wide spreading
Purple Splendour	Dark purple	Pointed leaves
Scarlet Wonder	Bright scarlet red	Compact and spreading
Shamrock	Yellow tinged green	Semi-dwarf spreader
Taurus	Bright red	Tall stately growth
Tiana	White, burgundy spotted	Similar to Sappho
Unique	Light yellow, pink flush	Round compact
Vulcan	Fire-red	Spreader

RHODODENDRONS AND AZALEAS FOR HOT AREAS

A lot of rhododendrons and a few azaleas will take considerable heat. However, they will only survive if you take care of other aspects of plant care, such as watering, mulching, and protecting against wind and direct and/or reflected afternoon sunshine. With a little extra care, these plants can become a part of your yard. The varieties listed below will be the more hardy types.

Albert Close (r)	Anah Kruschke (r)
Anna Rose Whitney (r)	Blue Peter (r)
Bravo (r)	Butterfly (r)
Caroline (r)	Catawbiense Album (r)
Chionoides (r)	Cunningham's Blush (r)
Cynthia (r)	Daphnoides (r)
Dora Amateis (r)	Fastuosum Flore Pleno (r)
Gomer Waterer (r)	Hallelujah (r)
Jean Marie de Montague (r)	Lord Roberts (r)
Madonna (a)	Mardi Gras (r)
Mollis vars. (a)	Nova Zembla (r)
PJM (r)	Trilby (r)

"When we list heat-tolerant rhodys, we mean warm climates, not necessarily in sun. The amount of sun they will stand depends upon the climate in which you live. In no case do we mean the south side of a wall in Arizona."—Harold Greer, Greer Gardens, Eugene, Oregon

RHODODENDRONS AND AZALEAS FOR ATTRACTIVE OR UNUSUAL FOLIAGE

The large flowering clusters and massed beauty are not the only enchanting parts of these plants. Many of them have foliage that is different from other plants. Some have the underside of their leaves covered with a mass of feltlike hairs called *indumentum*. The indumentum ranges in color from tan to brown and yellow. Or the foliage of some will be aromatic, thus giving the garden an unexpected fragrance. Here are some that will surprise you with indumentum or fragrance.

Atroflo (r)	Bow Bells (r)
Daphnoides (r)	Dora Amateis (aromatic)(r)
Fabia (r)	Good Times (a)
Great Lakes (r)	Leo (r)
May Day (r)	Mist Maiden (r)
Noyo Brave (r)	Odee Wright (r)
PJM (aromatic)(r)	*R. Carolinianum* (r)
R. Fictolacteum (r)	*R. Keleticum* (aromatic)(r)
Scarlet Wonder (r)	Sherwood Red (a)
Sir Charles Lemon (r)	White Dwarf (a)

RHODODENDRONS AND AZALEAS FOR COMPACT GROWTH

Some plants must be sheared frequently to make them compact. Others grow in a manner that shows them off as being compact sorts of plants. If the gardener can select the compact types to use in those parts of the garden that demand a controlled plant growth, pruning and maintenance chores will be diminished. Here are a few to get you started.

Dora Amateis (r)	Girard's Pink (a)
Gumpo (a)	Hi Gasa (a)
Hino-crimson (a)	Hinodegiri (a)
Impeditum (r)	Lorna (a)
Mardi Gras (r)	Mist Maiden (r)
Mrs. Furnival (r)	Molly Ann (r)
Noyo Brave (r)	Patty Bee (r)
Ramapo (r)	Red Bird (a)
Rosamundi (r)	Scarlet Wonder (r)
Unique (r)	Ward's Ruby (a)

The optimum single time for pruning a rhododendron or azalea is immediately after blooming. At that time you can prune back the terminal shoots to visible side buds, with assurance that the plant will have another set of blooms for the next spring. If you prune before the plants bloom, you lose that year's flowers. If you prune too late it may take another couple of years to make growth and set a flower bud.

SAMPLER OF RHODODENDRONS AND AZALEAS IN ORDER OF BLOOM

It is possible to have rhododendrons and/or azaleas in bloom from mid-spring to nearly mid-summer by selecting varieties with different blooming times. The following list is filled with types that bloom early, mid and late season. The entire flowering season can be made as long as three months by utilizing different varieties with overlapping blooming periods. There is such a wide array of both of these plants that the beginning gardener will be overwhelmed. Don't select only on the basis of flower, but consider also the growing habit, the foliage type, the color and shape of the leaves, and the overall form of the bush. Much of the information in this list came from Ted Van Veen and Harold Greer, both rhododendron growers and hybridizers for many years.

Very early (late February and through March)

Bric-a-brac (r)	Cheer (r)
Christmas Cheer (r)	Cilpinense (r)
Conemaugh (r)	Coral Bells (a)
Cornubia (r)	Else Frye (r)
Praecox (r)	Rosamundi (r)

Early

Anchorite (a)	Blue Diamond (r)
Blue Tit (r)	Cornubia (r)

Early (continued)

Hinodegiri (a)

Johanna (a)

PJM (r)

R. Moupinense (r)

Sherwood Red (a)

Hino Crimson (a)

Pioneer (r)

Purple Splendor (a)

Rose Greeley (a)

White Dwarf (a)

Midseason

Bow Bells (r)

Dora Amateis (r)

Everest (a)

Girard's Gomer Waterer (r)

Helen Close (a)

Hexe (a)

Louise Gable (a)

Moonstone (r)

Purple Gem (r)

Red Ruffles (a)

Rosaflora (a)

Sherwood Red (a)

Sunset Pink (a)

Unique (r)

Coral Bells (a)

Elsie Lee (a)

Hot Shot (a)

Hahn's Red (a)

Holland (a)

Jean Marie de Montague (r)

Mimi (a)

Nova Zembla (r)

Ramapo (r)

Rocket (r)

Sherwood Orchid (a)

Snow (a)

Sweet Briar (a)

Late

Aladdin (r)

Autumn Gold (r)

Cunningham's Blush (r)

Golden Lights (a)

Gumpo White (a)

Irene Koster (a)

Old Copper (r)

Polar Bear (r)

Summer Snow (r)

Trilby (r)

Vulcan (r)

Wilsoni (r)

Witchery (r)

Angelo (r)

Cannon's Double (a)

Evening Glow (r)

Gumpo Pink (a)

Ignatius Sargent (r)

Lee's Dark Purple (r)

Plum Beautiful (r)

Stewartsonian (a)

Summer Summit (r)

Tutti Frutti (a)

White Catawba (r)

Windsor Lad (r)

ROSES

Roses grow wonderfully well in the Pacific Northwest, both in the humid western parts and in the drier regions. When it comes to selecting, the new gardener sees a bewildering array of possibilities. There are so many varieties and so many kinds that compete for the space allotted in the landscape. We are fortunate in this region to have the International Rose Test Garden in Washington Park, and a gardener who visits Portland, Oregon, should take advantage of the opportunity to observe the best.

Roses are easy to plant, and if you place them in full sunlight in an area where air movement provides ventilation and in soil that is well drained and reasonably fertile, they will grow and bloom profusely. Most of the varieties that are adapted to the Pacific Northwest do best in full, all-day sunlight. Few of them do well in filtered shade, and those placed in deep shade will spend their lifetime trying to reach the light. Plant accordingly.

Roses are generally pruned in late winter in this region. Some light pruning can be done in November to keep the winter winds from whipping the plants about and loosening the roots. Along toward mid-February in the western half of this region or around mid-March in the eastern part, rose growers sharpen their shears and do the annual rose pruning. Most of the roses in this region develop flowers on new growth. Bush roses are usually pruned back to strong buds near the ground. Climbers and ramblers generally are pruned to remove some of the old canes while the newer canes are left to bear flowers. When training ramblers and climbers, provide as much horizontal training as possible to stimulate more flower production.

For more information about roses in your particular part of this region, contact the rose society in your state. Rose society members have learned by practice how to grow the best plants and how to make them flower to perfection. They are always willing to share their information. This chapter, which lists samplers of roses, is nowhere near complete. We have listed only a few in several categories, which will serve to launch you on your search for the best for your own garden.

ROSES FOR CUT FLOWERS

Roses have a beauty of form, substance, and structure that lends itself to many different kinds of arrangements. Some are better than others for use as cut flowers; they will retain their beauty and/or fragrance longer when handled properly. As you begin your rose garden, and begin finding ever more fragrant or increasingly beautiful types to use in those special niches in your landscape, you can add to this list.

Variety	Type	Color
Double Delight	Hybrid Tea	Red blend
Fragrant Cloud	Hybrid Tea	Orange-red
Graham Thomas	Shrub Rose	Dark yellow
Olympiad	Hybrid Tea	Medium red
Paradise	Hybrid Tea	Mauve
Peace	Hybrid Tea	Yellow blend
Prima Donna	Grandiflora	Deep pink
Royal Highness	Hybrid Tea	Light pink
Touch of Class	Hybrid Tea	Orange-pink

When cutting roses for use indoors or for showing, choose partially opened buds, cut them in early morning, and place them in a deep vase in cool water. Sometimes it helps to recut the stems under water. Various preservatives are suggested for keeping cut flowers fresh, but generally cool fresh water works best.

ROSES THAT ARE STRIPED

One of the newest of striped roses is the red-and-white hybrid tea variety 'George Burns' that was released in early 1996, just prior to the death of this noted comedian/actor. In the rose garden the stripes provide a comedy of their own, which you either like or prefer to see in someone else's yard. Whatever your feelings about stripes on roses, know that they can add another bit of interest to your landscape. Here are a few to try.

Variety	Type	Color
Candy Stripe	Hybrid Tea	Orange blend
Careless Love	Hybrid Tea	Pink blend
Earthquake	Moss	Red blend
Hurdy Gurdy	Moss	Red blend
Oranges and Lemons	Shrub	Orange blend
Pinstripe	Moss	Red blend
Rosa Mundi	Gallica	White and pink
Stars 'n Stripes	Moss	Red blend

ROSES THAT WILL GROW IN THE SHADE

Few roses will grow in less than six hours of sunlight; however, here are some that would be worth a try. These will tolerate dappled sunlight, bright shade, or whatever else you want to call a lack of full sunlight. Roses planted in less than ideal locations should be given a little extra care, perhaps a balanced fertilizer and a handful of bone meal at planting time, then make sure enough water is applied during the summer to keep them happy.

Variety	Type	Color
City of Belfast	Floribunda	Orange-red
The Fairy	Polyantha	Light pink
Playboy	Floribunda	Red blend
Rosa rugosa alba	Species	White
Rosa rugosa 'Delicata'	Species	Lilac pink
Rosa rugosa 'Martin Frobisher'	Species	Strawberries and cream
Rosa rugosa 'Robusta'	Species	Red
Rosa rugosa 'Roseraie de l'Hay'	Species	Purple-red
Sally Holmes	Shrub	White

"All roses need at least six hours of sunlight a day. Other than that they can be planted almost anywhere there is good drainage. All roses need a good program of pruning and fertilization, even the heirloom roses. Not all roses need fungicides; some even are damaged by them. I never spray for insects!"—Jane Anders, Portland Rose Society and Oregon Master Gardener, Portland

ROSES WITH GREAT HIPS

All plants in the genus *Rosa* make fruit in the same way: they bloom, the flower is fertilized, and the ovaries containing the seeds swell. This is true of apples, peaches, plums, and roses. In roses the resulting fruit that contains the seeds is called a **hip**. Some roses grow small, usually red, hips that are often eaten by small animals during winter. Others though, grow large and showy hips that stand out long after the plants have shed their leaves and gone into dormancy. These are the kinds that give enough winter color to make them additionally valued as a landscape item. Here are a few you might want to consider.

Variety	Type	Color
Bourbon Queen	Bourbon	Pink
Dortmund	Kordesii	Medium red
Meg	Climber	Apricot
Rosa rugosa alba	Species	White
Rosa rugosa 'Belle Poitevine'	Species	Lilac pink
Rosa rugosa 'Darts Dash'	Species	Purple-crimson
Rosa rugosa 'Purple Pavement'	Species	Violet-mauve
Rosa rugosa rubra	Species	Mauve
Treasure Trove	Rambler	Apricot

ROSES FOR EDGING LANDSCAPE AND GARDEN BEDS

With the wonderful array of sizes to which roses grow, it is no wonder that a list such as this would be developed. We don't list very many in this category and you might notice that those listed are all miniature. For more miniatures that could fit this group, see the lists of miniature roses that come later in this chapter.

Variety	Type	Color
Cinderella	Miniature	White
Cupcake	Miniature	Medium pink
Gourmet Popcorn	Miniature	White

ROSES THAT CLIMB

Roses are not really climbers insofar as they are able to support themselves by twining or holdfasts. But, many varieties grow long, pliant canes that can be trained onto supports. Plants that can be trained upward on a support of some sort give a vertical dimension to the landscape. You can place these plants upon a viewing trellis or along a fence that gives the garden visitor a better look at your plants, or they can also be used for screening or as dividers between garden rooms. For best bloom from your climbers, train them with as many horizontal runs as possible, for this is where the most flowers will be grown.

Climbers for the Pacific Northwest

Variety	Type	Color
Altissimo	Large flwg Climber	Medium red
Dortmund	Kordesii	Medium red
Dublin Bay	Large flwg Climber	Medium red
Golden Showers	Large flwg Climber	Medium yellow
Iceberg	Climbing Floribunda	White
Jeanne Lajoie	Climbing Miniature	Light pink
Royal Sunset	Large flwg Climber	Apricot blend
Zéphirine Drouhin	Bourbon	Medium pink

Rose gardens west of the Cascades

Variety	Type	Color
Altissimo	Large flwg Climber	Medium red
Dortmund	Kordesii	Medium red
Dublin Bay	Large flwg Climber	Medium red
Handel	Large flwg Climber	Red blend
Fred Loads	Large flwg Climber	Orange
Jeanne Lajoie	Climbing Miniature	Medium pink
Joseph's Coat	Large flwg Climber	Red blend
Royal Sunset	Large flwg Climber	Apricot blend

Shrub roses that train like a climber

Variety	Type	Color
Hanseat	Shrub	Pink (best in garden)
Mutabilis	China	Yellow to red
Radway Sunrise	Shrub	Orange blend

Schoner's Nutkana	Shrub	Pink blend
Schparrieshoop	Shrub	Light pink

SOME OF THE BEST FLORIBUNDA ROSES

Floribunda roses have many of the same desirable characteristics as hybrid teas—vivid colors and general hardiness. They are a valuable resource to the gardener who grows them, giving landscape beauty plus supplying lovely cut flowers. Here are some of the best.

For the Pacific Northwest

Variety	Color
Class Act	White
Europeana	Dark red
Iceberg	White
Margaret Merril	White
Playboy	Red blend
Playgirl	Medium pink
Sexy Rexy	Medium pink
Showbiz	Medium pink
Sunsprite	Dark yellow
Trumpeter	Orange

For rose gardens west of the Cascades

Variety	Color	Comments
Berlin	Deep red	Upright, disease resistant
Betty Prior	Pink	Upright
Dusky Maiden	Reddish mauve	Short, bushy
Festival Fanfare	Pale pink stripe	Very tall upright, disease resistant
Kirsten Poulsen	Pink	Upright, disease resistant
Lilac Charm	Pale mauve	Yellow stamens, disease resistant
Playboy	Red blend	Disease resistant
Playgirl	Medium pink	Medium growth
Playtime	Orange red	Medium to tall, disease resistant
Sarabande	Scarlet	Bushy habit, disease resistant

At age ninety, Ruth loves roses and her entire front yard is a well-filled rose garden. She says, "Their beauty was meant to be shared with people. I enjoy all those I meet through my roses. My favorite rose, if one can have a favorite, is Pink Favorite. It just keeps going, it is disease resistant, and has lots of blooms."— Ruth Donavon, Portland
(Authors' note: During the writing of this book our friend Ruth joined other gardeners in heaven to show them how to grow roses.)

ROSES FOR RAMBLING OR FOR TRAINING AS PILLARS

Ramblers do just that, and they pose a problem for those of us with small gardens, for they don't seem to want to remain "in their place." However, for the larger garden, or for the design that has definitive structures for training ramblers onto, they provide both interest and bloom, often in areas that no other flowering plant can satisfy. Pillars are a perfect accent for a place in the garden where height is needed. They create a vertical permanence and serve as the backbone of the design. Training to a pillar involves wrapping or braiding rose canes around the pillar with as many side shoots as possible growing in a horizontal plane to stimulate more blooms. Be as patient with ramblers as you are with climbers, for they both take several years to give their full potential.

Variety	Type	Color
Ramblers:		
Alberic Barbier	Rambler	Light yellow
American pillar	Rambler	Pink blend
Cl. Cécile Brünner	Climbing Polyantha	Light pink
Pillars:		
Altissimo	Large flwg Climber	Medium red
Cl. Iceberg	Climbing Floribunda	White

HYBRID TEAS FOR PACIFIC NORTHWEST GARDENS

Because so many new hybrids are brought to gardeners every year, it is a risk to try developing a list of these beauties because next year's will be even better. However, we canvassed some of the leading growers to find what varieties they felt were worth keeping from year to year and came up with the following suggestions. Add to them yourself as you find varieties that catch your eye, or that you test and find work very well in your garden and its microclimate. After all, that is what lists are for.

For Pacific Northwest gardens

Variety	Color
Dainty Bess	Light pink
Fragrant Cloud	Orange-red
Just Joey	Orange blend
Keepsake	Pink blend
Mr. Lincoln	Dark red
New Zealand	Light pink
Olympiad	Medium red
Paradise	Mauve
Peace	Yellow blend
Precious Platinum	Medium red
Sheer Elegance	Orange-pink

For rose gardens west of the Cascades

Variety	Color	Comments
Dainty Bess	Light pink	Magenta stamens, tall upright

Ellen Willmott	Light pink	Bushy
Frances Ashton	Deep pink	Upright, disease resistant
Irish Elegance	Orange blend	Sprawling bush
Irish Fireflame	Pink blend	Sprawling bush
Isobel	Pink blend	Upright
Mrs. Oakley Fisher	Deep yellow	Bushy

"If you are just starting a rose garden, you may want to study the types of roses that will meet the needs of your landscape plan. You will need to decide whether you want to have constant color in the landscape, a formal or informal garden with roses for cutting, a planting of different colors and styles, or a combination of cutting roses and landscape color. Roses can be used in nearly every part of the landscape as long as you have an open space with at least a half day of sunshine."—Edmund's Roses, Wilsonville, Oregon

ROSES THAT ARE FRAGRANT

A major reason for planting a rose is to enjoy its fragrance. Place your fragrant roses near the patio, deck, walkways—where on a warm summer evening you catch the aroma when you are nearby. The point is, if you are going to purchase a fragrant rose, don't waste this elegant feature by placing it far away from wherever you or your garden guests will be. Here are some to try.

Variety	Type	Color
Albéric Barbier	Rambler	Light yellow
Candy Stripe	Hybrid Tea	Orange blend
Careless Love	Hybrid Tea	Pink blend
Celestial	Alba	Light pink
Chrysler Imperial	Hybrid Tea	Dark red
Dainty Bess	Hybrid Tea	Light pink
Double Delight	Hybrid Tea	Red blend
Félicité Parmentier	Alba	Light pink
Fragrant Cloud	Hybrid Tea	Orange-red
Granada	Hybrid Tea	Red blend
Jacques Cartier	Polyantha	Medium red
Margaret Merril	Floribunda	White
Mme. Hardy	Damask	White
Mr. Lincoln	Hybrid Tea	Dark red
New Zealand	Hybrid Tea	Light pink
Old Pink Moss	Moss	Medium pink
Rosa Mundi	Gallica	White and pink
Rosa rugosa varieties	Species	Varies
Royal Sunset	Climber	Apricot blend
Sombreuil	Climber	White
Sunsprite	Floribunda	Dark yellow
Zéphirine Drouhin	Bourbon	Medium pink

MINIATURE ROSES

Just because you do not have a large enough garden for full-sized roses does not mean you can't grow any. The miniatures, scaled down versions of their larger relatives, give you the option of fitting roses into the small garden. And they are well adapted to being grown in containers. You can have a perfect, small, continuous-blooming rose to place in the special garden niche. Here are a few for your consideration.

Variety	Color	Comments
One bloom per stem varieties		
Child's Play	White with dark pink accent	Excellent exhibition, high centered bud, fast repeat
Jean Kenneally	Apricot ranging from pale to medium	Urn-shaped buds, upright to 36", some winter tenderness
Mary Marshall	Blend of yellow, pink, and orange	Very hardy, compact bushy habit, 26"
Minnie Pearl	Light pink and ivory blend	Sprawling habit, good for hanging basket, about 32"
Pacesetter	Pure white	Outstanding exhibition, upright habit to 34"
Rainbow's End	Deep yellow with scarlet tips	To 36", easy to grow, high-centered buds, fast repeat
Rise 'n' Shine	Medium yellow	Bushy, 30", semi-glossy foliage, exhibition quality, occasional flower clusters
Small, micro-miniature blooms		
Cinderella	Pure white bloom	Bushy compact, 10-12", ½" across, excellent for window box or container
Giselle	Dark pink accented with white stripes when open	Compact to 14", bloom urn-shaped and 1" in diameter
Red Minimo	Scarlet red	Upright to 32", intense flower color, excellent repeat
Climbers		
Radiant	Bright orange red	Double blooms, excellent repeat bloom, climbs 6'+

| Stolen Moment | Mauve | Urn-shaped buds, 7-9 petals, climbs to 5-6' |
| Work of Art | Orange blend with yellow accent | Vigorous, profuse bloom, climbs to 6' |

Five-petaled (single) blooms

Ain't Misbehavin	Very dark red	Compact, profuse, 24"
My Sunshine	Bright yellow	Profuse, long lasting, 28", glossy dark green foliage
Single's Better	Red shaded with plum	Sprawling, profuse bloom, fruity fragrance, heavily mossed

Multi-cluster bloomers

Buttons 'n' Bows	Bright soft pink	Compact to 24", bloom ½" diameter
Make Believe	Lilac to reddish purple	Profusion of semi-double 10-14 petal blooms, slow to fade
Whiteout	White with pink tinge	Upright to 34", blooms in clusters of 10 or more

Especially well suited for hanging baskets

My Honey	Deep orange	Sprawling habit, bloom large, borne singly and in sprays
Red Delight	Medium red	Can cascade or climb 6', requires regular pinching, quick repeater, excellent form
Touch O' Midas	Pastel blend of white, pink, and yellow	Drooping habit, profuse bloom, excellent form

"It seemed like it might be worthwhile to do some groupings of roses other than the typical exhibition varieties to provide information to those folks who might have other landscaping schemes in mind, or just as a way of letting folks know that not all miniatures are Hybrid Tea in form."—Jerry Justice, Justice Miniature Roses, Wilsonville, Oregon

ROSES THAT ARE THORNLESS

Anyone who plants roses in the garden will soon know that most of them have thorns that can prick, gouge, and draw sharp comments from the hardiest of gardeners. So it is a relief to have available to us some varieties that have no thorns. Here are a few to check out.

Variety	Type	Color
Smooth Prince	Hybrid tea	Light pink
Smooth Satin	Hybrid tea	Medium pink
Smooth Talk	Floribunda	White
Smooth Velvet	Hybrid tea	Dark red
Zéphirine Drouhin	Bourbon	Medium pink

SOME OF THE BEST GRANDIFLORA ROSES

These are generally vigorous plants, often ten feet tall, adorned with Hybrid Tea-type flowers, some with clusters of flowers, others with single-stemmed buds. Often the roses in this category are used for background, mass color, barrier, or simply to produce a lot of cut flowers. Here are some of the better ones for use in and around the Pacific Northwest, along with qualities that should be noted by the PNW gardener.

Audrey Hepburn (fragrant, disease resistant)
Caribbean (disease resistant)
Gold Medal (tender)
Lagerfeld (fragrant)
Love (disease resistant)
Prima Donna
Queen Elizabeth (disease resistant)
Tournament of Roses

"Some of the best roses can be found in the western part of the Pacific Northwest, in spite of the rainfall that is a part of the natural climate of this area. This dispels the commonly held myth that water on the leaves of roses is a major reason for foliage diseases. Humidity factors, ventilation, temperature, and sanitation are more important contributors to mildew and black spot."—
John Biewener, Portland Rose Society and Oregon Master Gardener

SUPERB ROSES THAT BLOOM ONCE A YEAR

Once-blooming roses put all their flowering energy into one profuse blooming period, in late spring to early summer, for four to six weeks.

Variety	Class	Color	Comments
Cécile Brünner	Polyantha	Light pink	
Celestial	Alba	Light pink	Fragrant
Félicité Parmentier	Alba	Light pink	Fragrant
Mme. Hardy	Damask	White	Fragrant

Heirloom roses that bloom once a year

Alba Semi-Plena	Alba	White	Fragrant
American Pillar	Wichuraiana	Pink	
The Bishop	Centifolia	Magenta purple	Fragrant
Blush Hip	Alba	Pink	Fragrant
Cabbage Rose	Centifolia	Pink	Fragrant
Celsiana	Damask	Soft pink	Fragrant
Chianti	English	Dark red	Fragrant
Mme. Plantier	Alba	Creamy white	Fragrant
Mrs. John McNabb	Rugosa	Pink	Fragrant
Rosa Mundi	Gallica	White/red stripe	

"If you grow only repeat flowering roses, you are missing out on some wonderful old varieties of great beauty and fragrance that are not duplicated in repeat bloomers. After all, as I often point out to customers, many of us give garden space to camellias, azaleas, and rhododendrons that have only one spring blooming period, so why not try some once-blooming roses?"—Louise Clements, Heirloom Old Garden Roses, St. Paul, Oregon

RUGOSA ROSES THAT DO WELL IN THE PACIFIC NORTHWEST

Rugosa roses are the members of the rose family that perform dependably under some of the more trying conditions. They may not be the most beautiful, but they will be the most hardy. They are prickly relatives of the Floribundas, and the robust cousins of the Hybrid Teas. They are the roses that you would plant for dependable color, both of foliage and flower, and rely upon for hardiness during the toughest of winters in this region.

Variety	Characteristics
Belle Poitevine	Sweet fragrance, large red hips, 5' × 5'
Blanc Double de Coubert	Hugely fragrant, excellent foliage, 5'+
Charles Albanel	Heady fragrance, good repeater, 3-4'
Dart's Dash	Rich fragrance, continual bloom, 3' × 3'
Delicata	Heavily fragrant, shade tolerant, 3'
Martin Frobisher	Prodigious clusters, shade tolerant, 5'
Purple Pavement	Nice fragrance, red hips, 3-4'
Red Max Graf	Very fragrant, groundcover, 3 × 10'
Robusta	Killer thorns, shade tolerant, 6'
R. rugosa alba	Heady fragrance, best edible rose, 6' × 6
Roseraie de l'hay	Rich fragrance, shade tolerant, 6'
Thérèse Bugnet	Very fragrant, repeat bloomer, 6'

"Rugosa roses are practically the perfect edible landscape plant. They require little pruning, no spraying, and are drought tolerant, as well as being beautiful to look at. Most are fragrant and many are tasty to eat. Several are shade tolerant."—Vern Nelson, PNW garden writer

ROSES THAT CAN BE USED AS GROUNDCOVERS

In recent years, roses have been developed that spread their canes more in a horizontal mode than vertical. When planted in groups, their combined growth provides a perfect groundcover to cover slopes or to form traffic-proof areas.

Variety	Color
Blooming Carpet	Rose pink
Dewdrops	White
Flower Carpet	Deep pink
Gourmet Pheasant	Light red
Happenstance	Light yellow
Rosa rugosa 'Red Max Graf'	Red
Snow on the Heather	White
Suma	Medium red

SHRUB ROSES THAT DO WELL IN THE PACIFIC NORTHWEST

Roses specifically bred for general landscape use are collectively labeled Shrub roses. The category encompasses a wide range of rose types which may be spreading or upright, have the ability to survive cold winters with no special protection, and provide attractive floral displays more or less constantly through the growing season. Most of them are repeat bloomers, and most are fragrant. Here are some to test in your own garden.

Variety	Type	Color
All That Jazz	Shrub	Orange pink
Ballerina	Hybrid Musk	Medium pink
Bonica	Shrub	Medium pink
Frau Karl Druschki	Hybrid Perpetual	White
Gartendirektor Otto Linne	Shrub	Light pink
Heidelberg	Shrub	Medium red
Lillian Austin	Shrub	Orange pink
Mary Rose	Shrub	Medium pink
Sally Holmes	Shrub	White

ROSES FOR HEDGES

Certain roses will make fine hedges that screen, form a barrier, or simply provide you with a multitude of flowers. For those of us who continually fight the rose diseases black spot and powdery mildew, be extra careful in selecting roses to fill a hedge. Make sure you work with your nurseryman or local rosarian to select those varieties that have the highest possible resistance to those diseases. Here are some that are suggested by rosarian John Biewener, Beaverton, Oregon.

Variety	Type	Color
China Doll	Polyantha	Medium pink
Iceberg	Floribunda	White

Rosa rugosa 'Purple Pavement'	Species	Violet-mauve
Rosa rugosa 'Robusta'	Species	Red
Simplicity	Floribunda	Medium pink
Sunsprite	Floribunda	Dark yellow
Trumpeter	Floribunda	Orange

ORNAMENTAL GRASSES

For years landscape gardeners have had ornamental grasses such as Pampas grass, blue fescue grass and a few native sedges for their use in developing the landscape. In the last dozen years a number of ornamental grasses have been found, hybridized, propagated, and sent into the landscape industry. They have many uses, as you will see when you investigate our following lists of grasses. While some ornamental grass nurseries list horsetail rush (*Equisetum* spp.) as an ornamental grass, we have purposely left it out of our lists because of its invasiveness and determination, especially in our coastal zone.

Arundo donax

GRASSES FOR SEASIDE GARDENS

Grasses in landscapes are not new, it is just that in some areas, particularly the western part of this region, there are so many native grasses that grow so rampantly that most gardeners spend a lot of time trying to get rid of them. In coastal areas, ornamental grasses must withstand the winds that come off the ocean, often in gusty masses, as well as the soil types that sometimes hold too much water and other times not enough to keep grasses happy. Here are some suggestions for this locale.

Name	Suggested use
Giant reed grass (*Arundo donax*)	Screen, background, cut flowers, specimen
Variegated giant reed (*Arundo donax* 'Versicolor')	Accent, specimen, cut flowers, perennial border
Feather reed grass (*Calamagrostis acutiflora* 'Karl Foerster')	Mass and groups, background, cut flowers
Palm sedge (*Carex muskingumensis*)	Groundcover, rock and water gardens, shade
Black sedge (*Carex nigra*)	Unique color seed head, specimen, container
Northern sea oats (*Chasmanthium latifolium*)	Perennial border, cut flowers, natural setting
Pampas grass (*Cortaderia selloana*)	Specimen, screen, background, cut flowers

Pink pampas grass (*C. selloana* 'Rosea')	Specimen, screen, background, cut flowers
Oregon tufted hair grass (*Deschampsia caespitosa*)	Mass planting, naturalizing, wetlands, groups
Golden hanging hairgrass (*D. caespitosa* 'Goldgehange')	Groundcover in mass, specimen, cut flowers, accent
Corkscrew rush (*Juncus effusus* 'Spiralis')	Pond, stream, bog garden, poor drainage
Findhorn lyme grass (*Leymus arenarius* 'Findhorn')	Metallic blue foliage, massing
Blue wild rye (*Leymus racemosus* 'Glaucus')	Group, massing groundcover, beach
Maiden grass (*Miscanthus sinensis* 'Gracillimus')	Specimen, cut flowers, screen, water feature
Malepartus silver grass (*M. sinensis* 'Malepartus')	Specimen, groups, cut flowers, water feature
Variegated Japanese silver grass (*M. sinensis* 'Variegatus')	Specimen, cut flowers, screen, perennial border
Zebra grass (*M. sinensis* 'Zebrinus')	Specimen, screen, groups, cut flowers, background
Red switch grass (*Panicum virgatum* vars.)	Groups, water features, perennial border, cut flowers
Variegated common reed (*Phragmites australis* 'Variegatus')	Containers, wet soils, mixed border
Dwarf cattails (*Typha minima*)	Pond, bog, containers

GRASSES THAT CAN BE USED FOR SCREENING

Screens can be used to stop the eye, to block out objectionable views, or to simply provide a boundary to the landscape. There are also many shrubs that can be used for this purpose and you can check the shrub chapter for those. However, for a different texture, appearance, color variation, and general plant type, give some of these a try where you need screening. Also check the list of grasses that grow to giant size, for many of them could be used as screens.

Feather Reed Grass

Name	Can also be used for
Feather reed grass (*Calamagrostis acutiflora* 'Karl Foerster')	Mass, groups, background, cut flowers
Pampas grass (*Cortaderia selloana*)	Specimen, background, cut flowers
Giant Chinese silver grass (*Miscanthus floridulus*)	Screen, background
Silver grass (*Miscanthus sinensis* and cultivars)	Groups, cut flowers, borders, containers
Moor grass (*Molinia arundinacea* and cultivars)	Specimen, groups
Fountain grass (*Pennisetum alopecuroides*)	Groups, mass, perennial border
Ravenna grass (*Saccharum ravennae* [*Erianthus*])	Specimen, background, cut flowers

GRASSES FOR HIGH DESERT CONDITIONS

Their drought tolerance and ability to withstand cold, dry winters make this group of ornamental grasses especially valuable to the gardener in the high and dry region of the Pacific Northwest. Nurserymen are propagating and cultivating these grasses because the trend in gardening is away from the use of more water-dependent plants and more to those that can live through normal dry periods without extra watering.

Name	Suggested use
Golden foxtail grass (*Alopecurus pratensis* 'Aureovariegatus')	Groups, massing, water gardens
Big blue stem (*Andropogon gerardii*)	Specimen, groups, mass, cut, screening
Quaking grass (*Briza media*)	Spring perennial border, specimen, cut, mass
Feather reed grass (*Calamagrostis acutiflora* 'Karl Foerster')	Mass, groups, background, cut flowers
Leather leaf sedge (*Carex buchananii*)	Perennial borders, group, mass, accent, rockery
Golden variegated Japanese sedge (*Carex morrowii* 'Aureovariegata')	Edging, groups, mass, specimen, rockery
Northern sea oats (*Chasmanthium latifolium*)	Perennial border, specimen, cut flowers
Large blue fescue (*Festuca amethystina*)	Groundcover, rock gardens, accent, specimen
Blue fescue (*F. glauca* 'Elijah Blue')	Dry areas, groundcover, edging
Sea blue (*F. glauca* 'Meerblau')	Mass, rock gardens, hanging baskets, edging
Idaho fescue (*F. idahohensis*)	Edging, accent, mass, rockery, native garden
Blue oat grass (*Helictotrichon sempervirens*)	Specimen, groups, mass, perennial borders
Prairie junegrass (*Koeleria pyramidalis*)	Groups, rock gardens, groundcover
Large blue hairgrass (*Koeleris glauca*)	Groups, mass, rock garden
Greater woodrush (*Luzula sylvatica*)	Evergreen perennial, woodland groundcover
Giant Chinese silver grass (*Miscanthus floridulus*)	Specimen, screen, background
Maiden grass (*M. sinensis* 'Gracillimus')	Specimen, cut, screen, potted, water feature
Early maiden grass (*M. sinensis* 'Graziella')	Specimen, screen, accent, groups
Sarabande miscanthus (*M. sinensis* 'Sarabande')	Groups, mass, water gardens, cut, accent
Silver feather Japanese silver grass (*M. sinensis* 'Silberfeder')	Specimen, cut, background, screen
Porcupine grass (*M. sinensis* 'Strictus')	Specimen, screen, cut, water feature
Variegated Japanese silver grass (*M. sinensis* 'Variegatus')	Specimen, cut, screen, perennial border
Zebra grass (*M. sinensis* 'Zebrinus')	Specimen, screen, groups, cut, background
Autumn red zebra grass	Cut, perennial border, specimen, group,

(*M. sinensis purpurescens*)	accent
Red switch grass	Groups, mass, perennial border, cut,
(*Panicum virgatum* 'Rehbraun')	water feature
Fountain grass (*Pennisetum alopecuroides*)	Groups, mass, specimen, perennial border

"In the high desert list are some sedges. Keep in mind that sedges are water plants and even though they will survive the dry, sunny climate of the high desert region, they will need water frequently if they are expected to thrive. To maintain their beauty and to enjoy them for a long time, provide a microclimate in your landscape that is condusive to their growth, put a water feature in your landscape, or set up a drip system to provide them with moisture."—Steve Schmidt, owner, American Perennials, Eagle Creek, Oregon

GRASSES THAT GROW TO GIANT SIZE

Giant grasses can be sited with other bold-textured, large-leafed perennials to create a garden of mystery, or to create an enticing landscape out of an otherwise flat rectangle of land. Large plant materials alter our perceptions of space by blurring boundaries, suggesting endless garden adventures by increasing the illusion of garden depth and providing sound and movement. Concealment, at least partially, also entices the imagination in the garden, and what better concealment than that provided by giant grasses? Here are a few to consider.

Name	Normal height in feet
Giant reed grass (*Arundo donax*)	7-15
Variegated reed grass (*Arundo donax* 'Versicolor')	5-7
Feather reed grass (*Calamagrostis acutiflora* 'Karl Foerster')	5-7
Toe toe grass (*Cortaderia richardii*)	5-8
Pampas grass (*Cortaderia selloana*)	8-15
Giant Chinese silver grass (*Miscanthus floridulus*)	8-12
Cabaret silver grass (*M. sinensis* 'Cabaret')	6-8
Cosmopolitan silver grass (*M. sinensis* 'Cosmopolitan')	6-8
Golden feather silver grass (*M. sinensis* 'Goldfeder')	5-6
Maiden grass (*M. sinensis* 'Gracillimus')	5-7
Early maiden grass (*M. sinensis* 'Graziella')	5-6
Dwarf zebra grass (*M. sinensis* 'Kirk Alexander')	5
Malepartus silver grass (*M. sinensis* 'Malepartus')	5-6
Silver feather Japanese silver grass (*M. sinensis* 'Silberfeder')	6-9
Porcupine grass (*M. sinensis* 'Strictus')	5-7
Variegated Japanese silver grass (*M. sinensis* 'Variegatus')	5-7
Zebra grass (*M. sinensis* 'Zebrinus')	6-8
Skyracer moor grass (*Molinia arundinacea* 'Skyracer')	7-8
Ravenna grass	9-12
(*Saccharum ravennae* [*Erianthus* is former genus name])	
Variegated cord grass (*Spartina pectinata* 'Aureomarginata')	5-6
Common cattail (*Typha latifolia*)	6-8

GRASSES THAT WILL REMAIN SMALL (DWARFS)

These grasses can be used in the garden to create interest, attract attention, provide contrast, and sometimes to define an area or zone. They can be worked into the landscape with companions of medium-sized shrubs and other herbaceous perennials, or can stand alone. Here are some that remain under three feet at maturity.

Name	Normal height in inches
Variegated sweet flag (*Acorus calamus* 'Variegatus')	24-36
Variegated Japanese sweet flag (*A. gramineus* 'Argenteostriatus')	6-12
Gold variegated Japanese sweet flag (*A. gramineus* 'Ogon')	10
Golden foxtail grass (*Alopecurus pratensis* 'Aureovariegatus')	12
Variegated bulbous oat grass (*Arrhenatherum bulbosum* 'Variegatum')	12
Quaking grass (*Briza media*)	18-24
Leather leaf sedge (*Carex buchananii*)	12-24
New Zealand hair sedge (*Carex comans*)	12-24
Bronze hair sedge (*C. comans* 'Bronze Form')	12-24
Golden fountain sedge (*C. dolichostachya* 'Gold Fountains')	12-24
Bowles's golden tufted sedge (*C. elata* 'Aurea')	24
Blue sedge (*C. flacca*)	6-18
Star sedge (*C. grayi*)	18-24
Golden variegated Japanese sedge (*C. morrowii* 'Aureovariegata')	24
Silver variegated Japanese sedge (*C. morrowii* 'Variegata')	18
Black sedge (*C. nigra*)	12
Variegated black sedge (*C. nigra* 'Variegata')	12
Variegated bird's foot sedge (*C. ornithopoda* 'Variegata')	6
Petrie's sedge (*C. petriei*)	12-18
Brick sedge (*C. testacea*)	12-24
Golden hair grass (*Deschampsia flexuosa* 'Tatra Gold')	6
Blue fescue (*Festuca glauca* vars.)	6-10
Variegated velvet grass (*Holcus mollis* 'Albovariegatus')	6-12
Japanese blood grass (*Imperata* 'Red Baron')	12-18
Fountain grass (*Pennisetum alopecuroides* 'Hameln')	18-24
Miniature fountain grass (*P. alopecuroides* 'Little Bunny')	12
Autumn moor grass (*Sesleria autumnalis*)	12-24
Blue wheat grass (*Elymus magellanicus*)	8-12

GRASSES THAT ARE VARIEGATED

Variegation in decorative plants makes them good candidates for lightening a dark area, or for bringing perceived light into a landscape where darker greens are predominant. Plants with variegations of white or light yellow are Nature's flashlights among the darker plants. Here are two dozen ornamental grasses that might brighten your landscape.

Name	Suggested use
Variegated sweet flag (*Acorus* spp.)	Perennial border, bog garden, container plant
Golden foxtail grass (*Alopecurus pratensis* 'Aureovariegatus')	Groups, massing, water gardens

Variegated bulbous oat grass (*Arrhenatherum bulbosum* 'Variegatum')	Border, edging, specimen, rock gardens
Variegated giant reed grass (*Arundo donax* 'Versicolor')	Accent, specimen, cut, perennial border
Variegated feather reed grass (*Calamagrostis acutiflora* 'Overdam')	Groups and massing
Golden fountain sedge (*Carex dolichostachya* 'Gold Fountains')	Rock gardens, wet areas, perennial border
Bowles's golden tufted sedge (*C. elata* 'Aurea')	Specimens, water gardens
Golden variegated Japanese sedge (*C. morrowii* 'Aureovariegata')	Edging, groups, mass, specimen, rockery
Silver variegated Japanese sedge (*C. morrowii* 'Variegata')	Group, mass, rock gardens, border
Variegated black sedge (*C. nigra* 'Variegata')	Specimen, containers, accent
Variegated birds foot sedge (*C. ornithopoda* 'Variegata')	Rock gardens, groups, edging, containers
Variegated manna grass (*Glyceria maxima* 'Variegata')	Ponds, streams, marshy areas, naturalizing
Variegated Japanese forest grass (*Hakonechloa macra* 'Aureola')	Groups, groundcover, accent
Cabaret silver grass (*Miscanthus sinensis* 'Cabaret')	Specimen, groups, screen
Cosmopolitan silver grass (*M. sinensis* 'Cosmopolitan')	Specimen, screen, groups
Golden feather silver grass (*M. sinensis* 'Goldfeder')	Specimen, screen, groups
Little dot silver grass (*M. sinensis* 'Punktchen')	Border, groups, mass
Porcupine grass (*M. sinensis* 'Strictus')	Specimen, cut, screen, perennial border
Variegated Japanese silver grass (*M. sinensis* 'Variegatus')	Specimen, cut, screen, perennial border
Zebra grass (*M. sinensis* 'Zebrinus')	Specimen, screen, groups, cut, background
Variegated purple moor grass (*Molinia caerulea* 'Variegata')	Specimen, mass, groups
Feesey's ribbon grass (*Phalaris arundinacea* 'Feesey')	Groundcover
Variegated common reed (*Phragmites australis* 'Variegatus')	Containers, wet soils, borders
Variegated cord grass (*Spartina pectinata* 'Aureomarginata')	Groups, mass, perennial border, accent

*A variegated grass that was left off this list is golden brome (*Bromus inermis* 'Skinners Gold'). One of its attributes is that it is a groundcover for difficult sites. According to nurseryman Steve Schmidt, "This will spread in the valley and coastal areas and could become a noxious weed. If I were going to use this grass it would preferably be in the dry areas of the Pacific Northwest where it would be less likely to spread." A word from the wise.*

GRASSES THAT WILL NOT TAKE OVER

Some grasses could become a problem in the landscape when they seed and begin to spread themselves throughout the garden. This is more often the case with native and pasture-type grasses. Here are thirty varieties (one of them an annual type) that shouldn't become weed problems in the landscape by overseeding themselves.

Carex

Name	Suggested use
Variegated Japanese sweet flag (*Acorus gramineus* 'Argenteostriatus')	Water garden, perennial border, containers, indoor
Big blue stem (*Andropogon gerardii*)	Specimen, mass, cut, screening
Quaking grass (*Briza media*)	Spring perennial border, specimen, cut, mass
Feather reed grass (*Calamagrostis acutiflora* 'Karl Foerster')	Mass, background, cut, combinations
Bronze hair sedge (*Carex comans* 'Bronze Form')	Rock gardens, mass, perennial border, accent
Golden fountain sedge (*C. dolichostachya* 'Gold Fountains')	Rock gardens, wet areas, border, perennial garden
Golden variegated Japanese sedge (*C. morrowii* 'Aureovariegata')	Edging, mass, specimen, rock gardens
Palm sedge (*C. muskingumensis*)	Groundcover, beneath trees, rock gardens
Northern sea oats (*Chasmanthium latifolium*)	Perennial border, specimen, cut
Pampas grass (*Cortaderia selloana*)	Specimen, screen, background, cut
Oregon tufted hair grass (*Deschampsia caespitosa*)	Mass, wet lands, naturalizing, groups
Blue fescue (*Festuca glauca* vars.)	Edging, accent, mass, groups, dry areas
Idaho fescue (*Festuca idahohensis*)	Edging, accent, rock gardens, naturalizing
Blue oat grass (*Helictotrichon sempervirens*)	Specimen, mass, groups, perennial borders
Maiden grass (*Miscanthus sinensis* vars.)	Specimen, cut, screen, containers
Small fountain silver grass (*M. sinensis* 'Kleine Fontane')	Borders, groups, mass, specimen
Nippon silver grass (*M. sinensis* 'Nippon')	Containers, compact, bronzy-red
Sarabande miscanthus (*M. sinensis* 'Sarabande')	Mass, groups, water gardens, cut, specimen
Silver feather Japanese silver grass (*M. sinensis* 'Silberfeder')	Specimen, mass, cut, background, screen
Porcupine grass (*M. sinensis* 'Strictus')	Specimen, cut, screen, perennial border
Variegated Japanese silver grass (*M. sinensis* 'Variegatus')	Specimen, cut, screen, perennial border
Zebra grass (*M. sinensis* 'Zebrinus')	Specimen, screen, cut, background
Autumn red Japanese grass (*M. sinensis purpurescens*)	Cut, perennial border, specimen, accent, group
Fountain grass (*Pennisetum alopecuroides*)	Mass, specimen, perennial border, group
Late blooming fountain grass (*P. alopecuroides* 'Moudry')	Group, mass, specimen, border

Ruby grass (*Rychelytrum neriglume*) (annual)	Accent, group, mass, cut, containers
Ravenna grass (*Saccharum ravennae*)	Specimen, background, screen, cut
Little blue stem (*Schizachyrium scoparium*)	Mass, group, cut, naturalizing
Autumn moor grass (*Sesleria autumnalis*)	Mass, groundcover, foreground, border
Giant feather grass (*Stipa gigantea*)	Specimen, group, perennial border, cut flowers

 "Deschampsia *and* Festuca *will reseed themselves, and over time could develop a lot of seedlings. But if a gardener is doing the normal bit of maintenance, these seedlings will be easily taken care of and present no threat to the landscape."—Steve Schmidt, owner, American Perennials Nursery, Eagle Creek, Oregon*

GRASSES THAT GROW TO BECOME HANDSOME SPECIMENS

Specimen plants provide focus, draw interest, sometimes provide an anchoring feature, and sometimes are the dominant feature that draws you into the garden. Pampas grass has been used as a hardy specimen in landscapes for years, often in dry valley and high desert regions, sharing specimen status with few other plants that have features through the winter. Here are a few specimens to consider in your own yard.

Name	Can also be used for
Giant reed grass (*Arundo donax*)	Screen, background, cut, near water
Variegated giant reed grass (*A. donax* 'Versicolor' ['Variegata'])	Accent, cut flowers, perennial border
Bowles's golden tufted sedge (*Carex elata* 'Aurea' ['Bowles's Golden'])	Drifts at water's edge, accent
Golden variegated Japanese sedge (*C. morrowii* 'Aureovariegata')	Edging, groups, mass, rock garden
Weeping sedge (*C. pendula*)	Mass, groundcover
Pampas grass (*Cortaderia selloana*)	Screen, background, cut flowers
Variegated Japanese forest grass (*Hakonechloa macra* 'Aureola')	Groups, groundcover, accent
Silver grass (*Miscanthus species* and cultivars)	Screen, cut, perennial border, accent
Ravenna grass (*Saccharum ravennae* [*Erianthus*])	Background, screen, cut flowers
Giant feather grass (*Stipa gigantea*)	Groups, perennial border, cut flowers

 Provide grass with the proper microclimate and place it in the soil for which it is adapted, along with a complete fertilizer (organic or chemical), then get out of the way, for it will grow and thrive. Grass growth can be regulated by the richness of its soil or by your addition of nitrogen and other elements.

ORNAMENTAL GRASSES THAT CAN BE USED AS GROUNDCOVERS IN PARTIAL SHADE

Few of the lawn-type grasses that are adapted to the Pacific Northwest will grow in shade. However, here is a listing of ornamental grasses that are rated as being tolerant of shade conditions. The amount of shade and the quality of light received (filtered, direct for several hours) will largely determine the success of the planting. Give them a try and rate them in your own garden.

Name	Comments
Golden foxtail grass (*Alopecurus pratensis* 'Aureovariegatus')	Groups, mass, water gardens
Variegated bulbous oat grass (*Arrhenatherum bulbosum* 'Variegatum')	Edging, specimen, rock gardens
Quaking grass (*Briza media*)	Spring perennial border, cut flowers
Feather reed grass (*Calamagrostis acutiflora* 'Karl Foerster')	Groups, background, cut flowers
Sedges (*Carex* spp.)	Perennial borders, accent, edging
Northern sea oats (*Chasmanthium latifolium*)	Perennial border, specimen, cut, near water
Oregon tufted hair grass (*Deschampsia caespitosa* and cultivars)	Groups, wet lands, naturalizing
Japanese forest grass (*Hakonechloa macra* and cultivars)	Groups, accent
Variegated velvet grass (*Holcus mollis* 'Albovariegatus')	Borders
Prairie junegrass (*Koeleria pyramidata* [cristata])	Groups, rock gardens
Wood rush (*Luzula* spp.)	Woodland settings, groups
Golden wood millet (*Millium effusum* 'Aureum')	Dwarf
Purple moor grass (*Molinia caerulea* and cultivars)	Specimen, groups
Oriental fountain grass (*Pennisetum orientale*)	Dwarf, specimen, group, combination
Ribbon grass (*Phalaris arundinacea* 'Feesey' and 'Picta')	Can take wet soils
Autumn moor grass (*Sesleria autumnalis*)	Groups, border, rockery, woodsy
Korean reed grass (*Stipa brachytricha* [Calamagrostis])	Small groups

ORNAMENTAL GRASSES THAT ARE DROUGHT TOLERANT

As water becomes ever more a part of the endangered resource list, gardeners everywhere are on the lookout for plants that can survive and possibly thrive on a minimum of water. When water rationing becomes a reality, here are some ornamental grasses that will be the survivors. Give them a place in your garden.

Name	Suggested use
Big blue stem (*Andropogon gerardii*)	Specimen, mass for naturalizing, cut, screen, highway planting
Variegated bulbous oat grass (*Arrhenatherum bulbosum* 'Variegatum')	Dwarf, border, edging, specimen, rock gardens, containers
Sideoats gramma (*Bouteloua* spp.)	Use with wild flowers, heather garden
Feather reed grass (*Calamagrostis acutiflora* 'Karl Foerster')	Mass, groups, background, cut flowers
Northern sea oats (*Chasmanthium latifolium*)	Perennial border, specimen, native setting, cut flowers
Large blue fescue (*Festuca amethystina*)	Groundcover, rock gardens, accent, specimen plant
Blue fescue (*F. glauca* and all cultivars)	Groundcover, edging, massing, rock gardens, hanging baskets, accent
Blue oat grass (*Helictotrichon sempervirens*)	Specimen, group, mass, perennial borders
Large blue hair grass (*Koeleria glauca*)	Groups, mass, rock gardens
Prairie junegrass (*K. pyramidata* [*cristata*])	Groups, rock gardens, groundcover
Blue wild rye (*Leymus racemosus* 'Glaucus')	Group, mass, groundcover
Maiden grass (*Miscanthus sinensis* 'Gracillimus')	Specimen, cut, screen, perennial border
Early maiden grass (*M. sinensis* 'Graziella')	Specimen, screen, accent, groups
Switch grass (*Panicum virgatum* vars.)	Group, mass, perennial borders, naturalizing, cut flowers
Feesey's ribbon grass (*Phalaris arundinacea* 'Feesey')	Groundcover
Ribbon grass (*Phalaris arundinacea* 'Picta')	Groundcover
Little blue stem (*Schizachyrium scoparium*)	Mass, groups, naturalizing, cut, groundcover
Autumn moor grass (*Sesleria autumnalis*)	Mass, foreground, border, rock gardens, forest setting
Indian grass (*Sorghastrum nutans* [*avenaceum*])	Cut, mass, group, specimen, perennial border

Take care of ornamental grasses just as you do other herbaceous perennials. They love a mulch that covers their crowns. They generally tolerate drought but will respond to any water you care to give them during the dry summer. They don't need regular transplanting or dividing if you have carefully planned your planting. Put them where they can grow to their normal size without crowding or interference from other plants.

GRASSES THAT ARE SHADE TOLERANT

Especially in the western part of the Pacific Northwest region, finding grasses that will stay alive in the shade of native trees and large shrubs is a challenge. Luckily in this group of ornamental grasses, there exists a rather large number of selections. Give some of them a try in places where your lawn grasses gave up long ago.

Name	Suggested use
Golden foxtail grass (*Alopecurus pratensis* 'Aureovariegatus')	Groups, mass, water gardens
Variegated bulbous oat grass (*Arrhenatherum bulbosum* 'Variegatum')	Border, edging, specimen, containers
Quaking grass (*Briza media*)	Spring perennial border, mass, cut, specimen
Feather reed grass (*Calamagrostis acutiflora* 'Karl Foerster')	Mass, groups, background, cut flowers
Sedges (*Carex* spp.)	Groundcover, accent, edging
Northern sea oats (*Chasmanthium latifolium*)	Perennial border, specimen, cut
Oregon tufted hair grass (*Deschampsia caespitosa* and cultivars)	Mass, groups, wet lands, specimen, cut
Japanese forest grass (*Hakonechloa macra* and cultivars)	Groups, groundcover, accent
Variegated velvet grass (*Holcus mollis* 'Albovariegatus')	Borders, groundcover
Prairie junegrass (*Koeleria pyramidata* (*cristata*))	Group, rock gardens, groundcover
Wood rushes (*Luzula* spp.)	Groundcover, groups, woodland sites
Golden wood millet (*Millium effusum* 'Aureum')	Dwarf, groundcover
Purple moor grass (*Molinia caerulea* and cultivars)	Specimen, groups, mass
Oriental fountain grass (*Pennisetum orientale*)	Specimen, groups, perennial beds
Feesey's ribbon grass (*Phalaris arundinacea* 'Feesey')	Groundcover
Ribbon grass (*Phalaris arundinacea* 'Picta')	Groundcover
Autumn moor grass (*Sesleria autumnalis*)	Group, mass, groundcover, rockery
Korean reed grass (*Stipa brachytricha*)	Small groups

No grasses are completely tolerant of shade. If you plant an ornamental clumping grass and a young shade tree within arms length of each other, the grass will outgrow the tree in the early years, but its days are numbered. Once the tree reaches maturity and becomes dense, the grass will become leggy and weak and will eventually give up because of the lack of light. Plan accordingly and put your grasses where they can receive sufficient light for life.

GRASSES THAT ARE TOLERANT OF WET AREAS

The classic growing conditions for grasses across the region are full sun, well-drained soils, and often soils that are likely to be dry much of the year. But it is true that some will grow in, or at least tolerate, wet soils. Here are some suggested types and varieties that have performed well in damp sites.

Name	Suggested use
Japanese sweet flag (*Acorus gramineus* and cultivars)	Perennial border, containers, bog garden
Golden foxtail grass (*Alopecurus pratensis* 'Aureovariegatus')	Groups, massing, water gardens
Giant reed grass (*Arundo donax* and cultivars)	Screen, background, cut, specimen
Feather reed grass (*Calamagrostis acutiflora* 'Karl Foerster')	Mass, groups, cut flowers
Sedges (*Carex* spp.)	Groundcover, rockery, under trees, perennial borders, accent
Northern sea oats (*Chasmanthium latifolium*)	Perennial border, specimen, cut
Oregon tufted hair grass (*Deschampsia caespitosa* and cultivars)	Mass, groups, specimen, cut, perennial border, accent, groundcover
Variegated manna grass (*Glyceria maxima* 'Variegata')	Ponds, streams, marshy areas, bogs
Rushes (*Juncus* spp.)	Ponds, streams, marshy areas, bogs
Wood rushes (*Luzula* spp.)	Dwarf grasses
Giant Chinese silver grass (*Miscanthus floridulus*)	Specimen, screen, background
Maiden grass (*Miscanthus sinensis* and cultivars)	Specimen, screen, perennial border, accent, groups, cut flowers
Moor grass (*Molinia caerulea* and cultivars)	Specimen, mass, groups
Tall moor grass (*Molinia arundinacea* and cultivars)	Specimen, groups
Switch grass (*Panicum virgatum* and cultivars)	Groups, mass, perennial border, containers, cut flowers
Feesey's ribbon grass (*Phalaris arundinacea* 'Feesey')	Groundcover
Ribbon grass (*Phalaris arundinacea* 'Picta')	Groundcover
Variegated common reed (*Phragmites australis* 'Variegatus')	Border, containers, wet soils
Variegated cord grass (*Spartina pectinata* 'Aureomarginata')	Groups, mass, perennial border, accent
Common cattail (*Typha latifolia*)	Groups, mass, cut

 You will notice as you scan through the lists of ornamental grasses that Karl Foerster's name is used as a variety name of feather reed grass. The German plantsman, collector, and hybridizer Karl Foerster was one of the first to discover the unique ability of grasses to lend form and grace to the landscape. He is quoted as calling grass "the hair of Mother Earth."

GRASSES FOR SPRING AND SUMMER FLOWERS AND FALL COLOR

Annual and perennial flowers are not the only plants that add color to the landscape. Grasses provide interesting spring and summer flowers as well as a palette of fall color. Here are some suggestions for adding a bit of interest during certain seasons with grasses.

Name	Comments
For spring flowers	
Quaking grass (*Briza media*)	Spring perennial border, specimen, cut, mass
Star sedge (*Carex greyi*)	Dwarf, mace-like flower
Weeping sedge (*Carex pendula*)	Mass, groundcover, small groups
Oregon tufted hair grass (*Deschampsia caespitosa* and cultivars)	Mass, groups, wet lands, naturalizing
Fescues (*Festuca* spp.)	Mass, specimen, perennial border
Blue oat grass (*Helictotrichon sempervirens*)	Specimen, groups, mass, border
Large blue hair grass (*Koeleria glauca*)	Groups, mass, rock gardens
Wood rush (*Luzula species* and cultivars)	Groundcover, groups, beneath trees
Giant feather grass (*Stipa gigantea*)	Specimen, groups, perennial borders, cut
For summer flowers	
Feather reed grass (*Calamagrostis acutiflora* 'Karl Foerster')	Mass, groups, background, cut flowers
Northern sea oats (*Chasmanthium latifolium*)	Perennial border, specimen, cut flowers
Pampas grass (*Cortaderia selloana* and cultivars)	Specimen, screen, background, cut
Love grass (*Eragrostis trichoides*)	Specimen, background, containers
Arabesque silver grass (*Miscanthus sinensis* 'Arabesque')	Compact grower
Silver feather Japanese silver grass (*M. sinensis* 'Silberfeder')	Specimen, mass, cut, background
Yaku Jima silver grass (*M. sinensis* 'Yaku Jima')	Groups, mass, combination
Purple moor grass (*Molinia caerulea* and cultivars)	Specimen, mass, groups
Moor grass (*M. arundinacea* and cultivars)	Specimen, groups
Red switch grass (*Panicum virgatum* vars.)	Groups, mass, perennial border, cut
Fountain grass (*Pennisetum alopecuroides* and cultivars)	Groups, mass, specimen, perennial border
Oriental fountain grass (*Pennisetum orientale*)	Dwarf specimen, edging, border, accent
Indian grass (*Sorghastrum nutans* (*avenaceum*))	Cut, mass, groups, specimen, border
Frost grass (*Spodiopogon sibiricus*)	Groups, specimen
Feather grass (*Stipa capillata*)	Groups, cut flowers
For fall colors	
Big blue stem (*Andropogon gerardii*)	Silver flowers; orange, purple, and red foliage

Gramma grasses (*Bouteloua curtipendula*, *B. gracilis*)	Purple
Northern sea oats (*Chasmanthium latifolium*)	Purplish foliage
Variegated Japanese forest grass (*Hakonechloa macra* 'Aureola')	Green, pink, and red
Japanese blood grass (*Imperata* 'Red Baron')	Intense red
Purple wood rush (*Luzula purpurea*)	Reddish purple with green
Maiden grass (*Miscanthus sinensis* 'Gracillimus')	Purple stem, yellow foliage
Flame grass (*M. sinensis purpurescens*)	Red, purple, yellow, and orange foliage
Purple moor grass (*Molinia caerulea* and cultivars)	Orange red
Malepartus silver grass (*Miscanthus sinensis* 'Malepartus')	Orange foliage
Red switch grass (*Panicum virgatum* vars.)	Intense red with yellow
Heavy Metal switch grass (*P. virgatum* 'Heavy Metal')	Bright yellow foliage
Feesey's ribbon grass (*Phalaris arundinacea* 'Feesey')	Blush pink with green and white
Ribbon grass (*P. arundinacea* 'Picta')	Blush pink
Indian grass (*Sorghastrum nutans* (*avenaceum*))	Yellow and orange
Korean reed grass (*Stipa brachytricha*)	Bright yellow

ORNAMENTAL GRASSES THAT MAKE GOOD GROUNDCOVERS IN FULL SUN

Check the lists for desert and for seaside to see which of these will fit into your particular climate or microclimate. Provide these grasses with reasonably good soil (well-drained for most of them), remove native grasses as they try to fill the gaps, and fertilize as they show a need. Add to the list as you try others.

Name	Can also be used for
Quaking grass (*Briza media*)	Spring perennial border, specimen, cut
Oregon tufted hair grass (*Deschampsia caespitosa* and cultivars)	Groups, wet lands, naturalizing
Fescue grass (*Festuca* spp.)	Edging, accent, rockery
Blue oat grass (*Helictotrichon sempervirens*)	Specimen, groups, perennial borders
Variegated velvet grass (*Holcus mollis* 'Albovariegatus')	Borders
Blue wild rye (*Leymus racemosus* 'Glauca')	Group, beach and seashore
Silver grass (*Miscanthus sinensis* and cultivars)	Specimen, groups, cut, perennial border
Fountain grass (*Pennisetum alopecuroides* and cultivars)	Groups, specimen, perennial border
Autumn moor grass (*Sesleria autumnalis*)	Group, foreground, borders, rockery

GRASSES AND WILDFLOWER MEADOW MIXTURES

Christy Hopkins of Hobbs & Hopkins Protime Lawn Seed, provided seed lists of their wild-flower mixtures that are used throughout the Pacific Northwest. Christy and husband Keith emphasize the importance of eradicating weeds, especially those that tend to dominate others, before planting. Once the weeds are taken care of, lightly disc or till shallowly so there is ample soil and seed contact. After planting, keep the area dampened until seeds have germinated and if Mother Nature does not provide enough water, provide moisture via irrigation until the plants are established. The fact that these plant selections are wild types does not mean that they can thrive without care from you. They are simply those flowering plants that are adapted to this region, that will, if given time and a modicum of care, provide you with color and interest.

Low profile wildflowers: all Pacific Northwest zones
Less than 24 inches tall in most plantings

Spurred snapdragon (*Antirrhinum majus*)   Bachelor button (*Centaurea cyanus*)
Clarkia (*Clarkia pulchella*)   Chinese houses (*Collinsia heterophylla*)
Coreopsis (*Coreopsis grandiflora*)   Pinks (*Dianthus* spp.)
Sweet William (*Dianthus barbatus*)   African daisy (*Dimorphotheca* spp.)
California poppy (*Eschscholzia californica*)   Wallflower (*Erysimum* spp.)
Baby's breath (*Gypsophila paniculata*)   Candytuft (*Iberis* spp.)
Blue flax (*Linum perenne*)   Alyssum (*Lobularia* spp.)
Dwarf lupine (*Lupinus* spp.)   Forget-me-not (*Myosotis* spp.)

Portland wildflowers used by City of Portland

White yarrow (*Achillea millefolium*)   Spurred snapdragon (*Antirrhinum majus*)
Columbine (*Aquilegia formosa*)   Bachelor button (*Centaurea cyanus*)
Shasta daisy (*Chrysanthemum maximum*)   Clarkia (*Clarkia pulchella*)
Chinese houses (*Colinsia heterophylla*)   Coreopsis (*Coreopsis grandiflora*)
Pinks (*Dianthus* spp.)   Delphinium (*D. grandiflorum*)
Wallflower (*Erysimum* spp.)   California poppy (*Eschscholzia californica*)
Blanket flower (*Gaillardia grandiflora*)   Baby's breath (*Gypsophila paniculata*)
Dame's rocket (*Hesperis matronalis*)   Candytuft (*Iberis sempervirens*)
Scarlet flax (*Linum grandiflorum* 'Rubrum')   Blue flax (*Linum perenne*)
Lobelia (*Lobelia* spp.)   Lupine (*Lupinus* spp.)
Baby blue eyes (*Nemophila menziesii*)   Evening primrose (*Oenothera* spp.)
Shirley poppy (*Papaver rhoeas*)   Black-eyed susan (*Rudbeckia hirta*)
Catchfly (*Silene* spp.)

"Early spring planting is best in the Pacific Northwest. Select a well-drained site and then figure out how to take care of weeds present or expected. Competition from weeds and grasses can be a challenge to a new wildflower planting."—Keith Hopkins, Protime Lawn Seed Co., Portland

A mix for gardeners who do not want California poppy ("Rita's Garden Mix")

Aster, mixed (*Aster* spp.)
Shasta daisy (*Chrysanthemum maximum*)
Chinese houses (*Colinsia heterophylla*)
Purple coneflower (*Echinacea purpurea*)
Strawflower (*Helichrysum bracteatum*)
Blue flax (*Linum perenne*)
Love in a mist (*Nigella damascena*)
Catchfly (*Silene* spp.)
Bachelor buttons (*Centauria cyanus*)
Godetia, dwarf and semi dwarf (*Clarkia amoena*)
African daisy (*Dimorphotheca* spp.)
Baby's breath (*Gypsophila paniculata*)
Scarlet flax (*Linum grandiflorum* 'Rubrum')
Baby blue eyes (*Nemophila menziesii*)
Shirley poppy (*Papaver rhoeas*)
Zinnia (*Zinnia* spp.)

Annual cut flower mix, also good to use for the annual overseeding of the wildflower patch

Love lies bleeding (*Amaranthus caudatus*)
Calendula (*Calendula* spp.)
Godetia (*Clarkia amoena*)
Coreopsis (*Coreopsis grandiflora*)
Chinese forget-me-not (*Cynoglossum amabile*)
Linaria (*Linaria* spp.)
Shirley poppy (*Papaver rhoeas*)
Zinnia (*Zinnia* spp.)
Crego aster mix (*Aster* spp.)
Bachelor button mix (*Centauria cyanus*)
Clarkia (*C. pulchella*)
Cosmos (*Cosmos* spp.)
Single baby's breath (*Gypsophila* spp.)
Blue lupine (*Lupinus* spp.)
Marigold (*Tagetes* spp.)

Perennial wildflower mix, for those long-lasting meadow and glade plantings

White yarrow (*Achillea millefolium*)
Ox-eye daisy (*Chrysanthemum leucanthemum*)
Sweet William (*Dianthus barbatus*)
Coneflower (*Echinacea purpurea*)
Dame's rocket (*Hesperis matronalis*)
Blue lupine (*Lupinus* spp.)
Columbine (*Aquilegia* spp.)
Coreopsis (*C. grandiflora*)
Foxglove (*Digitalis purpurea*)
Wallflower (*Erysimum* spp.)
Blue flax (*Linum perenne*)
Black-eyed susan (*Rudbeckia hirta*)

"Remember, don't plant too deep, ¼ to ½ inch at most. If nature doesn't provide sufficient rainfall, irrigation is recommended to keep the seeds moist during the establishment period. Wildflowers will establish without supplemental irrigation, but to maximize results, consistent moisture is necessary until establishment."—Christy Hopkins, Protime Lawn Seed Co., Portland

ORNAMENTAL GRASSES THAT PROVIDE CUT FLOWERS

The feathery plumes and golden spikes from some of these ornamental grasses give the flower arranger a resource that will be the envy of gardening friends. Most of them can be dried for saving, but the gardener who has some of these plants in the garden will never be lacking something for arrangement interest.

Name	Can also be used for
Quaking grass (*Briza media*)	Spring perennial border, specimen, mass
Feather reed grass (*Calamagrostis acutiflora* 'Karl Foerster')	Mass, groups, background

Ornamental Grasses That Provide Cut Flowers (continued)

Northern sea oats (*Chasmanthium latifolium*)	Perennial border, specimen, near water
Pampas grass (*Cortaderia selloana*)	Specimen, screen, background
Oregon tufted hair grass (*Deschampsia caespitosa* and cultivars)	Mass, specimen, groups, naturalizing
Silver grass (*Miscanthus* spp. and cultivars)	Specimen, borders, mass, screen
Switch grass (*Panicum virgatum* cultivars)	Groups, mass, specimen, containers
Fountain grass (*Pennisetum* spp. and cultivars)	Groups, mass, specimen, borders
Ravenna grass (*Saccharum ravennae* [*Erianthus*])	Specimen, background, screen
Indian grass (*Sorghastrum nutans* [*avenaceum*])	Mass, groups, specimen, perennial border
Feather grass (*Stipa species*)	Perennial border, mass, groups

VINES

The advantages of using vines are among the best kept gardening secrets. They are the best way to make use of a vertical garden surface. They serve as frosting on the cake of the well-planned garden. Those beautiful cottage gardens we see illustrated in our favorite gardening magazines are accented with vines. Small-space city gardens are softened by the use of vines. These climbers can be used to accent trellises, arbors, pergolas and posts. They can be planted to meander up an old tree trunk, sprawl over rocks to cover a bank, or cover an unsightly fence. Vines climb by aerial roots (ivy), leaf stalks (clematis), tendrils (passionvine) and twining stems (akebia). Clematis is one of the most common twiners. This vine winds to the right, or clockwise, while the morning glory turns to left, or counterclockwise. Why? Ask Mother Nature! Some vines need you to offer only support and they will do the rest; others will need a little coaxing to get them to go the direction you intend. Keep them where you want them and enjoy what they have to offer.

Morning Glories

We provide a list to help you choose a quick or temporary screen or backdrop. Climbing roses are also included in many lists. While they do not actually climb without being tied, they fit many vining categories nicely (see rose chapter). After you investigate the lists below, you will probably want to make a place for a vine, even if you don't have one now. Enjoy these vertical treasures of the gardening world.

VINES FOR ALKALINE SOIL

Vines grow in a wide range of soil pH. The following vines will do well in soils with a high pH without any special treatment. They will also do well in other soil types that are more acidic. One of the problems of growing in alkaline soils is the unavailability of iron, which then results in chlorosis (loss of green color in the leaf). Chlorosis can be dealt with by supplying soluble forms of iron; however, if you have alkaline soil your gardening activities will be less demanding if you select some of the following vines that will tolerate the higher soil pH ranges.

Actinidia (*Actinidia kolomikta*)	All PNW
Five-leaf akebia (*Akebia quinata*)	All PNW
Blueberry climber (*Ampelopsis brevipedunculata*)	All PNW
Climbing snapdragon (*Asarina antirrhinifolia*)	Annual
Dutchman's pipe (*Aristolochia durior*)	All PNW
Trumpet vine (*Campsis radicans*)	All PNW
Bittersweet (*Celastrus scandens*)	All PNW
Clematis (*Clematis*, some cultivars)	All PNW
Hyacinth bean (*Dolichos Lablab*)	Annual
English ivy (*Hedera helix*)	All PNW
Climbing hydrangea (*Hydrangea anomala petiolaris*)	All PNW
Morning glories (*Ipomoea* spp.)	Annual
Cardinal climber (*Ipomoea quamoclit*)	Annual
Perennial sweet pea (*Lathyrus latifolius*)	All PNW
Hall's honeysuckle (*Lonicera japonica* 'Halliana')	All PNW
Virginia creeper (*Parthenocissus quinquefolia*)	All PNW
Boston ivy (*Parthenocissus tricuspidata*)	All PNW
Silver lace vine (*Polygonum aubertii*)	All PNW
Climbing rose (*Rosa*, see rose chapter)	All PNW
Wisteria (*Wisteria* spp.)	All PNW

VINES FOR SHADE AND FULL SUN

A few vines will tolerate heavy shade. The first list will do well under a tree with a dense canopy or against the north side of a house. These vines will also do well in partial shade and will take full sun in cooler summer climates. The second list will do well in either sun or partial shade. Note the zones where you can expect them to tolerate these situations the best. If you see these vines growing vigorously in your neighborhood observe their exposure and choose your planting site accordingly. Gardening is not an exact science. It requires years of observation and experimentation to come up with winning plant selections for your particular location. For example, although clematis is listed as taking full sun, it prefers cool and shaded roots. The passionvine is considered a root-hardy perennial in milder PNW climates. In other words, it dies down in the winter but comes back from the roots in the spring.

Most annual vines require full sun. Don't forget to look at the annual vine list when deciding what vines will work in your sunniest exposures.

Shade

Five-leaf akebia (*Akebia quinata*)	All PNW
Blueberry climber (*Ampelopsis brevipedunculata*)	All PNW

Dutchman's pipe (*Aristolochia durior*) — All PNW
Clematis (*Clematis chrysocoma*) — All PNW
English ivy (*Hedera helix* var.) — All PNW
Honeysuckle (*Lonicera* spp.) — C, LV, LM, DV
Silvervein creeper (*Parthenocissus henryana*) — C, LV, LM, DV
Virginia creeper (*Parthenocissus quinquefolia*) — All PNW
Boston ivy (*Parthenocissus tricuspidata*) — All PNW
Schizophragma (*Schizophragma hydrangeoides*) — C, LV, LM, DV

Full sun or partial shade

Hardy kiwi (*Actinidia arguta*) — All PNW
Chinese gooseberry vine (*Actinidia deliciosa*) — All PNW
Actinidia (*Actinidia kolomikta*) — All PNW
Five-leaf akebia (*Akebia quinata*) — All PNW
Blueberry climber (*Ampelopsis brevipedunculata*) — All PNW
Dutchman's pipe (*Aristolochia durior*) — All PNW
Chinese trumpet creeper (*Campsis grandiflora*) — C, LV, LM, DV
Trumpet vine (*Campsis radicans*) — All PNW
American bittersweet (*Celastrus scandens*) — All PNW
Clematis (*Clematis* spp.) — All PNW
Cup-and-saucer vine (*Cobaea scandens*) — All PNW
Wintercreeper (*Euonymus fortunei radicans*) — All PNW
Hardenbergia (*Hardenbergia violacea* 'Happy Wanderer') — C
English ivy (*Hedera helix* var.) — All PNW
Japanese hop (*Humulus japonicus*) — All PNW
Common hop (*Humulus lupulus*) — All PNW
Climbing hydrangea (*Hydrangea anomala*) — All PNW
Spanish jasmine (*Jasminum grandiflorum*) — C, LV, LM
Winter jasmine (*Jasminum nudiflorum*) — C, LV, LM
Chilean bellflower (*Lapageria rosea*) — C, LV
Japanese honeysuckle (*Lonicera japonica* var.) — C, LV, LM, DV
Woodbine (*Lonicera periclymenum*) — C, LV, LM, DV
Chilean jasmine (*Mandevilla laxa*) — C, LV
Silvervein creeper (*Parthenocissus henryana*) — C, LV, LM, DV
Virginia creeper (*Parthenocissus quinquefolia*) — All PNW
Boston ivy (*Parthenocissus tricuspidata*) — All PNW
Incense passionvine (*Passiflora* 'Incense') — C, LV
Passionvine (*Passiflora alatocaerulea*) — C, LV
Silver lace vine (*Polygonum aubertii*) — All PNW
Climbing rose (*Rosa*, see rose chapter) — All PNW
Schizophragma (*Schizophragma hydrangeoides*) — C, LV, LM, DV
Jasmine (*Trachelospermum asiaticum*) — LV
Grape (*Vitis* spp.) — Varies
Wisteria (*Wisteria* spp.) — All PNW

Common Hop

Annual vines need only enough fertilizer to keep them healthy and vigorous through the summer. Perennial vines would benefit from a complete fertilizer once a year, however, if the vine is vigorous enough and is putting on sufficient new growth, why fertilize and cause yourself more work in pruning?

VINES HARDY IN ALL PNW ZONES

These vines are the tough guys of the Pacific Northwest. You can expect them to be vigorous, easy to grow, and reliable. It is possible for dieback to occur even with the most hardy plants. Nature sometimes deals us a severe winter. In this case, be patient and don't prune too soon. Wait for signs of life in your vine and then prune back to a live bud or a vigorous growing point.

> Hardy kiwi (*Actinidia arguta*)
> Actinidia (*Actinidia kolomikta*)
> Five-leaf akebia (*Akebia quinata*)
> Blueberry climber (*Ampelopsis brevipedunculata*)
> Trumpet vine (*Campsis radicans*)
> Chinese trumpet creeper (*Campsis grandiflora*)
> English ivy (*Hedera helix*)
> Baltic ivy (*Hedera helix* 'Baltica')
> Climbing hydrangea (*Hydrangea anomala*)
> Virginia creeper (*Parthenocissus quinquefolia*)
> Silver lace vine (*Polygonum aubertii*)
> Grape (*Vitis* spp.)
> Wisteria (*Wisteria* spp.)

A little-known vine that is a favorite of ours is the five-leaf akebia (Akebia quinata). It is attractive and graceful and provides interest outside of our office window. It grows up a wire on the southeast corner of the house. Its leaflets create a parasol for the fleshy little purple flowers that are borne on two stems, one male and one female, in late spring. It requires little in the way of fertilizer and pruning. Our biggest problem is to keep it from entwining the dinner bell hung nearby.

ANNUAL VINES

If you have a sunny area that could use a quick screen, attractive flowers, or a splash of color to provide a backdrop for other plants, why not choose an annual vine? Some may be difficult to find, but they are worth the search. Some nurseries do the germinating for you and offer annual vines potted and ready to go. Your seed catalogs are a good source for some of these less commonly used vines. Seeds can also be found in your local garden centers and nurseries. Look on the flower racks or specialty seed racks to find some of these gems. In the case of scarlet runner bean, the pods are edible. You can also let the pods dry on the vine to supply you with next year's seed. Love-in-a-puff has little balloon-like seed capsules that turn a rich brown in the fall. Don't hesitate to plant morning glory. The annual varieties are not the same as those that escape and become weeds. They will die down over the winter. Most annual vines will take full sun. It is fun to plant annual vines at the base of perennial vines to get interesting flower and foliage texture combinations.

> Madeira vine (*Anredera cordifolia*) (tuberous, hardy to C, LV, LM)
> Climbing snapdragon (*Asarina antirrhinifolia*)
> Creeping gloxinia (*Asarina scandens*)
> Love-in-a-puff (*Cardiospermum halicacabum*)
> Cup-and-saucer vine (*Cobaea scandens*)

Dwarf morning glory (*Convolvulus* 'Star of Yelta')
Ensign dwarf morning glory (*Convolvulus tricolor* 'Ensign')
Hyacinth bean (*Dolichos Lablab*)
Glory flower (*Eccremocarpus scaber* 'Anglia Hybrids')
Wild cucumber (*Echinocystis lobata*)
Glory lily (*Gloriosa superba*)
Hops (*Humulus japonicus* 'Variegatus')
Moonflower (*Ipomoea alba*)
Heavenly Blue morning glory (*Ipomoea nil* 'Heavenly Blue')
Crimson Glory morning glory (*Ipomoea purpurea* 'Crimson Glory')
Cardinal climber (*Ipomoea quamoclit* × *multifida*)
Crimson rambler morning glory (*Ipomoea tricolor*)
Luffa gourd (*Luffa aegyptiaca*)
Spanish flag (*Mina lobata*)
Sweet pea (*Lathyrus odoratus*)
Scarlet runner bean (*Phaseolus coccineus*)
Purple bell vine (*Rhodochiton atrosanguineum*)
Mexican flame vine (*Senecio confusus*)
Black-eyed susan vine (*Thunbergia alata*)
Orange clock vine (*Thunbergia gregorii*)
Garden nasturtium (*Tropaeolum majus*)
Canary bird flower (*Tropaeolum peregrinum*)
Tweedia (*Tweedia caerulea*)

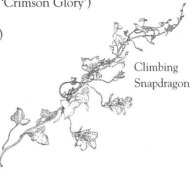

Climbing
Snapdragon

"The fun part of growing annual vines is seeing them grow several inches a day when the summer really heats up, and watching the hummingbirds and butterflies come to feed at the flowers. Besides being pretty, annual vines are very practical. I grow some, like scarlet runners or black-eyed susan vines, as flowering sunshades for the hot spots on the patio or greenhouse. Others I like to grow around the garden to hide a rather ugly fence and to add height where things are too flat. My all-time favorite is the purple hyacinth bean (Dolichos Lablab)."—Carolyn Clark, garden writer, Portland

VINES TOLERANT OF SOMETIMES SOGGY SITES

There are only a few vines that can thrive with wet feet. Those listed below are hardy all over the Pacific Northwest and do well in our region. The Dutchman's pipe, sometimes called the Dutchman's pipevine, is an interesting woody climber with large heart-shaped leaves and flaring, strangely formed blossoms favored by the pipevine swallowtail butterfly. Flowers are tube-shaped, brownish-purple with a yellowish green calyx. It does best in a northern exposure with its roots mulched in the winter.

Dutchman's pipe (*Aristolochia durior*)	All PNW
English ivy (*Hedera helix* var.)	All PNW
Common hop (*Humulus lupulus*)	All PNW
Japanese hop (*Humulus japonicus*)	All PNW
Golden hop (*Humulus lupulus* 'Aureus')	All PNW
Hall's honeysuckle (*Lonicera japonica* 'Halliana')	C, LV, LM, DV
Silver lace vine (*Polygonum aubertii*)	All PNW

VINES FOR THE BEACH

These vines will do well in coastal environments. That is not to say they will hold up under pounding salt wind conditions, but that they will thrive in the moderately moist conditions provided by the seashore garden. To protect from the wind you may have better results by planting these vines on the leeward side of your home. If you have an inland coastal garden, wind may not be a factor. Most of the vines listed will take full sun. A few vines listed will not do well in parts of the Pacific Northwest other than in a marine-influenced landscape. Happy Wanderer hardenbergia will grow only in coastal environments.

Note: There is one unique growing zone on the coast of southwestern Oregon. While all of the vines below will grow in this marine-influenced environment, it would be best to consult plant lists for Northern California for a much wider variety of plants that will thrive in this warmer climate.

Hardy kiwi (*Actinidia arguta*)
Actinidia (*Actinidia kolomikta*)
Five-leaf akebia (*Akebia quinata*)
Blueberry climber (*Ampelopsis brevipedunculata*)
Madeira vine (*Anredera cordifolia*) tuber
Chinese trumpet creeper (*Campsis grandiflora*)
Trumpet vine (*Campsis radicans*)
Clematis (*Clematis* spp.)
Hardenbergia (*Hardenbergia violacea* 'Happy Wanderer')
Persian ivy (*Hedera colchica* 'Dentata Variegata')
Goldheart English ivy (*Hedera helix* 'Goldheart')
Common hop (*Humulus lupulus*)
Golden hop (*Humulus lupulus* 'Aureus')
Variegated hop (*Humulus japonicus* 'Variegatus')
Japanese hop (*Humulus japonicus*)
Spanish jasmine (*Jasminum grandiflorum*)
Winter jasmine (*Jasminum nudiflorum*)
Chilean bellflower (*Lapageria rosea*)
Sweet pea (*Lathyrus odoratus*)
Japanese honeysuckle (*Lonicera japonica*)
Virginia creeper (*Parthenocissus quinquefolia*)
Passion vine (*Passiflora alatocaerulea*)
Silver lace vine (*Polygonum aubertii*)
Climbing rose (see rose chapter)
Garden nasturtium (*Tropaeolum majus*)
Wisteria (*Wisteria* spp.)

VINES FOR FALL COLOR

Few vines have good fall color; however, the ones in the list below can provide a colorful fall backdrop for larger evergreen shrubs. Golden hues of autumn vine foliage against dark green foliage of evergreen trees or large shrubs bring a rich seasonal contrast to the garden. In addition to good fall color, the blueberry climber provides clusters of greenish ivory to brilliant metallic blue berries in late summer and fall that attract the birds. Blueberry climber, grapes, and wisteria all are vigorous growers and require strong support. The Boston ivy and Virginia creeper need a wall on which to attach their disks that are developed at the ends of their tendrils.

Blueberry climber (*Ampelopsis brevipedunculata*)	All PNW
Climbing hydrangea (*Hydrangea anomala*)	All PNW
Honeysuckle (*Lonicera* spp.)	C, LV, LM, DV
Virginia creeper (*Parthenocissus quinquefolia*)	All PNW
Boston ivy (*Parthenocissus tricuspidata* var.)	All PNW
Grape (*Vitis* spp.)	Varies
Crimson glory vine (*Vitis coignetiae*)	All PNW
Wisteria (*Wisteria* spp.)	All PNW

FAVORITE VINES OF PNW GARDENERS

Here is a list of the favorite vines of the most avid gardeners we found throughout the Pacific Northwest. They are listed for the uniqueness of their foliage, flower, or fragrance. Each is worthy of a place in your garden. Go slowly though because you may wake up some morning and find the entire house engulfed with vines and you won't be able to open the doors! Find out why each of these vines is considered special. There are many other varieties and cultivars of the vines listed. For instance, Forest Farm in Williams, Oregon, has thirty different shrub and vining honeysuckles listed in their catalog.

Trumpet Vine

Actinidia (*Actinidia kolomikta*)	All PNW
Five-leaf akebia (*Akebia quinata*)	All PNW
Trumpet vine (*Campsis radicans*)	All PNW
Evergreen clematis (*Clematis armandii*)	C, LV, LM, DV
Jackman clematis (*Clematis jackmanii*)	All PNW
Anemone clematis (*Clematis montana*)	All PNW
Sweet autumn clematis (*Clematis paniculata*)	All PNW
Golden hop (*Humulus lupulus* 'Aureus')	All PNW
Climbing hydrangea (*Hydrangea anomala*)	All PNW
Winter jasmine (*Jasminum nudiflorum*)	C, LV, LM, DV
Goldnet honeysuckle (*Lonicera japonica* 'Aureoreticulata')	C, LV, LM, DV
Woodbine (*Lonicera periclymenum*)	C, LV, LM, DV
Passionvine (*Passiflora alatocaerulea*)	C, LV
Silver lace vine (*Polygonum aubertii*)	All PNW
Climbing rose (see rose chapter)	All PNW
Wisteria (*Wisteria* spp.)	All PNW

"We certainly respect the right of plants to just be without having any human use at all. The beauty and joy they bring to our lives is incalculable, but even an 'ugly' plant (can there be such a thing?) without an edible fruit or a fragrant flower has incredible importance to us all in the chain of which we are only one link (a link more dependent on plants than they are on us!). It is, nevertheless, interesting, and another perspective on history, to see the many and varied ways we've found to use plants."—Ray and Peg Prag, Forest Farm, Williams, Oregon

EVERGREEN VINES TO HOLD GROUND ON A SLOPE

Vines can be used as a trailing groundcover to hold topsoil in place. Don't expect them to hold large banks from major soil slippage. That is a job for tree roots. These vines will mound up on themselves and create interesting additions to your landscape. English ivy, Virginia creeper and trumpet vine have holdfast disks at the ends of their tendrils, so unless it is your plan, don't let them climb a tree or a wall. Periwinkle is really not a vine, but is considered a vining or trailing groundcover.

Trumpet vine (*Campsis radicans*)	All PNW
Wintercreeper (*Euonymus fortunei radicans*)	C, LV, LM, DV
English ivy (*Hedera helix*)	All PNW
Goldheart English ivy (*Hedera helix* 'Goldheart')	All PNW
Winter jasmine (*Jasminum nudiflorum*)	C, LV, LM, DV
Hall's honeysuckle (*Lonicera japonica* 'Halliana')	C, LV, LM, DV
Virginia creeper (*Parthenocissus quinquefolia*)	All PNW
Periwinkle (*Vinca major*)	All PNW
Dwarf periwinkle (*Vinca minor*)	All PNW

Consideration should be given to how much pruning time you want to spend on a vining plant. Don't choose a vigorous vine for a small space, as you will be spending all of your time trying to keep it within bounds. Some vines require heavy pruning to encourage new growth, others demand only moderate thinning to do their best. Do your homework and find out what your vine needs and what you can expect the vine to do in your growing zone.

VINES WITH SHOWY OR INTERESTING FLOWERS

Vines that grow in the Pacific Northwest can offer you brightly colored flowers with tropical-looking blooms or unexpected bursts of tiny colorful flowers. The Chilean jasmine has large trumpet-shaped flowers that are as powerfully fragrant as a gardenia. The akebia provides fleshy purple flowers protected by its five-part leaf. You will also discover that annual vines can provide quick-growing, interesting additions to the garden, many with large, sometimes fragrant flowers.

White

Madeira vine (*Anredera cordifolia*)		Tuber— C, LV, DV
Anemone clematis (*Clematis montana*)		All PNW
Sweet autumn clematis (*Clematis paniculata*)	White with pink	All PNW
Hyacinth bean (*Dolichos Lablab*)	White and purple	Annual
Moonflower (*Ipomoea alba*)		Annual
Spanish jasmine (*Jasminum grandiflorum*)		C, LV, LM
Chilean jasmine (*Mandevilla laxa*)		C, LV, LM, DV
Passion vine (*Passiflora alatocaerulea*)		C, LV
Silver lace vine (*Polygonum aubertii*)		All PNW
Wisteria (*Wisteria floribunda*)		All PNW

Purple, Lilac, and Blue

Five-leaf akebia (*Akebia quinata*)	Purple	All PNW
Cup-and-saucer vine (*Cobaea scandens*)	Violet	Annual
Hyacinth bean (*Dolichos Lablab*)	Purple and white	Annual
Hardenbergia (*Hardenbergia violacea*)	Lilac	C
Morning glory (*Ipomoea nil* 'Heavenly Blue')	Blue	Annual
Blue crown passionflower (*Passiflora alatocaerulea*)	Blue	Annual
Wisteria (*Wisteria floribunda*)	Purpl, blue, violet	All PNW
Chinese wisteria (*Wisteria sinensis*)	Purple	All PNW

Pink to Red

Actinidia (*Actinidia kolomikta*)	Pink and green (leaf)	All PNW
Trumpet vine (*Campsis radicans*)	Scarlet	All PNW
Chinese trumpet creeper (*Campsis grandiflora*)	Scarlet	C, LV, LM, DV
Scarlet clematis (*Clematis texensis*)	Red	All PNW
Cardinal climber (*Ipomoea quamoclit*)	Scarlet	Annual
Chilean bellflower (*Lapageria rosea*)	Rosy red	C, LV
Scarlet runner bean (*Phaseolus coccineus*)	Red	Annual
Bokahara fleece flower (*Polygonum baldschuanicum*)	Pink	All PNW
Mexican flame vine (*Senecio confusus*)	Orange-red	Annual

Yellow and Green

Dutchman's pipe (*Aristolochia durior*)	Yellowish green	All PNW
Common hop (*Humulus lupulus*)	Greenish	All PNW
Winter jasmine (*Jasminum nudiflorum*)	Yellow	C, LV, LM
Trumpet honeysuckle (*Lonicera sempervirens*)	Yellow to scarlet	C, LV, LM, DV
Berries Jubilee woodbine (*Lonicera periclymenum* 'Berries Jubilee')	Yellow	C, LV, LM, DV
Jasmine (*Trachelospermum asiaticum*)	Yellowish white	LV
Canary bird flower (*Tropaeolum peregrinium*)	Yellow	Annual

Come in Many Colors

Climbing snapdragon (*Asarina antirrhinifolia*)	Annual
Clematis (*Clematis* spp.)	All PNW
Climbing hydrangea (*Hydrangea anomala*)	All PNW
Sweet pea (*Lathyrus odoratus*)	All PNW
Honeysuckle (*Lonicera* spp.)	C, LV, LM, DV
Japanese honeysuckle (*Lonicera japonica*)	C, LV, LM, DV
Climbing rose (see rose chapter)	All PNW
Black-eyed susan vine (*Thunbergia alata*)	Annual
Garden nasturtium (*Tropaeolum majus*)	Annual
Japanese wisteria (*Wisteria floribunda*)	All PNW

Hyacinth Bean

VINES THAT REACH A LONG, LONG WAY

This grouping of vines gives you an idea of just how far a vine is likely to reach. When selecting a vine, choose wisely and make sure you have enough space. The most vigorous vines at the top of the list will require lots of room and support. It may also be wise to determine how these vines cling so that you can provide wires for twining, surfaces for holdfasts, or a surface for clinging. Not every vine available to gardeners in this region is listed, but the list will certainly give you a start. Determining how far a vine will grow is very dependent on your climate. In higher-rainfall areas your vine is sure to be very vigorous.

Fifty Feet or Longer
English ivy (*Hedera helix* spp.)	All PNW
Climbing hydrangea (*Hydrangea anomala*)	All PNW
Virginia creeper (*Parthenocissus quinquefolia*)	All PNW
Boston ivy (*Parthenocissus tricuspidata*)	All PNW
Grape (*Vitis* spp.)	Varies
Japanese wisteria (*Wisteria floribunda*)	All PNW

Forty Feet
Dutchman's pipe (*Aristolochia durior*)	All PNW
Chinese trumpet creeper (*Campsis grandiflora*)	All PNW
Trumpet vine (*Campsis radicans*)	All PNW
Crimson trumpet creeper (*Campsis tagliabuana*)	All PNW
Silvervein creeper (*Parthenocissus henryana*)	All PNW
Silver lace vine (*Polygonum aubertii*)	All PNW
Bokhara fleeceflower (*Polygonum baldschuanicum*)	All PNW

Twenty to Thirty Feet
Hardy kiwi (*Actinidia arguta*)	All PNW
Chinese gooseberry (*Actinidia deliciosa*)	C, LV, LM, DV
Blueberry climber (*Ampelopsis brevipedunculata*)	All PNW
Cup-and-saucer vine (*Cobaea scandens*)	Annual
Japanese hop (*Humulus japonicus*)	All PNW
Common hop (*Humulus lupulus*)	All PNW
Pink jasmine (*Jasminum polyanthum*)	C, LV
Japanese honeysuckle (*Lonicera japonica*)	C, LV, LM, DV
Passionvine (*Passiflora alatocaerulea*)	C, LV
Silver lace vine (*Polygonum aubertii*)	All PNW
Japanese hydrangea vine (*Schizophragma hydrangeoides*)	C, LV, LM, DV

Fifteen to Twenty Feet
Actinidia (*Actinidia kolomikta*)	All PNW
Five-leaf akebia (*Akebia quinata*)	All PNW
American bittersweet (*Celastrus scandens*)	All PNW
Armand clematis (*Clematis armandii*)	All PNW
Jackman clematis (*Clematis jackmanii*)	All PNW
Anemone clematis (*Clematis montana*)	All PNW
Wintercreeper (*Euonymus fortunei radicans*)	All PNW
Chilean jasmine (*Mandevilla laxa*)	C, LV, LM, DV
Climbing rose (see rose chapter)	All PNW

"Gardening in a vertical plane, through the use of vining plants, is becoming very popular because so many of us garden in limited spaces. Vertical gardens can be a part of a large garden, most of a small garden space, or on a deck in containers. When you run out of horizontal space for gardening, use vines, go vertical!"—Lucy Hardiman, Hardy Plant Society, Perennial Partners, Portland

CLIMBING AND TWINING VINES

These vines can easily find their way up to the sunlight and will twine their way around almost any kind of support. Give them support strong enough to hold their weight, which can be considerable when rain or snow adds to the plant's own bulk. Provide these vines with support on which they can climb. Sometimes they need a little help in determining which direction they will go. In the case of clematis, we provide a trellis for the main part of the plant, then we stretch wires that fan out and attach to the house gutter. As the new growth stretches, we wind it around one of the wires to spread it out. Climbers and twiners sometimes circle back over themselves if you don't provide a helping hand and direction. Lattice, netting, chicken wire, or string can provide a quick support system for annual and lightweight vines. For the woody sorts, give them the strong support needed to keep them from crashing down some stormy night.

Actinidia (*Actinidia kolomikta*)	All PNW
Five-leaf akebia (*Akebia quinata*)	All PNW
Blueberry climber (*Ampelopsis brevipedunculata*)	All PNW
Madeira vine (*Anredera cordifolia*)	Tuber - C, LV, DV
Dutchman's pipe (*Aristolochia durior*)	All PNW
Chinese trumpet creeper (*Campsis grandiflora*)	C, LV, LM, DV
Trumpet vine (*Campsis radicans*)	All PNW
American bittersweet (*Celastrus scandens*)	All PNW
Armand clematis (*Clematis armandii*)	All PNW
Clematis (*Clematis* spp.)	All PNW
Hyacinth bean (*Dolichos Lablab*)	Annual
Hardenbergia (*Hardenbergia violacea* 'Happy Wanderer')	C
Common hop (*Humulus lupulus*)	All PNW
Japanese hop (*Humulus japonicus*)	All PNW
Cardinal climber (*Ipomoea quamoclit*)	Annual
Chilean bellflower (*Lapageria rosea*)	C, LV
Japanese honeysuckle (*Lonicera japonica*)	C, LV, LM, DV
Chilean jasmine (*Mandevilla laxa*)	C, LV, LM, DV
Scarlet runner bean (*Phaseolus coccineus*)	Annual
Silver lace vine (*Polygonum aubertii*)	All PNW
Black-eyed susan vine (*Thunbergia alata*)	Annual
Jasmine (*Trachelospermum asiaticum*)	LV
Garden nasturtium (*Tropaeolum majus*)	Annual
Grape (*Vitis* spp.)	All PNW
Wisteria (*Wisteria* spp.)	All PNW

Cardinal Climber

CLEMATIS FOR EVERY SEASON

The most popular vine in the Pacific Northwest is the clematis. Most varieties will grow throughout the PNW region. They provide a profusion of flowers in a rainbow of colors and, depending on the variety selected, bloom from May to October. We have taken a random selection from nursery listings to develop this list. There are literally hundreds of clematis to entice you. Each vine has its own special attributes, such as profuse bloom, long flowering, exotic bloom, semi-double bloom, or striking stamens that contrast with the flower petals. Specialty nurseries carry the widest variety of clematis. Many nurseries publish catalogs that are good sources of information regarding these magnificent bloomers. If you find that one special clematis you are looking for, it is worth the hunt!

We have listed the Alpinas and Macropetalas that are best suited for the small garden. Their flowers are small, drooping bells. The large-flowered clematis bloom for a very long time and many will repeat bloom if pruned after they bloom. The Montanas are very vigorous climbers with bold foliage and profuse flowers in spring. The Viticella and related forms have smaller flowers and bloom throughout the summer.

Alpina and Macropetalas—small, lanternlike drooping flowers

Clematis alpina	Various colors
Clematis alpina 'Constance'	Deep rose pink
Clematis a. 'Helsingborg'	Purple-blue
Clematis a. 'Willy'	Pale lavender with pink at base
Clematis macropetala 'Floralia'	Pale blue
Clematis m. 'Markham's pink'	Pink
Clematis m. 'Rosy O' Grady'	Deep rose pink

Large flowering hybrids

Clematis 'Asao'	Dark pink
C. 'Barbara Jackman'	Purple-blue/red bar
C. 'Beauty of Richmond'	Pink/green bars
C. 'Belle of Woking'	Silvery blue
C. 'Carnaby'	White/red bar
C. 'Comtesse de Bouchaud'	Pink
C. 'Dr. Ruppel'	Rose red/deeper bar
C. 'Duchess of Sutherland'	Red
C. 'Edith'	White
C. 'Edo Murasaki' ('Edo Purple')	Purple
C. 'Elsa Spaeth'	Deep purple
C. 'Etoile de Malicorne'	Blue/mauve bar
C. 'Fireworks'	Purple blue/red bar
C. 'Fuji Musume' (Wisteria Maiden)	Wisteria blue
C. 'Gekkyuden'	Pale yellow
C. 'General Sikorski'	Medium blue
C. 'Gillian Blades'	White
C. 'Kakio' ('Pink Champagne')	Mauve pink
C. 'Lady Betty Balfour'	Purple blue/yellow eye
C. 'Lady Northcliffe'	Wedgwood blue
C. 'Lasurstern'	Lavender blue

C. 'Madame Grange'	Velvety, red-purple
C. 'Maureen'	Velvety, red-purple
C. 'Nelly Moser'	Mauve pink/carmine bar
C. 'Niobe'	Dark red
C. 'Proteus'	Double mauve pink
C. 'Richard Pennell'	Purple-blue
C. 'Royalty'	Semi-double purple
C. 'Sunset'	Intense red
C. 'The President'	Purple
C. 'Ville de Lyon'	Bright red

Montana—Anemone clematis

Clematis chrysocoma	Pale pink
Clematis montana 'Marjorie'	Double salmon pink
Clematis m. 'Pink Perfection'	Soft pink/fragrant
Clematis m. 'Rubens'	Lilac pink
Clematis m. 'Tetrarose'	Lilac pink/fragrant
Clematis spooneri	White
Clematis spooneri 'Rosea'	Shell pink

Viticella and Related Forms—small-flowering and bloom all summer

Clematis viticella 'Alba Luxurians'	White/touch of green
C. *v.* 'Betty Corning'	Pale lilac
C. *v.* 'Etoile Violette'	Rich purple/creamy stamens
C. *v.* 'Madame Julia Correvon'	Wine red
C. *v.* 'Minuet'	White/purplish margins
C. *v.* 'Polish Spirit'	Deep purple
C. *v.* 'Purpurea Plena Elegans'	Double red-violet
C. *v.* 'Royal Velours'	Velvety purple
C. *v.* 'Venosa Violacea'	White/purple veins

Other Species

Clematis armandii	White/evergreen
Clematis a. 'Apple Blossom'	Pink/evergreen
C. 'Jackmanii'	Deep violet
Clematis paniculata	Creamy white/fragrant
Clematis tangutica	Rich yellow
Clematis texensis 'Duchess of Albany'	Bright pink bells
Clematis × *triternata* 'Rubromarginata'	Small white/pink edge

 Clematis like conditions of full sun to partial shade, but do best if their roots are cool. In hottest climates it is advisable to put a few inches of mulch around the base of the plant or shade the base with other plants. Don't put a rock over the base, as it will absorb heat and make your vine very unhappy.

VINES FOR POOR, DRY SOILS

These will tolerate poor or dry soils if you spend the first year making sure they become well established. Especially in the higher and dryer eastern part of the Pacific Northwest, the first establishment year is most important in guaranteeing the longevity of the plant. Keeping the soil moist, fertilizing as needed, and generally nurturing the young plant insures its ability to please you with its performance.

Blueberry climber (*Ampelopsis brevipedunculata*)	All PNW
American bittersweet (*Celastrus scandens*)	All PNW
Hyacinth bean (*Dolichos Lablab*)	Annual
English ivy (*Hedera helix* varieties)	All PNW
Cardinal climber (*Ipomoea quamoclit*)	Annual
Japanese honeysuckle (*Lonicera japonica*)	All PNW
Hall's honeysuckle (*Lonicera japonica* 'Halliana')	All PNW
Silver lace vine (*Polygonum aubertii*)	All PNW
Wisteria (*Wisteria* spp.)	All PNW

 Some tender perennial vines are treated as annuals. In climates warmer than the Pacific Northwest they would live through the winter. All of these seasonal vines do well in containers for a moveable screen. Set a trellis in a large pot, and brace it towards the back of the pot with a small board or stone. For best results, fill the container with regular garden soil mixed with about 1/3 potting soil. Plant the seeds or potted vine at the base of the trellis, keep it adequately watered throughout the summer, and enjoy the flowers.

VINES FOR GOOD GROUNDCOVERS

Wintercreeper and the periwinkles are really not vines, but should be considered when searching for good vinelike groundcovers. Some of the best groundcovering vines are also those that are vigorous enough to take over when conditions are right. English ivy, for example, is one of the best for developing a groundcover that will smother out many weeds and give you a green, dense cover. However, often it escapes into the native plantings and shades out young woody plants as well.

Maintenance of groundcovers is high in their developing years. If you are not using a mulch or landscape cloth you'll get a chance to exercise your weeding muscles.

Five-leaf akebia (*Akebia quinata*)	All PNW
Wintercreeper (*Euonymus fortunei radicans*)	All PNW
English ivy (*Hedera helix* varieties)	All PNW
Japanese honeysuckle (*Lonicera japonica*)	All PNW
Virginia creeper (*Parthenocissus quinquefolia*)	All PNW
Boston ivy (*Parthenocissus tricuspidata*)	All PNW
Periwinkle (*Vinca major*)	C, LV, DV
Dwarf periwinkle (*Vinca minor*)	C, LV, DV

VINES WITH FRAGRANT FLOWERS

A vine that has flowers with fragrance is doubly enjoyed. Not only are the foliage and growth attractive, but it tells you by an aroma that the plant is doing well. Plant these where you can enjoy the plant as well as the scent. Scented vines can also be trained to grow far from their root zone to give fragrance elsewhere. Many of these vines can be used in containers, trained on a trellis attached to the container.

Honeysuckle

Five-leaf akebia (*Akebia quinata*)	All PNW
Madeira vine (*Anredera cordifolia*)	Tuber - C, LV, DV
Evergreen Armand clematis (*Clematis armandii*)	All PNW
Sweet autumn clematis (*Clematis paniculata*)	All PNW
Japanese hop (*Humulus japonicus*)	All PNW
Common hop (*Humulus lupulus*)	All PNW
Moonflower (*Ipomoea alba*)	Annual
Spanish jasmine (*Jasminum grandiflorum*)	C, LV, LM
Pink jasmine (*Jasminum polyanthum*)	C, LV
Sweet pea (*Lathyrus odoratus*)	Annual
Hall's honeysuckle (*Lonicera japonica* 'Halliana')	C, LV, LM, DV
Japanese honeysuckle (*Lonicera japonica* vars.)	C, LV, LM, DV
Woodbine (*Lonicera periclymenum*)	C, LV, LM, DV
Chilean jasmine (*Mandevilla laxa*)	C, LV, LM
Passionvine (*Passiflora alatocaerulea*)	C, LV
Incense passionvine (*Passiflora* 'Incense')	C, LV
Silver lace vine (*Polygonum aubertii*)	All PNW
Bokhara fleeceflower (*Polygonum baldschuanicum*)	All PNW
Climbing rose (see rose chapter)	All PNW
Jasmine (*Trachelospermum asiaticum*)	LV
Japanese wisteria (*Wisteria floribunda*)	All PNW
Silky wisteria (*Wisteria venusta* 'Violacea')	All PNW

EASY VINES FOR MAILBOX OR LAMPPOST

Here are some quick-covering smaller vines that will climb up your mailbox, fencepost, or small structures where you want some vertical interest. If you have room, you can even combine a couple of vines for contrast. If any of these climbers go beyond where you want them, just give them a trim. There are many other vines that may serve this purpose, but would require a lot of trimming on your part. As your plant collection grows, less maintenance becomes important.

Clematis hybrids, many named cultivars	All PNW
Gold Heart ivy (*Hedera helix* 'Gold Heart')	All PNW
Needlepoint ivy (*Hedera helix* 'Needlepoint')	All PNW
Winter jasmine (*Jasminum nudiflorum*)	C, LV, LM
Goldflame honeysuckle (*Lonicera Heckrottii*)	All PNW
Chilean jasmine (*Mandevilla laxa*)	C, LV, LM
Pink mandevilla (*Mandevilla* 'Alice du Pont')	C, LV, LM
Jasmine (*Trachelospermum asiaticum*)	LV
Purple leafed grape (*Vitis vinifera* 'Purpurea')	All PNW
Annual vines (see list)	All PNW

FAST-GROWING VINES FOR A QUICK SCREEN OR SHADE

Sometimes we have an unsightly surface that needs a little dressing up, or the need for a quick privacy screen. The following vines will do the job for you. There are only three annuals listed; the rest are woody perennials that will remain for years to provide interest in the garden. Some are quite vigorous. You might want to decide how far you want them to reach or how much pruning you are willing to do.

Blueberry climber (*Ampelopsis brevipedunculata*)	All PNW
Madeira vine (*Anredera cordifolia*)	C, LV, DV
Dutchman's pipe (*Aristolochia durior*)	All PNW
Chinese trumpet creeper (*Campsis grandiflora*)	All PNW
Trumpet vine (*Campsis radicans*)	All PNW
Cup-and-saucer vine (*Cobaea scandens*)	Annual
Sweet autumn clematis (*Clematis paniculata*)	All PNW
Japanese hop (*Humulus japonicus*)	All PNW
Common hop (*Humulus lupulus*)	All PNW
Morning glory (*Ipomoea nil* 'Heavenly Blue')	Annual
Sweet pea (*Lathyrus odoratus*)	Annual
Japanese honeysuckle (*Lonicera japonica*)	C, LV, LM, DV
Virginia creeper (*Parthenocissus quinquefolia*)	All PNW
Scarlet runner bean (*Phaseolus coccineus*)	Annual
Silver lace vine (*Polygonum aubertii*)	All PNW
Bokhara fleeceflower (*Polygonum baldschuanicum*)	All PNW
Grape (*Vitis* spp.)	Varies

VINES THAT CLIMB BY TENDRILS

You need to know how a vine climbs so that you can provide it with the proper support. Some vines need help getting started; others can simply be planted near a vertical surface and you had better jump back! These vines reach with tendrils that search out anything to wrap around. They are easy to encourage in the direction you want them to go.

Blueberry climber (*Ampelopsis brevipedunculata*)	All PNW
Hybrid clematis	All PNW
Sweet autumn clematis (*Clematis paniculata*)	All PNW
Cup-and-saucer vine (*Cobaea scandens*)	Annual
Glory lily (*Gloriosa superba*)	Annual
Perennial pea (*Lathyrus latifolius*)	All PNW
Sweet pea (*Lathyrus odoratus*)	All PNW
Virginia creeper (*Parthenocissus quinquefolia*)	All PNW
Passion vine (*Passiflora alatocaerulea*)	C, LV
Grapes (*Vitis* spp.)	All PNW

VINES THAT CLIMB BY CLINGING

These vines cling by discs or holdfasts that attach themselves to any surface. You may not want these vigorous climbers next to the house, as they can create a real headache when you want to paint or have repairs that need attention. These vines are best in areas where you can just let them run and go where they may without getting into too much trouble. Boston ivy and Virginia creeper have both tendrils and discs.

Chinese trumpet creeper (*Campsis grandiflora*)	All PNW
Trumpet vine (*Campsis radicans*)	All PNW
Wintercreeper (*Euonymus fortunei radicans*)	All PNW
English ivy (*Hedera helix* varieties)	All PNW
Climbing hydrangea (*Hydrangea anomala*)	All PNW
Virginia creeper (*Parthenocissus quinquefolia*)	All PNW
Boston ivy (*Parthenocissus tricuspidata*)	All PNW
Japanese hydrangea vine (*Schizophragma hydrangeodies*)	C, LV, LM, DV

"Vining plants transform the garden, take your eye upward, trick you into believing everything above you is part of your garden, too. They twine and sprawl and spill about, foliage and flower, binding and weaving your garden into the edges of the world. Vines walk the tightrope, fly the trapeze, loop the loop, reach, twine and dance. They are my garden's risk takers—and I swear I've heard them laugh!"—Jolly Butler, Master Gardener and wordsmith, Portland, Oregon

VINES WITH SHOWY FRUIT OR SEED PODS

When deciding to add seasonal interest to the garden, don't forget that vines can contribute some very unusual features. In late summer the blueberry climber offers clusters of berries in shades of greenish ivory to metallic blue, the hardy kiwi produces tempting fruit, and the hyacinth bean provides burgundy seed pods. Each vine on this list has something special to offer. Add them to your fall bouquets or just enjoy them as you stroll through your garden.

Hardy kiwi (*Actinidia arguta*)	All PNW
Chinese gooseberry vine (*Actinidia deliciosa*)	C, LV, LM, DV
Blueberry climber (*Ampelopsis brevipedunculata*)	All PNW
Love-in-a-puff (*Cardiospermum halicacabum*)	Annual
American bittersweet (*Celastrus scandens*)	All PNW
Chinese bittersweet (*Celastrus rosthornianus*)	All PNW
Hyacinth bean (*Dolichos Lablab*)	Annual
Woodbine (*Lonicera periclymenum*)	C, LV, LM, DV
Berries Jubilee woodbine (*Lonicera periclymenum* 'Berries Jubilee')	C, LV, LM, DV
Trumpet honeysuckle (*Lonicera sempervirens*)	C, LV, LM, DV
Scarlet runner bean (*Phaseolus coccineus*)	Annual
Grape (*Vitis* spp.)	Varies

Providing support—When training against a wall, make sure you provide a method of taking the vine down so you can paint or repair the supporting wall. In the case of kiwi and some of the other vigorous vines, a strong support system is necessary. For other lighter-weight vines something as simple as a teepee trellis made of branches from a contorted willow will do just fine. Keep in mind how the vine you selected will grow and give it adequate support.

A SAMPLER OF BLOOMS BY SEASON

Spring

Five-leaf akebia (*Akebia quinata*)	All PNW
Clematis (*Clematis* hybrids)	All PNW
Anemone clematis (*Clematis montana*)	All PNW
Winter jasmine (*Jasminum nudiflorum*)	C, LV, LM, DV
Sweet pea (*Lathyrus odoratus*)	All PNW
Goldflame honeysuckle (*Lonicera Heckrottii*)	All PNW
Climbing rose (see rose chapter)	All PNW
Periwinkle (*Vinca major*)	All PNW
Dwarf periwinkle (*Vinca minor*)	All PNW
Japanese wisteria (*Wisteria floribunda*)	All PNW

Summer

Dutchman's pipe (*Aristolochia durior*)	All PNW
Trumpet vine (*Campsis radicans*)	All PNW
Climbing hydrangea (*Hydrangea anomala*)	All PNW
Spanish jasmine (*Jasminum grandiflorum*)	C, LV, LM
Chilean bellflower (*Lapageria rosea*)	C, LV
Goldflame honeysuckle (*Lonicera Heckrottii*)	All PNW
Hall's honeysuckle (*Lonicera japonica* 'Halliana')	All PNW
Trumpet honeysuckle (*Lonicera sempervirens*)	All PNW
Chilean jasmine (*Mandevilla laxa*)	C, LV, DV
Silver lace vine (*Polygonum aubertii*)	All PNW
Bokahara fleeceflower (*Polygonum baldschuanicum*)	All PNW
Climbing rose (see rose chapter)	
All the annual vines except sweet pea	

Late Summer

Trumpet vine (*Campsis radicans*)	All PNW
Clematis (*Clematis* hybrids)	All PNW
Sweet autumn clematis (*Clematis paniculata*)	All PNW
Common hops (*Humulus lupulus*)	All PNW
Climbing hydrangea (*Hydrangea anomala*)	All PNW
Chilean bellflower (*Lapageria rosea*)	C, LV
Goldflame honeysuckle (*Lonicera Heckrottii*)	All PNW
Woodbine (*Lonicera periclymenum*)	C, LV, LM, DV
Silver lace vine (*Polygonum aubertii*)	All PNW
Bokahara fleece flower (*Polygonum baldschuanicum*)	All PNW
Climbing rose (see rose chapter)	All PNW

Fall

Clematis (*Clematis* hybrids)	All PNW
Climbing hydrangea (*Hydrangea anomala*)	All PNW
Chilean bellflower (*Laperia rosea*)	C, LV
Woodbine (*Lonicera periclymenum*)	C, LV, LM, DV
Silver lace vine (*Polygonum aubertii*)	All PNW
Bokahara fleeceflower (*Polygonum baldschuanicum*)	All PNW
Climbing rose (see rose chapter)	All PNW
Annual vines bloom until it gets cool or until frost	

EOUS
NIALS

S are generally classified as plants with
ar while the root system remains alive to
and the winter dieback separates these
nd trees. We are blessed in the Pacific
s that allow many herbaceous perennials
lists you will notice that we have includ-
as bulbs or rhizomatous plants. We felt,
along with herbaceous perennials. Check
d of perennial for your garden.

nnials, or if you are an old-timer who has
grown iris and peony and pampas grass forever but would like to know more about some of the
newer introductions, get in touch with the Hardy Plant Society or associate yourself with local
nurseries that grow some particular perennial that attracts your interest. As you peruse the lists
in this chapter, you will also be exposed to many native perennials that have been found useful in landscaping. To learn more about them, join your local Native Plant Society. There are
many avenues for learning more about these plants, including your local garden center, your
local county agent, botanical gardens, and nearby nurserymen. We hope to encourage your
participation in the world of perennials by introducing you to at least some of the names and
characteristics of different kinds.

Herbaceous perennials are very adaptable to whatever conditions exist in your garden.
We list some that grow in alkaline soil, some that take shade, others that prefer full sun, those
we know of that reseed themselves, along with about thirty other lists to tell you more about
these plants. And of course we don't list nearly all of them in any one category. That is so you
can add to the lists, thereby making them even more valuable to yourself and your gardening
friends. Enjoy these!

HERBACEOUS PERENNIALS FOR WET SITES

One person's landscape problems may be another's opportunity to use some striking plant materials, such as bear's-breeches or dinosaur food, along with large-leafed ferns or bamboo. Don't look at wetness as being a disadvantage; rather use that design challenge to do some great things. Lots of natives will fit this bill, as will some shrubs and trees that can withstand standing water. Most of the plants included in this list will do well in partial to full shade; however Helen's flower and bee balm will do better in sun or very light shade.

Bear's-breeches (*Acanthus mollis*)	C, LV, LM, DV
Sweet flag (*Acoris gramineus*)	All PNW
Goatsbeard (*Aruncus dioicus*)	All PNW
Giant reed (*Arundo donax*)	All PNW
Astilbe (*Astilbe × arendsii* varieties)	LV, LM, DV
Water arum (*Calla palustris*)	C, LV, LM
Marsh marigold (*Caltha palustris*)	All PNW
Camas lilies (*Camassia* spp.)	C, LV, LM, DV
Turtle heads (*Chelone* spp.)	All PNW
Bugbane (*Cimicifuga* spp.)	All PNW
Pampas grass (*Cortaderia selloana*)	C, LV, LM, DV
Cobra lily (*Darlingtonia californica*)	C, LV, LM
Umbrella plant (*Darmera peltatum*)	C, LV, LM, DV
Flowering spurge (*Euphorbia corollata*)	C, LV, LM, DV
Meadow sweet (*Filipendula* spp.)	All PNW
Dinosaur food (*Gunnera* spp.)	C, LV, LM, DV
Helen's flower (*Helenium autumnale*)	All PNW
Plantain lily (*Hosta* spp.)	All PNW
Japanese iris (*Iris ensata*)	All PNW
Yellow flag (*Iris pseudacorus*)	All PNW
Kirengeshoma (*Kirengeshoma koreana, K. palmata*)	C, LV, LM, DV
Cardinal flower (*Lobelia cardinalis*)	C, LV, LM
Corsican mint (*Mentha requienii*)	C, LV, LM, DV
Monkey flower (*Mimulus hybridus*)	All PNW
Bee balm (*Monarda* spp.)	All PNW
Forget-me-not (*Myosotis scorpioides*)	C, LV, LM, DV
Royal fern (*Osmunda regalis*)	C, LV, LM, DV
Redwood sorrel (*Oxalis oregana*)	C, LV, LM
New Zealand flax (*Phormium tenax*)	C, LV, LM
Solomon's seal (*Polygonatum odoratum*)	LV, LM, DV
Blue star creeper (*Pratia pedunculata*)	C, LV, LM, DV
Bronze leaf rodgersia (*Rodgersia* spp.)	C, LV, LM, DV
Periwinkle (*Vinca minor*)	C, LV, LM

 Sites that have water on them all year could be planted via the container method used for planting water lilies in ponds. Using a good potting mix with at least one-third by volume of well-rotted compost, plant in a container that will eventually decompose—pulp, paper, or scrap wood. Place the potted plant in the wet site, pressing the container into the soil, then let nature take over. With time the container will decay, the plant will send roots into the surrounding soil and become a plant on a small mound in your wet site.

HERBACEOUS PERENNIALS THAT CAN TAKE NEGLECT

N̲ot all gardens will be tended on schedule, nor do all gardeners want a landscape that requires constant care. That is why we developed this list, for those that would like to go fishing or visiting or golfing, rather than prune and coddle and look after a yard full of plants. These listed below can take care of themselves for a long while and still provide color, interest, texture, and healthy plants to the landscape. Now before you rush out and replant the entire yard with these, take the time to learn what they demand. If you don't provide the necessities, such as reasonably fertile soil, good drainage, the right amount of sunlight or shade, and protection from the elements, they will die from neglect. Learn also that some are hard to get started (gas plant for example), while others are lurking in their pots waiting for you to turn your back so they can invade the entire yard (creeping jennie and bishop's weed are two fine examples of potential invaders). Plan first for the kind of garden you want, provide the correct microclimate, plant at the proper time and in the approved manner, give care where absolutely needed, and enjoy the plants that will not demand a great deal of you.

Plant	Zone
Common yarrow (*Achillea millefolium*)	All PNW
Bishop's weed (*Aegopodium podagraria*)	All PNW
Blue starflower (*Amsonia tabernaemontana*)	C, LV, LM, DV
Heartleaf bergenia (*Bergenia cordifolia*)	C, LV, LM, DV
Bellflower (*Campanula lactiflora*)	All PNW
Shasta daisy (*Chrysanthemum maximum*)	All PNW
Corydalis (*Corydalis lutea*)	C, LV, LM
Crocus (*Crocus* spp.)	All PNW
Hardy cyclamen (*Cyclamen hederifolium*)	All PNW
Bleeding heart (*Dicentra formosa*)	All PNW
Gas plant (*Dictamnus albus*)	All PNW
Common snowdrop (*Galanthus nivalis*)	All PNW
Sweet woodruff (*Galium odoratum*)	All PNW
Whirling butterflies (*Gaura lindheimeri*)	All PNW
Helen's flower (*Helenium autumnale*)	All PNW
Evergreen candytuft (*Iberis sempervirens*)	All PNW
Lychnis (*Lychnis coronaria*)	All PNW
Creeping Jennie (*Lysimachia nummularia*)	All PNW
Redwood sorrel (*Oxalis oregana*)	C, LV, LM
Sedum (*Sedum* spp.)	All PNW
Lamb's ears (*Stachys byzantina*)	All PNW
Violet (*Viola wittrockiana*)	All PNW

Common Yarrow

"Although the above list shows there are many herbaceous perennials that can tolerate neglect, all perennials benefit from a little care. An organic mulch over the perennial bed, a bit of deadheading of old flower heads, cutting back and removing old dead foliage in late fall that might carry overwintering fungus disease spores, digging and dividing when necessary—all of these will enhance the health and growth of your perennials. They provide the beauty and interest, it is up to you to keep them happy." —Jim and Audrey Metcalf, Honeyhill Nursery, Portland, Oregon

HERBACEOUS PERENNIALS FOR AUTUMN COLOR

Comments about autumn color bring to mind maple leaves, sumac, and sweetgum, but there is an incredible list of plants that show a good display of brightly colored foliage or a last show of blossoms just as they die down in the fall. Here are some suggestions from Linda Beutler, designer and Master Gardener, for you to try in your own microclimate.

Garlic chives (*Allium tuberosum*)	All PNW
Parrot flower (*Alstroemeria psittacina*)	C, LV, LM, DV
Japanese anemone (*Anemone hybrida*)	All PNW
Aster (*Aster frikartii*)	All PNW
Blue beard (*Caryopteris clandonensis*)	All PNW
Centauria (*Centauria hypoleuca* 'John Coutts')	C, LV, LM
Jupiter's beard (*Centranthus ruber*)	C, LV, LM
Corydalis (*Corydalis lutea*)	C, LV, LM
Helen's flower (*Helenium autumnale*)	All PNW
Daylily (*Hemerocallis* 'Stella d'Oro')	All PNW
Rubrum lily (*Lilium* × 'Uchida')	All PNW
Blue cardinal flower (*Lobelia syphilitica*)	C, LV, LM, DV
Pink Flamingo lobelia (*Lobelia syphilitica* 'Pink Flamingo')	C, LV, LM, DV
Oswego tea (*Monarda didyma*)	All PNW
Border penstemon (*Penstemon* × *gloxinioides* 'Scarlet Queen')	All PNW
African Queen cape fuchsia (*Phygelius capensis* 'African Queen')	C, LV, LM
Black-eyed susan (*Rudbeckia hirta*)	All PNW
Gentian sage (*Salvia patens*)	C, LV
Bog sage (*Salvia uliginosa*)	C, LV
Kaffir lily (*Schizostylis coccinea* 'Oregon Sunset')	C, LV, LM
Lamb's ears (*Stachys byzantina* 'Primrose Heron')	All PNW
Japanese toad lily (*Tricyrtis formosana*)	C, LV, LM, DV

"What fun to spend a rainy few evenings revisiting the friends in my garden, remembering their many sterling qualities. Making the 'autumn color list' has helped me track the process that took a rose collection and cutting garden and turned it into an integrated mixed border. Of course right now [March] it is a soggy mess."—Linda Beutler, floral designer and Master Gardener, Portland, Oregon

HERBACEOUS PERENNIALS FOR CUT FOLIAGE

There are certain plants that provide background and interest to flower arrangements, and many of them are herbaceous perennials. In this list we have tried to find the ones that will give a point of interest, along with the ability to last for as long as possible after cutting. Characteristics of those in this list include the rigid form of *Alchemilla*, unusual color of *Hosta*, soft texture of *Stachys* and *Verbascum*, and shape of *Iris* and *Polystichum*. You will also find fragrance in some foliage of herbaceous perennials (see the list of those with fragrant foliage).

Lady's-mantle (*Alchemilla mollis*)	C, LV, LM, DV
Silver king artemesia (*Artemesia ludoviciana albula*)	All PNW
Dusty miller (*Artemesia stellerana*)	All PNW

Plantain lily (*Hosta* spp.)	All PNW
Iris (*Iris* spp.)	All PNW
Lavender (*Lavandula* spp.)	C, LV, LM, DV
Solomon's seal (*Polygonatum biflorum*)	C, LV, LM
Variegated Solomon's seal (*Polygonatum odoratum* 'Variegatum')	C, LV, LM
Sword fern (*Polystichum munitum*)	C, LV, LM
Rue (*Ruta graveolens*)	All PNW
False Solomon's seal (*Smilacina racemosa*)	C, LV, LM
Lamb's ears (*Stachys byzantina*)	All PNW
Meadow rue (*Thalictrum* spp.)	All PNW
Vancouveria (*Vancouveria chrysantha*)	C, LV
Mullein (*Verbascum* spp.)	All PNW

HERBACEOUS PERENNIALS FOR CUT FLOWERS

While you might think this was an easy list to prepare, we tried to find the best choices. Most gardeners like to bring bouquets indoors to make the home environment more enjoyable, and when they search for the elements for making an arrangement, nearly all flowers are fair game. Some though will perform longer than others after they are cut from the parent plant. Others provide fragrance that remains long after the freshness of the blossom disappears. Most, if you learn as much about the plant in question as can be found, are easy to grow and will flower if given the right microclimate. As you get into the habit of using herbaceous perennials, both in the landscape and as cut flowers, you will find it fun and profitable to experiment with new and different types. Use this list to start your cutting garden, and add to it as you find more.

Purple Coneflower

Peruvian lily (*Alstromeria* spp.)	C, LV, LM, DV
Masterwort (*Astrantia major*)	C, LV, LM, DV
Canterbury bell (*Campanula medium*)	All PNW
Bachelor's buttons (*Centaurea cyanus*)	All PNW
Chrysanthemum (*Chrysanthemum morifolium*)	All PNW
Shasta daisy (*Chrysanthemum maximum*)	All PNW
Feverfew (*Chrysanthemum parthenium*)	All PNW
Coreopsis (*Coreopsis grandiflora*)	All PNW
Montbretia (*Crocosmia crocosmiiflora*)	C, LV, LM, DV
Delphinium (*Delphinium belladonna*)	All PNW
Candle delphinium (*Delphinium elatum*)	All PNW
Purple coneflower (*Echinacea purpurea*)	All PNW
Freesia (*Freesia* vars.)	C, LV
Blanket flower (*Gaillardia grandiflora*)	All PNW
Gladiola (*Gladiola* spp.)	All PNW
Baby's breath (*Gypsophila paniculata*)	All PNW
Coral bells (*Heuchera sanguinea*)	All PNW
Iris (*Iris* spp.)	All PNW
Gayfeather (*Liatris spicata*)	All PNW
Lily (*Lilium* spp.)	All PNW
Statice (*Limonium* spp.)	All PNW
Peony (*Paeonia lactiflora*)	All PNW
Pincushion flower (*Scabiosa atropurpurea*)	C, LV, LM, DV
Calla lily (*Zantedeschia* spp.)	C, LV, LM, DV

FAVORITE HERBACEOUS PERENNIALS FOR THE WESTERN PART OF PNW

This list was prepared by Elizabeth Howley, head of the Horticulture Department at Clackamas Community College and past president of the Hardy Plant Society in Oregon.

Bear's-breeches (*Acanthus mollis*)	Big bold leaves and striking flowers add architectural definition to the garden
Monkshood (*Aconitum* spp.)	Remarkable perennial for mid to late summer bloom with tall strong stems
Blue starflower (*Amsonia* spp.)	Striking flowers held atop remarkable foliage that offers vertical definition to the garden and unique foliage texture
Goatsbeard (*Aruncus dioicus*)	Great fluffy sprays of flowers borne atop 3-to 4-foot tall stems, a lovely winter accent when frost covers stems and flower heads
Astilbe (*Astilbe* spp.)	Some dramatic bicolor flowers are available in the genus, along with dramatic foliage color
False indigo (*Baptisia australis*)	Remarkable pest-free plants supporting pealike flowers atop 3-foot stems
Marsh marigold (*Calthia palustris*)	A native plant adapted to wet stream sides with bright yellow flowers
Black snakeroot, Cohosh (*Cimicifuga racemosa*)	Finely divided leaves support sweetly scented bottle-brush flowers; the plant has many medicinal uses
Fairy bells (*Dierama* spp.)	Graceful bells are held on tall arching stems above a clump of grass-like foliage
Mayflower (*Epigea reptans*)	Sweet smelling, low growing; a great addition for the shady site
Bishop's hat (*Epimedium*)	Foliage shapes, color patterns and tiny graceful flowers add to the charm of this genus
Daylily (*Hemerocallis*)	For their summer bloom and reliable return to the garden, these old-fashioned varieties, along with newer selections, merit attention
Peony (*Paeonia*)	Thousands of remarkable flower and leaf forms are available to make a big splash in the perennial border
Garden phlox (*Phlox paniculata*)	This genus offers some dramatic late summer bloomers that brighten the border when others have finished
Perennial salvia (*Salvia* spp.)	So many remarkable species are available with great foliage; are suitable to hot garden sites
Columbine meadow rue (*Thalictrum aquilegifolium*)	Flowers resembling delicate puffs are held high above the attractive foliage on this reliable garden plant

Violet (*Viola*)

These edible blooms are some of the most familiar plants for the perennial border; some newer ones are highly scented

"No garden should be without some iris for cut flowers and for sinking your nose into the childhood scent of grape juice available from some of the old-fashioned purple selections."—Elizabeth Howley, Clackamas Community College, Oregon City, Oregon

HERBACEOUS PERENNIALS THAT BLOOM IN WINTER OR EARLY SPRING

With careful selection, one can have in the landscape harbingers of spring that bloom long before the buds swell on woody plants. Winter ends several months apart between the zones of this region, yet you will see that some of these are listed for all zones. This is because each reacts to soil temperature in whatever zone it might grow, and when the ground warms to that plant's required level, up it comes. Those listed here bloom before leaves arrive, or soon after. Next spring look around your community and add others to your list.

Rockcress (*Arabis sturii*)	All PNW
Wild ginger (*Asarum caudatum*)	C, LV, LM, DV
Common aubretia (*Aubretia deltoidea*)	All PNW
Basket-of-gold (*Aurinia saxatilis*)	All PNW
Glory of the snow (*Chionodoxa luciliae*)	All PNW
Lily-of-the-valley (*Convallaria majalis*)	All PNW
Crocus (*Crocus* spp.)	All PNW
Hardy cyclamen (*Cyclamen coum*)	All PNW
Winter aconite (*Eranthus hyemalis*)	All PNW
Fawn lily (*Erythronium californicum*)	All PNW
Euphorbia (*Euphorbia characias*)	C, LV, LM, DV
Giant snowdrop (*Galanthus elwesii*)	All PNW
Common snowdrop (*Galanthus nivalis*)	All PNW
Christmas rose (*Helleborus niger*)	All PNW
Lenten rose (*Helleborus orientalis*)	All PNW
Common hyacinth (*Hyacinthus orientalis*)	All PNW
Candytuft (*Iberis sempervirens*)	All PNW
Creeping phlox (*Phlox stolonifera*)	All PNW
Primrose (*Primula* × *juliana*)	All PNW
Bethlehem sage (*Pulmonaria saccharata*)	All PNW
Bloodroot (*Sanguinaria canadensis*)	LM, DV, HD
Foamflower (*Tiarella wherryi*)	All PNW
Trillium (*Trillium grandiflorum*)	All PNW
Violet (*Viola* spp.)	C, LV, LM
Barren strawberry (*Waldsteinia fragarioides*)	C, LV, LM

THE BEST HELLEBORES FOR PACIFIC NORTHWEST GARDENS

Ray must admit that hellebores have never been at the top of his list of plants, but after being exposed to them through friends Audrey and Jim Metcalf of Honeyhill Nursery in Portland, and through other nurseries, such as Siskiyou Rare Plant Nursery in Medford, Oregon, and Forest Farm Nursery in Williams, Oregon, he knows they should be listed as a valuable herbaceous plant that will bring your garden to life in the months when nothing else is ready to bloom (besides, they are among Jan's favorite plants).

Christmas Rose

Corsican hellebore (*H. argutifolius*)	suitable for shade	C, LV, LM, DV
Bear's foot hellebore (*H. foetidus*)	suitable for shade	All PNW
Purple-red hellebore (*H.* × *atrorubens*)	very early	C, LV, LM, DV
Christmas rose (*Helleborus niger*)	best if left undisturbed	All PNW
Lenten rose (*Helleborus orientalis*)	wide color range	All PNW

"Hellebores are very easy to grow. I add a little bonemeal and a generous shovelful of compost to new planting holes and water the plants well during their first year. Don't spend another winter without the company of hellebores. They're great consolers, bringing light in a dark season."—Barbara Ashmum, gardener, writer, and teacher, Portland, Oregon

HERBACEOUS PERENNIALS FOR STRIKING GROUNDCOVER

Groundcover plants can be woody or of softer material, such as herbaceous perennials. Steve Carruthers, Portland landscape architect, sent along the following suggestions for groundcovering plantings using herbaceous perennials. Add them to your list of plants for this purpose.

Carpet bugle (*Ajuga reptans*)	All PNW
Lady's mantle (*Alchemilla pectinata*)	C, LV, LM
Sandwort (*Arenaria* spp.)	C, LV, LM, DV
Common thrift (*Armeria maritima*)	All PNW
Wild ginger (*Asarum europaeum*)	C, LV, LM, DV
Basket-of-gold (*Aurinia saxatilis*)	All PNW
Snow-in-summer (*Cerastium tomentosum*)	All PNW
Ice plant (*Delosperma cooperi*)	C, LV, LM, DV
Bishop's hat (*Epimedium grandiflorum*)	C, LV, LM, DV
Mrs. Robb's spurge (*Euphorbia amygdaloides* 'Robbiae')	C, LV, LM, DV
Sweet woodruff (*Galium odoratum*)	All PNW
Cranesbill (*Geranium macrorrhizum*)	All PNW
Sun rose (*Helianthemum nummularium* vars.)	C, LV, LM, DV
Hosta (*Hosta* spp.)	All PNW
Variegated houttuynia (*Houttuynia cordata* 'Variegata')	All PNW
Pink Pewter (*Lamium maculatum* 'Pink Pewter')	All PNW
Silver lamium (*Lamium maculatum* 'Beacon Silver')	All PNW

False lily-of-the-valley (*Maianthemum dilatatum*)	All PNW
Ozark sundrops (*Oenothera missourensis*)	All PNW
Blue-eyed Mary (*Omphalodes verna*)	LV, LM, DV
Creeping phlox (*Phlox stolonifera*)	All PNW
Moss pink (*Phlox subulata*)	All PNW
Polygonum (*Polygonum affine*)	C, LV, LM, DV
London pride saxifrage (*Saxifraga umbrosa*)	All PNW
Goldmoss sedum (*Sedum acre*)	All PNW
Lamb's ears (*Stachys byzantina*)	All PNW
Foamflower (*Tiarella wherryi*)	All PNW
Barren strawberry (*Waldstenia fragarioides*)	C, LV, LM, DV

HERBACEOUS PERENNIALS FOR DRY SITES

These are the herbaceous perennials that are the best for planting in sites that will be dry most of the time. However, keep in mind that water will be necessary during that first growing season to allow these to become established. Once they are "at home" in your dry site, they can grow and thrive without much attention to watering other than during the worst of droughts.

Red Beauty yarrow (*Achillea millefolium* 'Red Beauty')	All PNW
Atlas daisy (*Anacyclus depressus*)	All PNW
Silver Mound artemesia (*Artemesia schmidtiana* 'Silver Mound')	All PNW
Blue false indigo (*Baptisia australis*)	C, LV, LM, DV
Perennial cornflower (*Centaurea montana*)	C, LV, LM, DV
Jupiter's beard (*Centranthus ruber*)	C, LV, LM, DV
Snow-in-summer (*Cerastium tomentosum*)	All PNW
Coreopsis (*Coreopsis grandiflora*)	All PNW
Golden Showers (*Coreopsis verticillata* 'Golden Showers')	C, LV, LM, DV
Moonbeam coreopsis (*Coreopsis verticillata* 'Moonbeam')	All PNW
Foxglove (*Digitalis purpurea*)	All PNW
Red wood spurge (*Euphorbia amygdaloides* 'Rubra')	C, LV, LM, DV
Dwarf blanket flower (*Gaillardia* 'Goblin')	All PNW
Whirling Butterflies (*Gaura lindheimeri* 'Whirling Butterflies')	All PNW
Baby's breath (*Gypsophila* spp.)	All PNW
Sun rose (*Helianthemum nummularium* vars.)	C, LV, LM, DV
Autumnalis candytuft (*Iberis sempervirens* 'Autumnalis')	C, LV, LM, DV
Pink hardy gloxinia (*Incarvillea delavayi*)	C, LV, LM, DV
Red-hot poker (*Kniphofia uvaria*)	C, LV, LM, DV
Evening primrose (*Oenothera* spp.)	All PNW
Pine-leafed penstemon (*Penstemon pinifolius*)	All PNW
Mersea Yellow penstemon (*Penstemon pinifolius* 'Mersea Yellow')	All PNW
Rocky Mountain penstemon (*Penstemon strictus*)	All PNW
Russian sage (*Perovskia atriplicifolia*)	All PNW
Hardy purple sage (*Salvia superba* 'Blue Queen')	C, LV, LM
Silver lavender cotton (*Santolina chamaecyparissus*)	All PNW
Green lavender cotton (*Santolina virens*)	All PNW
Sedum (*Sedum* spp. selected varieties)	C, LV, LM, DV
Dusty miller (*Senecio cineraria*)	All PNW

HERBACEOUS PERENNIALS FOR SHADY SITES

In the western part of the Pacific Northwest, shade becomes a problem when trying to come up with something that will grow in the shade of so many trees. In the eastern part, most plants would like some shade every now and then. Many plants will grow in shade. Just look at the natural growth along the highways through the forests. This list will give you some plants to think about. But do consider how much competition these plants will have among the roots of trees and large shrubs, for in many instances it is not the shade that prevents the growth of plants, but the competition for water and minerals. Avoid the plants that have invasive roots with many surface feeder roots (avoid the trees that we listed in the tree chapter as being impossible to grow anything beneath). Also check the list of shrubs that are listed as shade-loving.

Sweet Violet

Bishop's weed (*Aegopodium podagraria*)	All PNW
Anemone (*Anemone* selected spp.)	C, LV, LM, DV
Goatsbeard (*Aruncus dioicus*)	C, LV, LM, DV
European ginger (*Asarum europaeum*)	C, LV, LM, DV
Astilbe (*Astilbe* spp. and selected varieties)	C, LV, LM, DV
Siberian bugloss (*Brunnera macrophylla*)	All PNW
Dalmation bellflower (*Campanula portenschlagiana*)	C, LV, LM, DV
Blue cohosh (*Caulophyllum thalictroides*)	All PNW
Lily-of-the-valley (*Convallaria majalis*)	All PNW
Blue panda corydalis (*Corydalis flexuosa*)	C, LV, LM, DV
China Blue corydalis (*Corydalis flexuosa* 'China Blue')	All PNW
Corydalis (*Corydalis lutea*)	C, LV, LM, DV
Hardy cyclamen (*Cyclamen* spp.)	C, LV, LM
Bleeding heart (*Dicentra* spp.)	All PNW
Fringed bleeding heart (*Dicentra eximia*)	All PNW
Luxuriant bleeding heart (*Dicentra* 'Luxuriant')	All PNW
Bishop's hat (*Epimedium* spp.)	All PNW
Fawn lily (*Erythronium californicum*)	All PNW
White mist flower (*Eupatorium coelestinum* 'Album')	C, LV, LM, DV
Hellebore (*Helleborus* spp.)	All PNW
Coral bells (*Heuchera* spp.)	All PNW
Plantain lily (*Hosta* spp.)	C, LV, LM, DV
Lamium (*Lamium* spp.)	C, LV, LM, DV
Cranesbill (*Geranium macrorrhizum*)	All PNW
Yellow archangel (*Lamiastrum galeobdolon* vars.)	C, LV, LM, DV
Golden grounsel (*Ligularia dentata*)	All PNW
Othello ligularia (*Ligularia dentata* 'Othello')	C, LV, LM, DV
Redwood sorrel (*Oxalis oregana* vars.)	C, LV, LM
Lungwort (*Pulmonaria* spp.)	All PNW
Meadow rue (*Thalictrum* spp.)	All PNW
Foam flower (*Tiarella* spp.)	C, LV, LM, DV
Wake robin (*Trillium grandiflorum, T. ovatum*)	C, LV, LM, DV
Violets (*Viola* spp.)	C, LV, LM, DV

HERBACEOUS PERENNIALS THAT MAKE GOOD AQUATIC MARGIN PLANTS

Plants in this list include those suitable for the margins of a pond or an active wetland site. These plants prefer having their roots in saturated or flooded soils, though many can withstand a bit of dry soil. These plants also provide flower color and foliage textures throughout the growing season. If your landscape includes a pond or a wetland, give some of these a try. In harsh winters, consider some of these as replaceable annual plants; however, if given protection during the coldest part of the winter, all may survive to grow and bloom again next spring.

Variegated acorus (*Acorus gramineus* vars.)
Yellow marsh marigold (*Caltha palustris*)
Yellow double-flowering marsh marigold (*Caltha palustris flora plena*)
Slough sedge (*Carex stipata*)
Cottongrass (*Eriophorum angustifolium*)
Chameleon plant (*Houttuynia cordata variegata*)
Pennywort (*Hydrocotyle umbellata*)
Yellow flag (*Iris pseudacorus*)
Blue iris (*Iris versicolor*)
Blue spreading rush (*Juncus patens*)
Cardinal flower (*Lobelia cardinalis*)
Yellow monkey flower (*Mimulus lewesii*)
Purple pickerelweed (*Pontaderia cordata*)
Narrow-leafed arrowhead (*Sagittaria gramineus*)
Arrowhead (*Sagittaria latifolia*)
Lizard's tail (*Saururus cernuus*)
Zebra rush (*Scirpus zebrinus*)
Golden-eyed grass (*Sisyrinchium californicum*)
Dwarf cattail (*Typha minima*)
Variegated cattail (*Typha variegata*)

Iris versicolor

HERBACEOUS PERENNIALS WITH VERTICAL, SPIKY FLOWERS

Form in the garden comes from the shapes of trees and shrubs, the growth shape of herbaceous perennials, and from the contrasts of flower forms. The vertical spikes of flowers leads your eye upwards, on to the next taller plant, or when used in the back of a flower bed, upwards to the sky, or into the trees behind. When we started selecting the herbaceous perennials for this list, we tried to differentiate between spikelike flowers and plumes. That is why *Liatrus* and pampas grass are left off, since they both provide flower stalks that are plumelike. You can add them back if you like, and by all means add others that come to mind. Here are some to begin with.

Foxglove

Bear's-breeches (*Acanthus mollis*)	C, LV, LM, DV
Garden monkshood (*Aconitum napellus*)	All PNW
Astilbe (*Astilbe chinensis*)	C, LV, LM
Peach-leafed bluebell (*Campanula persicifolia*)	All PNW
Bugbane (*Cimicifuga* spp.)	All PNW
Delphinium (*Delphinium elatum* vars.)	All PNW
Twinspur (*Diascia rigescens*)	C, LV
Gas plant (*Dictamnus albus*)	All PNW
Foxglove (*Digitalis* spp.)	All PNW
Gladiolus (*Gladiola grandiflora* hybrids)	All PNW
Hyssop (*Hyssopus officinalis*)	All PNW
Red-hot poker (*Kniphofia uvaria*)	All PNW
English lavender (*Lavandula angustifolia*)	All PNW
French lavender (*Lavandula dentata*)	C, LV
Spanish lavender (*Lavandula stoechas*)	C, LV, LM, DV
Rocket ligularia (*Ligularia stenocephala* 'The Rocket')	C, LV, LM, DV
Toadflax (*Linaria purpurea* 'Cannon Went')	All PNW
Cardinal flower (*Lobelia cardinalis*)	All PNW
Lobelia (*Lobelia syphilitica*)	C, LV, LM, DV
Lupine (*Lupinus* spp.)	All PNW
Catmint (*Nepeta faassenii*)	All PNW
Beard tongue (*Penstemon* spp.)	Varies
Russian sage (*Perovskia* 'Blue Spire')	All PNW
False dragonhead (*Physostegia virginiana*)	All PNW
Snakeweed (*Polygonum bistorta* 'Superbum')	All PNW
Primrose (*Primula vialii*)	All PNW
Hardy purple sage (*Salvia superba* 'Blue Queen')	All PNW
Hardy pink sage (*Salvia superba* 'Rose Queen')	All PNW
Checkerbloom (*Sidalcea malviflora*)	C, LV, LM, DV
Foamflower (*Tiarella wherryi*)	All PNW
Moth mullein (*Verbascum chaixii*)	All PNW
Purple mullein (*Verbascum phoeniceum*)	All PNW
Speedwell (*Veronica* spp.)	All PNW
Yucca (*Yucca filamentosa*)	All PNW

"Lobelias are real eye-catchers in the border garden. We grow our lobelias in full sun in moist, fertile, well-drained soil. As is all too often the case with our favorite flowers, the slugs love them as well. Hummingbirds also love them, so perhaps there is a balance in nature."—Maurice Horn, partner-owner, Joy Creek Nursery, Scappoose, Oregon

HERBACEOUS PERENNIALS FOR SOUTHWESTERN IDAHO

According to Dr. Michael Colt, Idaho extension horticulturist, herbaceous perennials do quite well in southwest Idaho because the winter period is distinct and cold (Zone 5 around Boise/Caldwell/Nampa). Mulching and late fall watering aid survival for the newly planted, and placing Zone 5 plants in the more severe microclimates insures a thriving garden. Here are his selections.

Michael's favorite 20

Allium	Especially *Allium giganteum*
Hollyhock	*Alcea rosea nigra*
Heartleaf bergenia	*Bergenia cordifolia*
Delphinium	Avoid Pacific hybrids, join the Delphinium Society
Foxgloves	*Digitalis purpurea*
Purple coneflower	*Echinacea purpurea* 'Magnus'
Geranium	*Geranium* 'Johnson's Blue'
Daylily	*Hemerocallis* 'Stella d' Oro' for beginners
Coral bells	*Heuchera*
Hosta	Choose varieties which lack iron chlorosis-like appearance
Iris	*Iris sibirica* does especially well here
Spike gay feather	*Liatris spicata*
Lily	*Lilium* 'Enchantment' for beginners
Lychnis	*Lychnis coronaria, L. chalcedonica*
Bee balm	*Monarda didyma* 'Cambridge Scarlet'
Peony	*Paeonia*
Poppy	*Papaver orientale*
Phlox	*Phlox paniculata* 'Brighteyes'
Rudbeckia	*Rudbeckia fulgida* 'Goldsturm'
Sedum	*Sedum telephium* 'Autumn Joy'

"The most important phase in producing a satisfactory herbaceous perennial garden is the soil preparation before planting. Most soils need to have the rocks harvested at least down to two inches and then be amended with the addition of lots of compost. It takes several years for most herbaceous perennials to come into their glory, and so you need to insure your wait is justified by sufficient and proper soil preparation beforehand. There are many choices from more than a hundred perennial genera. When you add many more species and lots of cultivars, the possibilities are staggering for gardeners in southwest Idaho."—Dr. Michael Colt, University of Idaho extension horticulturist, Parma, Idaho

HERBACEOUS PERENNIALS FOR ALKALINE SOILS

Most of the flowering annuals and herbaceous perennials have a wide tolerance to soil acidity or alkalinity. Some will do better in acid soils and some definitely need the calcium found in alkaline soils. Listed here are those that are happy with soils that are on the alkaline side of the scale. Also, most of the grasses listed in the ornamental grass chapter are tolerant of soils that are alkaline. So too are most of the annuals listed in the chapter on annuals. Check also with local sources of information, both to learn about your soils and to ask about specific plants that may not be listed here.

Variegated bishop's weed (*Aegopodium podagraria* 'Variegatum')	All PNW
Wall rockcress (*Arabis caucasica*)	All PNW
French tarragon (*Artemisia dracunculus*)	All PNW
Silver king artemisia (*Artemisia ludoviciana albula*)	All PNW
Common aubretia (*Aubretia deltoidea*)	All PNW
Shasta daisy (*Chrysanthemum maximum*)	All PNW
Dusty miller (*Chrysanthemum ptarmiciflorum*)	All PNW
Coreopsis (*Coreopsis grandiflora, C. lanceolata*)	All PNW
Globe thistle (*Echinops exaltatus*)	All PNW
Fleabane (*Erigeron speciosus*)	All PNW
Crane's bill (*Erodium macradenum roseum*)	C, LV, LM, DV
Wallflower (*Erysimum cheiri*)	LV, LM, DV, HD
Blanket flower (*Gaillardia grandiflora*)	All PNW
Baby's breath (*Gypsophila paniculata*)	All PNW
Perennial sunflower (*Helianthus maximilianii*)	LM, DV, HD
Daylily (*Hemerocallis* spp.)	All PNW
Iris (*Iris* spp.)	All PNW
Gayfeather (*Liatris spicata*)	All PNW
Perennial blue flax (*Linum perenne*)	All PNW
California bluebell (*Phacelia campanularia*)	DV, HD
Creeping phlox (*Phlox subulata*)	All PNW
Lupine (Russell lupines)	All PNW
Sedum (*Sedum* spp.)	All PNW
Lamb's ears (*Stachys byzantina*)	All PNW

HERBACEOUS PERENNIALS FOR DRY SHADE SITES

The western part of the Pacific Northwest is blessed with trees, many of them quite large. They provide shade that is welcomed during the hot summer, but for many of the flowering perennials it may be more than they can tolerate. Also, trees are heavy users of groundwater, often to the detriment of shallowly rooted soft-foliaged plants. Luckily there are a few plants that will tolerate the shade along with droughty conditions, and some of them are listed below. Before you plant the entire backlot with them, check them out carefully, for some, such as Claridge Druce geranium, can become rather overbearing. Give any that you plant some help with an occasional watering and feeding.

Japanese anemone (*Anemone hybrida*)	All PNW
Campanula (*Campanula lactiflora*)	All PNW

Jupiter's beard (*Centranthus ruber*)	C, LV
Bleeding heart (*Dicentra spectabilis*)	All PNW
Hen-and-chicks (*Echeveria* selected spp.)	C, LV, LM
Bishop's hat (*Epimedium* spp.)	All PNW
White snakeroot (*Eupatorium rugosum*)	All PNW
Euphorbia (*Euphorbia amygdaloides*)	C, LV, LM, DV
Claridge Druce geranium (*Geranium oxonianum* 'Claridge Druce')	All PNW
Hellebore (*Helleborus foetidus*)	All PNW
Daylily (*Hemerocallis* selected spp.)	All PNW
Gladwin iris (*Iris foetidissima*)	All PNW
Lamium (*Lamium* spp.)	All PNW
Yellow archangel (*Lamium galeobdolon*)	All PNW
Lily turf (*Liriope gigantea*)	C, LV, LM
Rose mallow (*Malva moschata*)	All PNW
London pride saxifrage (*Saxifraga umbrosa*)	All PNW
Fringe cups (*Tellima grandiflora*)	C, LV, LM, DV
Foamflower (*Tiarella cordifolia*)	All PNW

Perennials should be watered heavily when they are first planted, to settle the plants and get good contact beween their roots and surrounding soil. During summer, most perennials need to be watered as the soil dries. Occasional deep waterings are better than short, frequent waterings. A two- to three-inch organic mulch will cut down on watering and weeding. In cold winters when the soil freezes, add mulch to cover the plants' roots after the soil is frozen. This will keep the roots from freezing and thawing through the variable winter of the Pacific Northwest.

HERBACEOUS PERENNIALS THAT HAVE SEEDS BIRDS LOVE

Herbaceous perennials can be used to attract birds in late fall and winter without putting up a feeding station. Just plant some of the following plants and leave the seedheads on instead of cutting them back when cold weather arrives. Then, if you have arranged things properly, watch the siskins and finches and chickadees dart from the coneflowers to the globe thistles and coreopsis. Here are a few of the plants that the birds love to explore to find their seeds.

Aster (*Aster* spp.)	All PNW
Shasta daisy (*Chrysanthemum maximum*)	All PNW
Coreopsis (*Coreopsis grandiflora*)	All PNW
Purple coneflower (*Echinacea purpurea*)	All PNW
Globe thistle (*Echinops exaltatus*)	All PNW
Fleabane (*Erigeron speciosus*)	All PNW
Blanket flower (*Gaillardia grandiflora*)	All PNW
Four o'clock (*Mirabilis jalapa*)	C, LV, LM
Evening primrose (*Oenothera erythrosepala*)	All PNW
Garden penstemon (*Penstemon gloxinioides*)	All PNW
Thick-leaf phlox (*Phlox carolina*)	All PNW
Gloriosa daisy (*Rudbeckia hirta*)	All PNW

HERBACEOUS PERENNIALS WITH AROMATIC FOLIAGE

A garden can be planned to provide aroma in several ways. The usual method is by selecting plants with aromatic flowers. It is also possible though to intersperse the planting with plants whose foliage gives off an aroma through contact with those who pass by. Some, like the scented geraniums (which are grown as annuals in most of the Pacific Northwest), could be placed where it is easy to rub the leaves and obtain the aroma. Others, like Corsican mint, can be planted among stepping stones where feet brushing by release the minty aroma. Here are a few that you might try, and as you find others, add them to the list.

Common yarrow (*Achillea millefolium*)	All PNW
Wormwood (*Artemesia* spp.)	All PNW
Chamomile (*Chamaemelum nobile*)	All PNW
Feverfew (*Chrysanthemum parthenium*)	All PNW
Gas plant (*Dictamnus albus*)	All PNW
Chameleon plant (*Houttuynia cordata*)	All PNW
English lavender (*Lavandula angustifolia*)	C, LV, LM, DV
Lemon balm (*Melissa officinalis*)	All PNW
Peppermint (*Mentha piperita*)	All PNW
Corsican mint (*Mentha requienii*)	C, LV, LM, DV
Spearmint (*Mentha spicata*)	All PNW
Bee balm (*Monarda didyma*)	All PNW
Oregano (*Oregano vulgare*)	All PNW
Rosemary (*Rosmarinus officinalis*)	C, LV, LM, DV
Pineapple sage (*Salvia elegans*)	C
Common sage (*Salvia officinalis*)	All PNW
Lemon thyme (*Thymus citriodorus*)	All PNW
Caraway-scented thyme (*Thymus herba-barona*)	All PNW

EXTRA VIGOROUS ONES TO WATCH FOR

The perennials in this list are vigorous when planted in their proper place and may become a problem staying in the boundaries you plan. You might have to pull some sprouts or pluck a few seedlings or spend some regular time digging out invasive roots. On the other hand, they can be just the ticket for covering banks that erode or for establishment on hillsides that might slide in wet times or for growing a mass of foliage in a particularly difficult site. Remember, a weed is but a plant out of place, which means that some of these might even become weeds. Check the growth habit of the plant you are considering to see if the plant is right for your situation. You might also check the list of those we say can take neglect.

Yarrow (*Achillea millefolium*)	All PNW
Bishop's weed (*Aegopodium podagraria*)	All PNW
Jupiter's beard (*Centranthus ruber*)	C, LV, LM
Lily-of-the-valley (*Convallaria majalis*)	All PNW
Crown vetch (*Coronilla varia*)	All PNW
Sweet woodruff (*Galium odoratum*)	All PNW
Whirling Butterflies (*Gaura lindheimeri* 'Whirling Butterflies')	All PNW
Daylily (*Hemerocallis* hybrids)	All PNW

Dead nettle (*Lamium maculatum*)	All PNW
Creeping Jennie (*Lysimachia nummularia*)	All PNW
Loosestrife (*Lysimachia punctata*)*	All PNW
Purple loosestrife (*Lythrum virgatum*)*	All PNW
Mint (*Mentha* spp.)	All PNW
Chinese lanterns (*Physalis alkekengi*)	All PNW
False dragonhead (*Physostegia virginiana*)	All PNW
Japanese knotweed (*Polygonum cuspidatum*)	All PNW
Self heal (*Prunella* spp.)	All PNW
Matilija poppy (*Romneya coulteri*)	All PNW
Violet (*Viola wittrockiana*)	All PNW

* See box below

> Both common loosestrife and purple loosestrife are so invasive that one or both have been placed on the noxious weed list in several western states. If you use these in your landscape, they should be restricted in some manner. It would be best to keep both of them out of your neighborhood.

HERBACEOUS PERENNIALS THAT ATTRACT HUMMINGBIRDS

Creating a garden that will attract hummingbirds ensures a pleasant encounter with these fascinating creatures. Plan your garden to include nectar flowers, tubular flowering forms, and brightly colored flowers. Hummers eat half their weight daily in nectar and the tiny insects drawn to it. As they feed on the nectar, they also pollinate the flowers. This list contains some of the herbaceous perennials that hummingbirds like.

Columbine (*Aquilegia formosa*)	All PNW
Canna (*Canna* spp.)	All PNW
Montbretia (*Crocosmia crocosmiiflora*)	C, LV, LM, DV
Delphinium (*Delphinium elatum*)	All PNW
Foxglove (*Digitalis purpurea*)	All PNW
Blanket flower (*Gaillardia grandiflora*)	All PNW
Coral bells (*Heuchera sanguinea*)	All PNW
Hyssop (*Hyssopus officinalis*)	All PNW
Red-hot poker (*Kniphofia uvaria*)	All PNW
Cardinal flower (*Lobelia cardinalis*)	All PNW
Lupine (*Lupinus* Russell hybrids)	All PNW
Red monkey flower (*Mimulus cardinalis*)	C, LV, LM, DV
Pink monkey flower (*Mimulus lewisii*)	All PNW
Bee balm (*Monarda didyma*)	All PNW
Garden penstemon (*Penstemon gloxinioides*)	All PNW
Gloriosa daisy (*Rudbeckia hirta*)	All PNW
Hummingbird flower (*Zauschneria californica*)	C, LV, LM, DV

Bee Balm

HERBACEOUS PERENNIALS FOR FULL SUN
ALL DAY

Perennials that can take full sun are the hardiest, and often the showiest, plants in the garden. However, you the gardener must keep in mind that full sun in eastern Washington and Idaho is much brighter than full sun in western Oregon. Some of the plants listed for all PNW zones might not look so colorful in the western half of this region as in the more sunny eastern parts. The listing here is general, and we hope you will look around your own neighborhood before consigning your selected plants to shadeless gardens. Look also in the ornamental grass chapter for other full-sun-loving perennial plants.

Dianthus

Yarrow (*Achillea* spp.)	All PNW
Wormwood (*Artemesia* spp.)	All PNW
Aster (*Aster frikartii* 'Monch')	All PNW
Cupid's dart (*Catananche caerulea*)	All PNW
Painted daisy (*Chrysanthemum coccineum*)	All PNW
Shasta daisy (*Chrysanthemum maximum*)	All PNW
Candle delphinium (*Delphinium elatum*)	All PNW
Pinks (*Dianthus* spp.)	All PNW
Purple coneflower (*Echinacea purpurea*)	All PNW
Euryops (*Euryops acraeus*)	C, LV
Blanket flower (*Gaillardia grandiflora*)	All PNW
Whirling Butterflies (*Gaura lindheimeri* 'Whirling Butterflies')	All PNW
Johnson's Blue geranium (*Geranium* 'Johnson's Blue')	C, LV, LM, DV
Russell Prichard geranium (*Geranium* 'Russell Prichard')	C, LV, LM, DV
Baby's breath (*Gypsophila paniculata*)	All PNW
Sun rose (*Helianthemum nummularium* vars.)	C, LV, LM, DV
Daylily (*Hemerocallis* spp.)	All PNW
Evergreen candytuft (*Iberis sempervirens*)	All PNW
Inula (*Inula royleana*)	All PNW
Crimson pincushion flower (*Knautia macedonica*)	All PNW
Statice (*Limonium latifolium*)	All PNW
Perennial blue flax (*Linum perenne*)	All PNW
Plume poppy (*Macleaya cordata*)	All PNW
Mallow (*Malva alcea*)	All PNW
Four o'clock (*Mirabilis jalapa*)	LV, LM, DV
Catmint (*Nepeta faassenii*)	All PNW
White cup flower (*Nierembergia repens*)	C, LV, LM
Mexican evening primrose (*Oenothera berlandieri* 'Siskiyou')	All PNW
Sundrops (*Oenothera tetragona*)	All PNW
Garden penstemon (*Penstemon gloxinioides*)	All PNW
Russian sage (*Perovskia* 'Blue Spire')	All PNW
Cape fuchsia (*Phygelius* spp.)	C, LV, LM, DV
Gloriosa daisy (*Rudbeckia hirta*)	All PNW
Sage (*Salvia* selected spp.)	Varies
Variegated sedum (*Sedum sieboldii* 'Variegatum')	All PNW
Stonecrop (*Sedum spathulifolium*)	All PNW
Dragon's Blood sedum (*Sedum spurium* 'Dragon's Blood')	All PNW

Dusty miller (*Senecio cineraria*)	C, LV, LM, DV
Lamb's ears (*Stachys byzantina*)	All PNW
Mother of thyme (*Thymus praecox arcticus*)	All PNW
Woolly thyme (*Thymus pseudolanuginosus*)	All PNW
Pansy (*Viola wittrockiana*)	All PNW

"Sedums prefer full sun except in the hottest zones where some shade on the roots may be necessary. Grow small sedums on the lean side as the foliage takes on beautiful coloration when the plants are stressed. The larger clumping varieties are excellent for late summer bloom in the border."—Scott Christy, partner-owner, Joy Creek Nursery, Scappoose, Oregon

HERBACEOUS PERENNIALS USED AS "EVERLASTINGS"

Quite a number of herbaceous perennials can be used to make dried arrangements by cutting and saving the flowers, generally after they have passed mid-bloom. Some can be cut and hung upside down in some sort of dry, airy storage area where they can be completely dried. Others may need treatment of some sort, perhaps burying in sand or silica gel to dry, or being treated with glycerin to maintain flower structure or color. In any case, those on this list work well as "everlastings."

Yarrow (*Achillea filipendulina*)	All PNW
Pearly everlasting (*Anaphalis margaritacea*)	All PNW
Pussy toes (*Antennaria dioica* vars.)	All PNW
Masterwort (*Astrantia major, A. maxima*)	C, LV, LM, DV
Tassel flower (*Brickellia grandiflora*)	All PNW
Cupid's dart (*Catananche caerulea*)	All PNW
Globe centaurea (*Centaurea macrocephala*)	All PNW
Jupiter's beard (*Centranthus ruber*)	C, LV
Feverfew (*Chrysanthemum parthenium*)	All PNW
Bouquet delphinium (*Delphinium grandiflorum*)	All PNW
Sweet William (*Dianthus barbatus*)	All PNW
Chinese pink (*Dianthus chinensis*)	All PNW
Globe thistle (*Echinops exaltatus*)	All PNW
Lizard tail (*Eriophyllum staechadifolium*)	All PNW
Cudweed (*Gnaphalium californicum*)	All PNW
English lavender (*Lavandula angustifolia*)	C, LV, LM, DV
Lavender hybrids (*Lavandula intermedia* hybrids)	C, LV, LM, DV
Gayfeather (*Liatris spicata*)	All PNW
Statice (*Limonium latifolium*)	All PNW
Silver dollar plant (biennial) (*Lunaria annua*)	All PNW
Stock (*Matthiola incana*)	All PNW
Chinese lantern plant (*Physalis alkekengi*)	All PNW
Pincushion flower (*Scabiosa caucasia*)	All PNW
Goldenrod (*Solidago* spp.)	All PNW
Lamb's ears (*Stachys byzantina*)	All PNW

HERBACEOUS PERENNIALS THAT BLOOM SIX WEEKS OR MORE

The problem with many herbaceous perennials is that they don't bloom for long periods of time, unlike most of the annual flowers that we depend on for color most of the summer. However, there are some that do give long-term flower color. Like many of the flowering softer plants, they should be tended periodically to remove old, faded blooms (which often stimulates more blossoms). Other plants to consider in the category of long-term bloom are the ornamental grasses, of which many put up plumes that remain until the hardest winter storms hit. The plants listed here are ones that we know will bloom for long periods; you should add to the list as you run across others.

Yarrow (*Achillea* spp.)	All PNW
Lady's mantle (*Alchemilla* spp.)*	All PNW
Windflower (*Anemone* spp.)	C, LV, LM, DV
Goatsbeard (*Aruncus dioicus*)	C, LV, LM, DV
Aster (*Aster* spp.)*	All PNW
Boltonia (*Boltonia asteroides*)	All PNW
Dalmation bellflower (*Campanula portenschlagiana*)	All PNW
Jupiter's beard (*Centranthus ruber*)	C, LV
Turtleheads (*Chelone* spp.)	All PNW
Feverfew (*Chrysanthemum parthenium*)*	All PNW
Coreopsis (*Coreopsis grandiflora*)	All PNW
Coreopsis (*Coreopsis verticillata*)	C, LV
Corydalis (*Corydalis lutea*)	C, LV, LM, DV
Gaura (*Gaura lindheimeri*)	All PNW
Geranium (*Geranium endressii*)	All PNW
Geranium (*Geranium sanguineum*)	All PNW
Baby's breath (*Gypsophila paniculata*)*	All PNW
Common sneezeweed (*Helenium autumnale*)*	All PNW
Sun rose (*Helianthemum nummularium* vars.)*	C, LV, LM, DV
Christmas rose (*Helleborus niger*)	All PNW
Lenten rose (*Helleborus orientalis*)	All PNW
Evergreen candytuft (*Iberis sempervirens*)*	All PNW
Tree mallow (*Lavatera thuringiaca* 'Barnsley')	C, LV, LM
Mexican evening primrose (*Oenothera berlandieri* 'Siskiyou')	All PNW
Jerusalem sage (*Phlomis fruticosa*)*	All PNW
Balloon flower (*Platycodon grandiflorus*)*	All PNW
Primrose (*Primula japonica* 'Miller's Crimson')	All PNW
Polyanthus primrose (*Primula polyantha*)	All PNW
Matilija poppy (*Romneya coulteri*)	All PNW
Pincushion flower (*Scabiosa caucasica*)	All PNW
Autumn Joy sedum (*Sedum telephium* 'Autumn Joy')	All PNW
Checkerbloom (*Sidalcea malviflora*)	C, LV, LM, DV
Sunny Border Blue veronica (*Veronica* hybrids 'Sunny Border Blue')	All PNW

* Will bloom again if cut back after blossoming

HERBACEOUS PERENNIALS FOR ROCK GARDENS

Rock gardens are an extracurricular activity for the average gardener, sometimes developed where a problem of the terrain exists. For some of the woody materials that supply the backbone of most of the landscape, check the shrub chapter and the list for rock gardens. For the color of the rock garden, though, here are the ones that will make yours the center of attention. The color of foliage or the seasonal flowers, often followed by dry florets or colorful leaves, make the rock garden a very important part of the landscape.

Rock jasmine (*Androsace* spp.)	All PNW
Fan columbine (*Aquilegia flabellata*)	All PNW
Mountain rock cress (*Arabis alpina*)	LV, LM, DV, HD
Rock cress (*Arabis sturii*)	All PNW
Sandwort (*Arenaria* spp.)	C, LV, LM, DV
Common thrift (*Armeria maritima*)	All PNW
Alpine aster (*Aster alpinus*)	All PNW
Common aubrieta (*Aubrieta deltoidea*)	All PNW
Basket of gold (*Aurinia saxatilis*)	All PNW
English daisy (*Bellis perennis*)	All PNW
Bellflower (*Campanula fragilis*)	All PNW
Snow in summer (*Cerastium tomentosum*)	All PNW
Glory-of-the-snow (*Chionodoxa luciliae*)	All PNW
Indian carpet sweet William (*Dianthus barbartus* 'Indian Carpet')	All PNW
Twinspur (*Diascia* spp.)	C, LV
Dryas (*Dryas* spp.)	LV, LM, DV, HD
Winter aconite (*Eranthis hyemalis*)	All PNW
Creeping wallflower (*Erysimum kotschyanum*)	All PNW
Bronze fennel (*Foeniculum vulgare*)	All PNW
Common snowdrops (*Galanthus nivalis*)	All PNW
Gentian (*Gentiana* spp.)	LV, LM, DV, HD
Oregon gentian (*Gentiana oregana*)	C, LV, LM, DV
Cranesbill geranium (*Geranium sanguineum* 'Dwarf Form')	All PNW
Rupturewort (*Herniaria glabra*)	All PNW
Hosta 'Blue Moon'	All PNW
H. 'Sea Sprite'	All PNW
H. 'Shining Tot'	All PNW
H. 'Sum and Substance'	All PNW
Gibraltar candytuft (*Iberis gibraltarica*)	All PNW
Lewisii (*Lewisii* spp.)	LV, LM, DV, HD
Golden flax (*Linum flavum*)	All PNW
Lithodora (*Lithodora diffusa*)	LV, LM, DV
Evening primrose (*Oenothera missourensis*)	All PNW
Moss pink (*Phlox subulata*)	All PNW
Perennial carpeting plant (*Raoulia australis*)	C, LV, LM, DV
Rock soapwort (*Saponaria ocymoides*)	All PNW
London pride saxifrage (*Saxifraga umbrosa*)	All PNW
Variegated sedum (*Sedum sieboldii* 'Variegatum')	All PNW
Mother of thyme (*Thymus praecox*)	All PNW

HERBACEOUS PERENNIALS THAT ATTRACT BUTTERFLIES

While butterflies are attracted to many flowers, those listed below are sure to lure them to your garden if there are any within flying distance. To make sure they come and then to insure that they remain for as long as possible, plant these herbaceous perennials in large masses. Be aware that butterflies will lay eggs, which hatch into caterpillars that like to eat. And they eat the leaves of many different kinds of flowers. Avoid pesticides that might leave residues and harm the caterpillars, else no more butterflies will come.

Nectar plants for butterflies

Butterfly weed (*Asclepias tuberosa*)	All PNW
Aster (*Aster* spp.)	All PNW
Bachelor's button (*Centaurea cyanus*)	All PNW
Jupiter's beard (*Centranthus ruber, C. ruber* 'Albus')	All PNW
Daisy (*Chrysanthemum* spp.)	All PNW
Sun Ray coreopsis (*Coreopsis* hybrid 'Sun Ray')	All PNW
Tiny Rubies pink (*Dianthus gratianopolitanus* 'Tiny Rubies')	All PNW
Purple coneflower (*Echinacea purpurea*)	All PNW
Orange fleabane (*Erigeron aurantiacus*)	All PNW
Seaside daisy (*Erigeron glaucus*)	C, LV, LM, DV
Perennial candytuft (*Iberis sempervirens*)	All PNW
White blazing star (*Liatris spicata* 'Snow White')	All PNW
Statice (*Limonium latifolium*)	All PNW
Bee balm (*Monarda* spp.)	All PNW
Catmint (*Nepeta faassenii*)	All PNW
Summer phlox (*Phlox paniculata*)	All PNW
Gloriosa daisy (*Rudbeckia hirta*)	All PNW
Hardy purple sage (*Salvia* × *superba* 'Blue Queen')	All PNW
Hardy pink sage (*Salvia* × *superba* 'Rose Queen')	All PNW
Golden Baby goldenrod (*Solidago canadensis* 'Golden Baby')	All PNW
Betony (*Stachys macrantha*)	All PNW

Host plants for larvae (caterpillars)

Butterfly weed, milkweed (*Asclepias* spp.)	All PNW
Aster (*Aster* spp.)	All PNW
Dwarf Russell hybrid lupine (*Lupinus* Russell hybrids)	All PNW
Checkerbloom (*Sidalcea malviflora*)	C, LV, LM, DV
Verbena (*Verbena rigida*)	All PNW
Royal Robe violet (*Viola odorata* 'Royal Robe')	C, LV, LM, DV

HOSTAS THAT CAN GROW AND THRIVE IN FULL SUN

Now, before you make a run on the nearest hosta nursery, look over your landscape situation. Hostas are not going to make it in hot, full sunlight in Boise, Idaho, or Burns, Oregon, unless you adapt a microclimate that provides the coolness and moisture that they need. With a little garden microclimate knowledge, however, you can place the following hostas in some of your full-sun locations, with expectation that they will do very well. And, as you run across others, add them to the list too.

Full-sun Hostas

Hosta 'Blue Umbrellas'	Background	Blue or blue-green
H. 'Citation'	Speciman	Variegated white/gold
H. 'Fall Bouquet'	Edger	Dark green
H. 'Fringe Benefit'	Background	Variegated green/white
H. 'Gold Drop'	Small	Gold
H. 'Gold Edger'	Edger	Chartreuse to gold
H. 'Grand Master'	Groundcover	Variegated blue-green/white
H. 'Green Fountain'	Groundcover	Green
H. 'Green Wedge'	Background	Light green to gold
H. 'Invincible'	Edger	Glossy green
H. 'Midas Touch'	Groundcover	Gold
H. 'On Stage'	Specimen	Variegated green/white
H. 'Sea Drift'	Background	Green
H. 'Shade Fanfare'	Groundcover	Variegated green/gold/cream
H. 'Shining Tot'	Small	Deep green
H. 'Spritzer'	Specimen	Variegated
H. 'Sum and Substance'	Background	Chartreuse to gold
H. *tardiflora*	Edger	Dark green
H. *tortifrons*	Specimen	Green
H. 'Vanilla Cream'	Edger	Chartreuse to gold to cream
H. 'Vera Verde'	Groundcover	Variegated green/cream

When using hostas in the landscape, give each sufficient room to grow. Use height as an indicator for spacing. At least double the height of each plant will be needed for normal growth. For example, if a plant is listed at twelve to twenty-four inches in height, give it from twenty-four to forty-eight inches of growing space.

Hostas for mass planting

H. 'Francee'	Groundcover	Variegated green/white
H. 'Grand Master'	Groundcover	Variegated bluegreen/white
H. 'Green Fountain'	Groundcover	Green
H. 'Ground Master'	Groundcover	Variegated green/white
H. 'Hadspen Blue'	Groundcover	Blue
H. 'Invincible'	Edger	Glossy green
H. 'Shade Master'	Groundcover	Gold
H. *ventricosa* 'Aureo-marginata'	Groundcover	Variegated green/yellow
H. 'Vera Verde'	Groundcover	Variegated green/cream

"Hostas are very adaptable plants that grow and excel under conditions of partial to almost full shade. Leaves, which last a long time after cutting, are widely used in arrangements. The yellows and golds are at their best with a little more morning sun. They enjoy enriched organic soils and a high-nitrogen fertilizer, such as 10-5-5. Summer watering is essential for best growth."—Al and Dorothy Rogers, Caprice Farm Nursery, Sherwood, Oregon

HERBACEOUS PERENNIALS THAT RESEED THEMSELVES

Wouldn't it be great to put a plant in the garden that could keep itself going by reseeding every year? For some of us maybe, but there are others who like to keep a well-manicured garden, and the seedlings that come up from these plants might become a nuisance. Therefore, you can use this list for two reasons; one, to plant with some certainty plants which will reseed themselves, or two, to avoid planting the kinds that insist on having dozens of their progeny around them. In either case, this list will tell you a little more about the energy that abounds in this world of plants.

Anise hyssop (*Agastache foeniculum*)	C, LV, LM, DV
Oriental garlic (*Allium tuberosum*)	All PNW
Columbine (*Aquilegia* spp.)	All PNW
Basket-of-gold (*Aurinia saxatilis*)	All PNW
Brunnera (*Brunnera macrophylla*)	All PNW
Peach-leafed bellflower (*Campanula persicifolia*)	All PNW
Jupiter's beard (*Centranthus ruber*)	C
Coreopsis (*Coreopsis grandiflora*)	All PNW
Corydalis (*Corydalis* spp.)	C, LV, LM, DV
Sweet William (*Dianthus barbatus*)	All PNW
Foxglove (*Digitalis purpurea* 'Excelsior')	All PNW
Purple coneflower (*Echinacea purpurea*)	All PNW
Blanket flower (*Gaillardia grandiflora*)	All PNW
Common snowdrop (*Galanthus elwesii*)	All PNW
Sweet woodruff (*Galium odoratum*)	LV, LM, DV, HD
Claridge Druce geranium (*Geranium oxonianum* 'Claridge Druce')	All PNW
Dame's rocket (*Hesperis matronalis*)	All PNW
Statice (*Limonium latifolium*)	All PNW
Silver dollar plant (*Lunaria annua*) (biennial)	All PNW
Crown pink (*Lychnis coronaria*)	All PNW
Four o'clock (*Mirabilis jalapa*)	C, LV, LM, DV
Forget-me-not (*Myosotis scorpioides*)	All PNW

Columbine

HERBACEOUS PERENNIALS FOR SUN ON THE "EASTSIDE"

Tom and Inger Burns, owners and operators of Klamath Basin Perennials, a hardy flowering plant nursery, provided this list of herbaceous perennials that they know from experience will do well in their region. As you find others that work well for your gardens in the mid to eastern portion of the Pacific Northwest, add to their suggestions.

Yarrow (*Achillea* spp.)	All PNW
Daylily (*Hemerocallis* spp.)	All PNW
Siberian iris (*Iris siberica* vars.)	All PNW
Lupine (*Lupinus* selected species)	All PNW
Mint (*Mentha* selected species)	All PNW
Bee balm (*Monarda didyma*)	All PNW
Russian sage (*Perovskia atriplicifolia*)	All PNW
Sedum 'Autumn Joy' (*Sedum telephium*)	All PNW
Thyme (*Thymus* spp.)	All PNW
Crater Lake veronica (*Veronica latifolia* 'Crater Lake')	All PNW

"We on the 'Eastside' have very little good information available on culture. We end up getting lumped in with Northwesterners of all categories, when our climate is dry and hot in summer, cold in winter, and we can have frost any day of the year because of our altitude, Chiloquin being at 4200 feet elevation. We have a small nursery just outside Chiloquin and are trying to help people realize that in fact you can have a very nice flower garden here. There are, of course, hundreds of plants that will make it here, but I'm listing just a few of my favorites. Oh yes, it is a must for anyone living in the Klamath Basin to have Veronica 'Crater Lake' in their garden."—Inger Burns, Klamath Basin Perennials, Chiloquin, Oregon

HERBACEOUS PERENNIALS WITH FRAGRANT FLOWERS

Fragrance in the herbaceous perennial garden is as natural as bees making honey. However, not all perennials have aroma in their flowers; some attract pollinating insects by color or form. Many gardeners purchase plants whose fragrance reminds them of gardens they enjoyed as children. Garden lilies and herbaceous peonies are highly valued for their sweet fragrance, yet there are others equally aromatic. We have listed those that are adaptable across most of the Pacific Northwest zones. As you begin looking for others, you will find ones that will become memories for your children when they become gardeners.

Lady bells (*Adenophora lilifolia*)	All PNW
Peruvian lily (*Alstroemeria* hybrids)	All PNW
Jupiter's beard (*Centranthus ruber*)	C, LV, LM
Lily-of-the-valley (*Convallaria majalis*)	All PNW
Chocolate cosmos (*Cosmos atrosanguineus*)	C, LV, LM, DV
Crocus (*Crocus chrysanthus*)	All PNW
Chinese pink (*Dianthus chinensis*)	All PNW
Cheddar pink (*Dianthus gratianopolitanus*)	All PNW
Cottage pink (*Dianthus plumarius*)	All PNW
Fragrant white pink (*Dianthus plumarius* 'Itsaul White')	All PNW
Tiny Rubies pink (*Dianthus* 'Tiny Rubies')	All PNW
Wallflower (*Erysimum cheiri*)	C, LV, LM
Alpine wallflower (*Erysimum alpinum*)	C, LV, LM, DV
Variegated wallflower (*Erysimum linifolium* 'Variegatum')	C
Lemon daylily (*Hemerocallis lilioasphodelus*)	All PNW
Purple sweet rocket (*Hesperis matrionalis*)	All PNW
Fragrant hosta (*Hosta plantagenea*)	All PNW
Common hyacinth (*Hyacinthus orientalis*)	All PNW
Lily (*Lilium* spp.)	All PNW
Stock (*Matthiola* spp.)	All PNW
Herbaceous peony (*Paeonia lactiflora*)	All PNW
Sweet William phlox (*Phlox divaricata*)	All PNW
Summer phlox (*Phlox paniculata*)	All PNW
Moonlight primrose (*Primula alpicola*)	LV, LM, DV, HD
Matilija poppy (*Romneya coulteri*)	All PNW
Fragrant goldenrod (*Solidago odora*)	All PNW
Sweet violet (*Viola odorata*)	All PNW

Wallflower

HERBACEOUS PERENNIAL BORDER IN CORVALLIS

Mary Fran Fryer, Master Gardener in Benton County (Oregon), contributed her suggestions for a perennial border planting that would fit the environs of the Low Valley Zone of western Oregon and Washington. These are plants that have been proven for this area and that will fit many gardens of the Pacific Northwest. Add to the list as you find others that suit your conditions.

Lady's mantle (*Alchemilla mollis*)	C, LV, LM, DV
Artemesia (*Artemesia* hybrid 'Powis Castle')	All PNW
Aster (*Aster* × *frikartii* 'Monch')	All PNW
Jupiter's beard (*Centranthus ruber*)	C, LV
Montbretia (*Crocosmia* hybrids 'Lucifer')	C, LV, LM, DV
Coreopsis (*Coreopsis grandiflora*)	All PNW
Coreopsis (*C. verticillata*)	C, LV
Daylily (*Hemerocallis* hybrids)	All PNW
Hosta (*Hosta* spp.)	All PNW
Pincushion flower (*Scabiosa caucasica*)	All PNW
Autumn Joy sedum (*Sedum spectabile* 'Autumn Joy')	All PNW

Mary Fran's unusual but easy plants in the perennial border

Angelica (*Angelica archangelica*)	All PNW
Corydalis (*Corydalis lutea*)	C, LV, LM, DV
European sea kale (*Crambe cordifolia*)	C, LV, LM
Angel's fishing rod (*Dierama pulcherrium*, *D. pendulum*)	C, LV
Globe thistle (*Echinops exaltatus* 'Taplow Blue')	All PNW
Gaura (*Gaura lindheimeri*)	All PNW
Desdemona ligularia (*Ligularia dentata* 'Desdemona')	C, LV, LM
Jerusalem sage (*Phlomis fruticosa*)	C, LV, LM, DV
Matilija poppy (*Romneya coulteri*)	All PNW
Mullein (*Verbascum dumuslosum*, *V.* 'Silver Lining')	All PNW

"Regarding Autumn Joy sedum, lots of interest nearly all year; rosettes of succulent leaves appear in early spring, then clusters of flowers on upright heads appear in soft pinks and gradually darken over the summer. Leave these dried stalks for winter interest and trim off in late winter or early spring. This succulent takes dryness, sun, and shuns pests and diseases."—Mary Fran Fryer, writer, horticulturist, Master Gardener, Corvallis, Oregon

HERBACEOUS PERENNIALS FOR PACIFIC NORTHWEST COASTAL REGIONS

Bill Rogers, OSU extension agent since 1980, is officed in Newport, Oregon, in the middle of Oregon's coastal region. Here are some perennials that are suggested by Bill and other experts. Don't forget the spring-blooming bulbs that could blend with the perennials below.

Sand verbena (*Abronia latifolia*)
Yarrow (*Achillea millefolium*)
Beachgrass (*Ammophila arenaria*)

English daisy (*Bellis perennis*)
Brunnera (*Brunnera macrophylla*)
Jupiter's beard (*Centranthus ruber*)
Seaside daisy (*Erigeron glaucus* 'Olga')
Bog gentian (*Gentiana bisetae*)
Lupine (*Lupinus littoralis*)
New Zealand flax (*Phormium tenax* and hybrids)

Sedum (*Sedum spathulifolium*)
Speedwell (*Veronica* spp.)

Bear's breeches (*Acanthus mollis*)
Monkshood (*Aconitum* spp.)
Sandhill sage
   (*Artemesia pycnocephala*)
Bergenia (*Bergenia* spp.)
Bighead sedge (*Carex macrocephala*)
Rye grass (*Elymus mollis*)
Beach strawberry (*Fragaria chiloensis*)
Daylily (*Hemerocallis* spp.)
Sword fern (*Nephrolepis exaltata*)
Black knotweed
   (*Polygonum paronychia*)
Dusty miller (*Senecio cineraria*)

"When designing sites in a coastal region, landscapers must select plants that not only survive the winter weather but also withstand salt-laden winds, cool summer temperatures, and fog. These plants must also be able to grow in a wide range of soils that tend to be very acidic. Successful coastal gardeners use features in the landscape to reduce wind speed and to increase temperatures. For example, very attractive gardens are grown on the southeast (leeward) side of homes fronting the ocean. Existing trees and shrubs also can provide special spots that are well protected from the winds."—Bill Rogers, Oregon State University extension agent, Newport, Oregon

A SAMPLER OF HERBACEOUS PERENNIAL BLOOM THROUGH THE SEASONS

Winter/Very Early Spring

Pasque flower (*Anemone pulsatilla*)
Wild ginger (*Asarum caudatum*)
English daisy (*Bellis perennis*)
English wallflower (*Cheiranthus cheiri*)
Crocus (*Crocus* spp.)
Winter aconite (*Eranthis hyemalis*)
Euphorbia (*Euphorbia* spp.)
Common snowdrop (*Galanthus nivalis*)
Hyacinth (*Hyacinthus orientalis*)
Cowslip lungwort (*Pulmonaria angustifolia*)
Buttercup (*Ranunculas repens* 'Pleniflorus')
Bloodroot (*Sanguinaria canadensis*)
Trillium (*Trillium grandiflorum*)

Rock cress (*Arabis alpina* 'Snowcap')
Common aubrieta (*Aubrieta deltoidea*)
Heartleaf bergenia (*Bergenia cordifolia*)
Glory-of-the-snow (*Chionodoxa luciliae*)
Leopard's bane (*Doronicum cordatum*)
Fawn lily (*Erythronium californicum*)
Giant snowdrop (*Galanthus elwesii*)
Christmas rose (*Helleborus niger*)
Primrose (*Primula polyantha*)
Bethlehem sage (*Pulmonaria saccharata*)
Rosemary (*Rosmarinus officinalis*)
Foamflower (*Tiarella wherryi*)
Violet (*Viola odorata*)

Spring

Poppy flower anemone (*Anemone coronaria*)
Basket of gold (*Aurinia saxatilis*)
Sea thrift (*Armeria maritima*)
Lily-of-the-valley (*Convallaria majalis*)
Bishop's hat (*Epimedium grandiflorum*)
Lenten rose (*Helleborus orientalis*)
Evergreen candytuft (*Iberis sempervirens*)
Lupine (*Lupinus polyphyllus* 'Russell Strain')
Daffodil (*Narcissus* spp.)
Herbaceous peony (*Paeonia lactiflora*)
Moss pink (*Phlox subulata*)
Jacob's ladder (*Polemonium caeruleum*)
Primrose (*Primula auricula*)
False Solomon's seal (*Smilacina racemosa*)

Columbine (*Aquilegia hybrids*)
Mountain sandwort (*Arenaria montana*)
Tussock bellflower (*Campanula carpatica*)
Pinks (*Dianthus* spp.)
Geum (*Geum quellyon*)
Coral bells (*Heuchera sanguinea*)
Lupine (*Lupinus* spp.)
German catchfly (*Lychnis viscaria*)
Peony (*Paeonia lactiflora*)
Oriental poppy (*Papaver orientale*)
Balloon flower (*Platycodon grandiflorus*)
Solomon's seal (*Polygonatum* spp.)
Rock soapwort (*Saponaria ocymoides*)
Barren strawberry (*Waldsteinia fragarioides*)

Summer

Yarrow (*Achillea filipendulina*)
Pearly everlasting (*Anaphalis margaritacea*)

Cupid's dart (*Catanache caerulea*)
Snow-in-summer (*Cerastium tomentosum*)
Delphinium (*Delphinium cardinale*)
Blanket flower (*Gaillardia aristata*)
Spanish lavender (*Lavandula stoechas*)
Perennial flax (*Linum perenne*)
Creeping jennie (*Lysimachia nummularia*)
Evening primrose (*Oenothera erythrosepala*)
Iceland poppy (*Papaver nudicaule*)
False dragonhead (*Physostegia virginiana*)
Pincushion flower (*Scabiosa caucasis*)
Lamb's ears (*Stachys byzantina*)

Anise hyssop (*Agastache foeniculum*)
Peach-leaf bellflower
    (*Campanula persicifolia*)
Shasta daisy (*Chrysanthemum maximum*)
Coreopsis (*Coreopsis grandiflora* vars.)
Globe thistle (*Echinops exaltatus*)
Lamium (*Lamium maculatum* hybrids)
Gayfeather (*Liatris* spp.)
Cardinal flower (*Lobelia cardinalis*)
Bee balm (*Monarda didyma*)
Ozark sundrops (*Oenothera missourensis*)
Beard tongue (*Penstemon* spp.)
Gloriosa daisy (*Rudbeckia hirta*)
Gentian salvia (*Salvia patens*)
Speedwell (*Veronica latifolia* 'Royal Blue')

Autumn

Japanese anemone (*Anemone hybrids*)
Boltonia (*Boltonia asteroides*)
Bugbane (*Cimicifuga* spp.)
Montbretia (*Crocosmia crocosmiiflora*)
Purple coneflower (*Echinacea purpurea*)
Daylily (*Hemerocallis* spp.)
Althea (*Malva sylvestris*)
Black-eyed susan (*Rudbeckia fulgida*)
Autumn Joy sedum
    (*Sedum telephium* 'Autumn Joy')
Moss campion (*Silene schafta*)

Michaelmas daisy (*Aster* 'novi-belgii')
Italian bellflower (*Campanula isophylla*)
Fall crocus (*Crocus speciosus*)
Carnation (*Dianthus carophyllus*)
Baby's breath (*Gypsophila paniculata*)
Red-hot poker (*Kniphofia caulescens*)
Chinese lantern (*Physalis alkekengi*)
Salvia (*Salvia azurea grandiflora*)
Indian Chief sedum
    (*Sedum telephium* 'Indian Chief')
Peruvian verbena (*Verbena peruviana*)

ANNUALS

Annual flowering plants are what we use to finish out the gardening picture each year. They are destined to flourish for a couple of months—growing from seeds or little transplants to maturity—and in the process from birth to old age give us the beauty of their flowers and foliage, form, and texture. They are the accessories that help the garden give us excitement, color, aroma, and charm. Enjoy them, for their time is limited. Select them carefully so their color and texture add to whatever you want to emphasize, be it a wide sweep of petunias or a file of marigolds.

Most of us purchase these plants as "bedding plants," transplantable young specimens that can be successfully set in our soils and be expected to grow properly. If you are in this category, wait until the soil has warmed enough for these young plants to be happy. Planting marigolds too early means that their foliage usually turns purple and they seem to shrink until the soil finally warms to the right temperature for their tiny roots to grow. If you are into growing your own transplants from seed, don't plant the seeds indoors more than six weeks before the last killing frost in your area. If you plant them indoors too early, before you can safely plant them outside, you have a house full of foliage and a lot of "leggy" plants.

When you plant, remember that young plants need phosphorus (the second number on a bag of fertilizer) for their energy source, and it needs to be placed near the young plant or seed row. A handful of bone meal, for example, in the planting row will supply this need. Then, know that these plants need nitrogen and potassium as well, so supply this in a complete fertilizer or an organic source of these elements alongside the row or five or six inches away from the newly planted plants. Then water both the plant and the fertilizer into the soil.

Calliopsis

Because annual varieties are transitory—here this year and replaced next—check with your local retail nursery for the newest and best in your area. The lists that follow are provided for specific needs. We hope they will help you to make wise choices in your garden.

ANNUALS FOR SUNNY, HOT, AND DRY

Annual flowers and vegetables are rather shallowly rooted, and few can make it through the entire growing season without being watered, either from rainfall or at scheduled irrigation times. So, even though we list the following as being those that will tolerate hot, dry, sunny locations, they should be given water regularly during the drier and hotter part of the summer. Besides, if you keep these plants in top growing condition by feeding and watering, they will reward your efforts by growing interesting foliage and showy flowers.

Madagascar periwinkle (*Catharanthus roseus*)
Spider flower (*Cleome hasslerana*)
Yellow cosmos (*Cosmos sulphureus*)
African daisy (*Dimorphotheca sinuata*)
Snow-on-the-mountain (*Euphorbia marginata*)
Baby's breath (*Gypsophila paniculata*)
Cardinal climber (*Ipomoea quamoclit*)
Flax (*Linum grandiflorum* 'Rubrum')
Four o'clock (*Mirabilis jalapa*)
Moss rose (*Portulaca grandiflora*)
Gloriosa daisy (*Rudbeckia hirta*)
Nasturtium (*Tropaeolum majus*)

Sweet sultan (*Centaurea moschata*)
Cosmos (*Cosmos bipinnatus*)
Calliopsis (*Coreopsis tinctoria*)
California poppy (*Eschscholzia californica*)
Blanketflower (*Gaillardia pulchella*)
Strawflower (*Helichrysum bracteatum*)
Statice (*Limonium sinuatum*)
Ice plant (*Mesembryanthemum crystallinum*)
Annual phlox (*Phlox drummondii*)
Castor bean (*Ricinus communis*)
Stonecrop (*Sedum* spp.)
Zinnia (*Zinnia* spp.)

 Climatic regions such as those found in Yakima, Washington; Bend, Oregon; and Boise, Idaho, which fit the "sunny, hot, and dry" category above, also have extreme ranges of day and night temperatures. They have growing seasons somewhat shorter than those of gardening areas in the western part of the Pacific Northwest. A new gardener to those areas would be wise to check with the local extension office to learn more about the many facets of local gardening conditions.

ANNUALS THAT WILL RESEED THEMSELVES

In some cases the idea of self-sowing plants might be okay, but in others it might lead to a weediness that affects the neatness of an annual garden. If yours is a lengthy growing season, it would be possible to transplant seedlings that sprout from seeds dropped by their parent plant in mid-summer to another spot in the garden and add color elsewhere in the landscape. Anyway, here are some flowers that will leave seeds behind when they finish their season.

Calendula (*Calendula officinalis*)
Bachelor's button (*Centaurea cyanus*)
Sweet William (*Dianthus barbatus*)
Blanketflower (*Gaillardia pulchella*)
Four o'clock (*Mirabilis jalapa*)
Shirley poppy (*Papaver rhoeas*)

Madagascar periwinkle (*Catharanthus roseus*)
Cleome (*Cleome hasslerana*)
California poppy (*Eschscholzia californica*)
Statice (*Limonium sinuatum*)
Nicotiana (*Nicotiana alata*)
Nasturtium (*Tropaeolum majus*)

 Gardeners can successfully save seed from many annuals. The stage of development is the crucial factor in determining viability of seed. The pods or fruits should be very dry with no trace of green remaining before being harvested. Place pods in a paper bag in a warm, dry place until the seeds are shed. Separate seed from chaff, dry seeds thoroughly, and store them in a closed container in the refrigerator until early spring when they can be planted.

ANNUALS WHOSE FLOWERS ATTRACT HUMMINGBIRDS

In other chapters in this book we have listed other plants as being attractive to hummingbirds. There are also some annuals that may help your efforts. Using annuals to attract the hummers means that you need to replant each year to maintain that attraction. As you continue this process of planting to attract, you may find there are better places to make your plantings so the hummingbirds are more easily viewed, or find that they are not being attracted to your plantings because they are too near cats and other predators. Annuals will allow you to make changes easily. Here are some of the attractive annuals.

Hollyhock (*Alcea rosea*)
Spider flower (*Cleome hasslerana*)
Monkey flower (*Mimulus hybridus*)
Geranium (*Pelargonium* spp.)
Sage (*Salvia* spp.)

Clarkia (*Clarkia* spp.)
Rosamond lobelia (*Lobelia erinus* 'Rosamond')
Tobacco plant (*Nicotiana sylvestris*)
Scarlet runner bean (*Phaseolus* spp.)
Zinnia (*Zinnia* spp.)

ANNUALS REPORTED TO BE RESISTANT TO SLUGS

One of the more voracious garden animals in the Pacific Northwest, and one that causes gardeners to tear their hair out, is the garden slug. They come in several shapes and sizes, and as with all animals, there are differences among them in their dietary choices. The gray garden slug is notorious for getting an early start in the landscape and garden. Numerous control measures have been tried, none with absolute success. They can be drowned in beer, salted like pretzels, squirted with ammonia, and still they come. Baits have been used for years. Sometimes they work, but during dull, rainy weather they don't. Here is a plant list prepared by Master Gardeners in Seattle, Washington, suggested for use in high-slug-populated areas. (Note: some of these will need some sort of protection while they are in the tender emerging stages. Once they are into their first or second true leaf, they are hardy enough to withstand the slug invasion.)

Floss flower (*Ageratum houstonianum*)
Snapdragon (*Antirrhinum majus*)
Swan River daisy (*Brachycome iberidifolia*)
Canterbury bell (*Campanula medium*)
Cosmos (*Cosmos* spp.)
Sweet alyssum (*Lobularia maritima*)
Stock (*Matthiola incana*)
Love-in-a-mist (*Nigella damascena*)
Phlox (*Phlox drummondii*)
Scarlet sage (*Salvia splendens*)
Nasturtium (*Tropaeolum majus*)

Summer forget-me-not (*Anchusa capensis*)
African daisy (*Arctotis hybrids*)
Calendula (*Calendula officinalis*)
Bachelor's button (*Centaurea cyanus*)
Pinks (*Dianthus* spp.)
Money plant (*Lunaria annua*)(biennial)
Forget-me-not (*Myosotis sylvatica*)
Shirley poppy (*Papaver rhoeas*)
Moss rose (*Portulaca grandiflora*)
Pincushion flower (*Scabiosa atropurpurea*)
Pansy (*Viola* spp.)

 There are no guarantees in life. The list above is not one that was researched by scientists, but simply a compilation of those plants that gardeners in the Pacific Northwest have had luck with. A hungry slug will probably eat any plant available, but like us they like some better than others. Generally, they seem to avoid plants with milky sap or with hairy leaves. New leaves are always preferred over the old ones, so the main time to protect your plants is during their young seedling stages. Good luck!

ANNUALS EASILY GROWN FROM SEED

All annuals are grown from seed, but some will come earlier and easier than others. We have listed the ones that we feel can be planted successfully out of doors whenever the ground warms in your area. The key here is warm ground! One of the best gifts a friend can give a gardener is a soil thermometer so he or she can tell when the soil temperature is up to 45 or 50 degrees F before planting the seeds of flowering plants. If you plant too early and the ground is cold and wet, the seeds will rot. Do keep in mind that your local retail nursery will have the newest hybrids, and is there to fill your needs should your seeds not germinate like you expected.

Poppy

Ageratum (*Ageratum houstonianum*)
Bachelor's button (*Centaurea cyanus*)
Cosmos (*Cosmos bipinnatus*)
Sweet William (*Dianthus barbatus*)
Snow-on-the-mountain (*Euphorbia marginata*)
Strawflower (*Helichrysum bracteatum*)
Sweet pea (*Lathyrus odoratus*)
Lupine (*Lupinus hartwegii*)
Nicotiana (*Nicotiana alata*)
Gloriosa daisy (*Rudbeckia hirta*)
Nasturtium (*Tropaeolum majus*)

Calendula (*Calendula officinalis*)
Cleome (*Cleome hasslerana*)
Chinese forget-me-not (*Cynoglossum amabile*)
California poppy (*Eschscholzia californica*)
Blanketflower (*Gaillardia pulchella*)
Annual mallow (*Lavatera trimestris*)
Sweet alyssum (*Lobularia maritima*)
Four o'clock (*Mirabilis jalapa*)
Shirley poppy (*Papaver rhoeas*)
Marigold (*Tagetes* spp.)
Zinnia (*Zinnia elegans*)

> *Annuals bloom for one season then they die. If you are lucky enough to reside in a region where winters are usually mild, plant spring-blooming annuals in the fall and they will give you color much earlier that those that are planted in spring. Plant summer-blooming annuals after the last killing frost. To save time in either case, purchase high-quality plants from your local retail nursery.*

ANNUALS FOR BEGINNING GARDENERS

First-time gardeners often are lead by the colorful seed packets and flower picture cards on transplants, sometimes to their dismay. Things just don't seem to work out as expected. Some plants are tough enough to withstand being planted too early, or in the wrong exposure, but some are not. Here is a list suggested by Ed Markham, horticulturist in Kent, Washington, for three distinct planting times in the Pacific Northwest. These can be bought by the flat or in individual pots. Of course the planting time is only one of the many critical keys to success, others include good soil of the proper fertility, good drainage, lots of organic matter in the soil, and a shot of fertilizer early and another about midway in the growing season.

Group 1—These generally can be planted successfully from late February.

English daisy (*Bellis perennis*)
Sweet pea (*Lathyrus odoratus* 'Royal')
Stock (*Matthiola incana* 'Midget,' 'Legacy')
Salvia (*Salvia farinacea* 'Sapphire')

Dwarf pinks (*Dianthus chinensis* × *barbatus*)
Lobelia (*Lobelia erinus*)
Salvia (*Salvia coccinea* 'Lady in Red')
Pansy (*Viola wittrockiana* vars.)

Group 2—Don't even think about planting these until the top several inches of soil is 50 degrees F or warmer, usually around the middle of May.

Fibrous-rooted begonia
(*Begonia semperflorens*)

Celosia (plume type) (*Celosia plumosa*)

Cosmos (*Cosmos bipinnatus*)

New Guinea impatiens
(*Impatiens* 'New Guinea' hybrids)

Alyssum 'Easter Bonnet'
(*Lobularia maritima*)

Love-in-mist (*Nigella damascena*)

Viola (*Viola cornuta* hybrids)

Catchfly (*Viscaria occidentalis*)

Begonia 'Non Stop' (*Begonia tuberhybrida*)

Coleus (*Coleus* spp. and hybrids)

Dahlia dwarf (*Dahlia hybridus*)

Busy Lizzie (*Impatiens walleriana*)

Nicotiana (*Nicotiana alata*)

Marigold (*Tagetes* spp.)

Verbena 'Homestead Blue' (*Verbena* spp.)

Group 3—These can be planted in late summer, to give color in fall and into winter.

English daisy (*Bellis perennis*)

Ornamental kale (*Brassica*)

Stock (*Mathiola incana* vars.)

Pansy (*Viola wittrockiana* vars. Maxim, Universal, Challon)

Ornamental cabbage (*Brassica*)

Dwarf pinks (*Dianthus chinensis* × barbatus)

Johnny jump-ups (*Viola cornuta* hybrids)

"The best gardeners respect the Northwest's long, cold, late springs. Observe these planting dates carefully for the happiest gardening. Don't be tempted to plant too early by those stores pushing impatiens and Salvia splendens, begonia and marigolds. You'll only have to buy plants twice. Patience, patience, Northwest gardeners." — Ed Markham, horticulturist, "Chief Red Sneaks," Kent, Washington

ANNUALS FOR SHADY GARDENS

If yours is a yard with lots of dense shade, you might want to check the list for annuals that do well in containers and move them around to take advantage of any sunlight that occurs. If yours is a semi-shaded yard, there are some annual plants that will do well there. We have listed those that have proved themselves in the Pacific Northwest. As you find others, add them to your list.

Ageratum (*Ageratum houstonianum*)

English daisy (*Bellis perennis*)

Basketflower (*Centaurea americana*)

Clarkia (*Clarkia unguiculata*)

Chinese forget-me-not
(*Cynoglossum amabile*)

Annual candytuft (*Iberis umbellata*)

Lobelia (*Lobelia erinus*)

Forget-me-not (*Myosotis sylvatica*)

Scarlet sage (*Salvia splendens*)

Pansy (*Viola tricolor* var. *hortensis*)

Begonia (*Begonia* spp.)

Amethyst flower
(*Browallia americana*)

Sweet sultan (*Centaurea moschata*)

Coleus (*Coleus blumeii*)

Heliotrope (*Heliotrope arborescens*)

Busy Lizzie (*Impatiens wallerana*)

Four o'clock (*Mirabilis jalapa*)

Nicotiana (*Nicotiana alata* 'Grandiflora')

Wishbone flower (*Torenia fournieri*)

Four O'clock

ANNUALS THAT ATTRACT BUTTERFLIES

It is possible to grow nectar flowers for butterflies in anything from window boxes to wildflower meadows. Nectar-rich wildflowers include asters, bleeding heart, milkweed, columbine, goldenrod, Indian paintbrush, iris, larkspur, lupine, nettle, sedum, thistle, and yarrow. Listed below are some of the non-native annuals that will also supply nectar for the butterflies. Also, check the tree, shrub, and herbaceous perennial chapters for other plants that will attract these lovely insects.

Dahlia (*Dahlia* spp.)
Snapdragon (*Antirrhinum majus*)
Pinks (*Dianthus* spp.)
Globe thistle (*Echinops exaltatus*)
Busy Lizzie (*Impatiens wallerana*)
Statice (*Limonium* spp.)
Money plant (biennial)(*Lunaria annua*)
Marigold (*Tagetes* spp.)

Cosmos (*Cosmos bipinnatus*)
Bachelor's button (*Centaurea cyanus*)
Sweet William (*Dianthus barbatus*)
Heliotrope (*Heliotropium arborescens*)
Sweet pea (*Lathyrus odoratus*)
Sweet alyssum (*Lobularia maritima*)
Geranium (*Pelargonium* spp.)
Zinnia (*Zinnia* spp.)

Remember too that the offspring of the butterfly must have something to feed upon as well. Here are some annuals that will host the caterpillars.

Hollyhock (*Alcea rosea*)(biennial)
Sunflower (*Helianthus annuus*)
Lupine (*Lupinus hartwegii*)

Snapdragon (*Antirrhinum majus*)
Annual mallow (*Lavatera trimestris*)
Nasturtium (*Tropaeolum majus*)

"The Pacific Northwest is blessed with more than 150 species of butterflies. A little more than half of these species are found only in the eastern part of the region. In Oregon about 30 species are found only on the western side of the state. Home gardeners don't need a large yard to provide the basics for butterfly survival. All they need are nectar plants, larval host plants, resting areas, sun, and water. For more information about butterfly habitat, consult the **Handbook for Butterfly Watchers,** *by Robert Michael Pyle, or* **Butterfly Gardening,** *published by Sierra Club Books and the National Wildlife Federation."—Gail Gredler, Yamhill County home horticulturist, Oregon State University Extension Service*

ANNUALS THAT ARE SUITABLE FOR CUT FLOWERS

Most every plant produces a flower that can be picked and kept for awhile in a vase. A gardener, especially one who likes to arrange flowers, could pluck and arrange dandelions and foxtail grass and love the effect. However, we have put together this list to give you some suggestions for annuals that will make a long enough stem and that will hold up for several days or more indoors. As you run across others, add them to your list.

Snapdragon (*Antirrhinum majus*)
Calendula (*Calendula officinalis*)

Blue-eyed African daisy (*Arctotis stoechadifolia*)
China aster (*Callistephus chinensis*)

Basketflower (*Centaurea americana*)

Clarkia (*Clarkia unguiculata*)

Calliopsis (*Coreopsis tinctoria*)

Dahlia (*Dahlia* spp.)

Blanket flower (*Gaillardia pulchella*)

Annual baby's breath
(*Gypsophila elegans*)

Sweet pea (*Lathyrus odoratus*)

Bells of Ireland (*Moluccella laevis*)

Painted tongue (*Salpiglossis sinuata*)

Pincushion flower
(*Scabiosa atropurpurea*)

Bluelace flower (*Trachymene coerulea*)

Pansy (*Viola tricolor* vars.)

Sweet sultan (*Centaurea moschata*)

Larkspur (*Consolida ambigua*)

Cosmos (*Cosmos* spp.)

China pink (*Dianthus chinensis*)

Globe amaranth (*Gomphrena globosa*)

Annual candytuft (*Iberis umbellata*)

Stock (*Matthiola incana*)

Love-in-a-mist (*Nigella damescena*)

Sage (*Salvia* spp.)

Marigold (*Tagetes* spp.)

Nasturtium (*Tropaeolum majus*)

Zinnia (*Zinnia* spp.)

ANNUALS THAT ATTRACT BENEFICIAL INSECTS

As your gardening expertise grows, you might discover that there are systematic interactions between plants and animals. Plants attract insects of various kinds. If you have planted the right plants, you have lots of predatory insects attracted to pollen or nectar. The predatory types often have larval stages that parasitize, or feed upon, other insects. So, with a little careful planning, Mother Nature can help keep pest problems under some control. One last thing: In order for this to work you must be tolerant of a few bugs, because if there are no plant pests to feed upon, the predators fly on to someone else's garden. Here are a few annuals and the beneficial insects that they attract.

Hollyhock (*Alcea rosea*)	Bees
Snapdragon (*Antirrhinum majus*)	Bees
Calendula (*Calendula officinalis*)	Hoverflies
China aster (*Callistephus chinensis*)	Hoverflies
Marguerite (*Chrysanthemum frutescens*)	Hoverflies
Sweet William (*Dianthus barbatus*)	Hoverflies, butterflies
Globe thistle (*Echinops ritro*)	Bees, butterflies
Buckwheat (*Fagopyrum esculentum*)	Parasitic wasps, tachinid flies, bees
Strawflower (*Helichrysum bracteatum*)	Hoverflies, various others
Sweet alyssum (*Lobularia maritima*)	Tachinid flies, syrpids, chalcids
Black-eyed susan (*Rudbeckia hirta*)	Hoverflies, various others
African marigold (*Tagetes erecta*)	Bees, butterflies
French marigold (*Tagetes patula*)	Bees, hoverflies
Nasturtium (*Tropaeolum minus*)	Hoverflies, various others

"This year plant a border of plants or scatter plants within your garden or orchard. Select plants that will have a succession of bloom from spring through fall. This will provide for the requirements of many adult species of beneficial insects. It will also provide beauty to your landscape." —Ted L. Swensen, botanist (retired), Portland Community College

ANNUALS WITH EXTENDED BLOOMING PERIODS

The annuals in this list will begin blooming early in the spring and continue through most of the growing season. They will do even better if you take the time to remove old, faded blooms (deadheading). Some, like the petunias, will give many more flowers if you trim them back periodically when they begin to get leggy. Don't forget to give them a midseason feeding too, either with a light side-dressing of a dry fertilizer, or by watering with a liquid form of complete fertilizer.

Madagascar Periwinkle

Fibrous begonia
  (*Begonia semperflorens*)
Calendula (*Calendula officinalis*)
Plume cockscomb (*Celosia argentea*)
Calliopsis (*Coreopsis tinctoria*)
African daisy (*Gazania* spp.)
Impatiens (*Impatiens wallerana*)
Edging lobelia (*Lobelia erinus*)

Portulaca (*Portulaca grandiflora*)
Scarlet sage (*Salvia splendens*)
Creeping zinnia (*Sanvitalia procumbens*)
French marigold (*Tagetes patula*)
Wishbone flower (*Torenia fournieri*)

Browallia (*Browallia* spp.)

Madagascar periwinkle (*Catharanthus roseus*)
Spiderflower (*Cleome hasslerana*)
Cosmos (*Cosmos* spp.)
Globe amaranth (*Gomphrena globosa*)
Mallow (*Lavatera trimestris*)
Flowering tobacco
  (*Nicotiana alata* 'Grandiflora')
Blue sage (*Salvia farinacea*)
Pincushion flower (*Scabiosa atropurpurea*)
African marigold (*Tagetes erecta*)
Jewels of ophir (*Talinum paniculatum*)
Zinnia (*Zinnia* spp.)

On East Burnside Street in Portland live the two most avid gardeners we know. They live in a white, two-story, traditional turn-of-the-century farmhouse. It is surrounded by pavement, concrete, and the hum of the urban environment. Ernest and Elsie Hays have created an oasis for busy city dwellers. Each year they circle their small yard with brilliant annuals that bloom profusely among their roses and vegetables. At ninety-two and eighty-nine, Ernest and Elsie have been gardening together for sixty-nine years. Elsie says they met when she was ten. Their love of flowers shows in their prolific-blooming pansies, seed dahlias, snapdragons, annual candytuft, and a myriad of other brightly colored blooms.

They visit over the fence with passers-by, sharing their gardening expertise and receiving compliments on their lovely yard. They enjoy the children that seem interested enough in their garden to ask, "What is that? How do you grow this?" Elsie says that Ernest has a surefire concoction that makes their garden beautiful every year. Ernest says, "I use this big garbage can and I mix in chicken manure, super phosphate, fish meal, bone meal, garden lime, sulfate of ammonia, and potash and fill the can with water. After I stir it up it comes out to be an analysis of about a 10-8-6. I use one quart to a gallon when I water." The proportions of this mix are Ernest's secret. Gardening keeps this wonderful couple young. —Elsie and Ernest Hayes, gardeners, Portland, Oregon

ANNUALS FOR MOIST AND COOL CONDITIONS

The western part of the Pacific Northwest, and especially some of the coastal areas, usually will be cool and damp in the first half of the normal growing season. Later it turns hot and dry. All of this means that the gardener must be able to select plants that will tolerate cooler, wetter conditions and will later adapt to hot and dry ones. Luckily, we have a few listed for you to start with. Add to the list as you find others that are as adaptable.

Mask flower (*Alonsoa warscewiczii*)   Bugloss (*Anchusa capensis*)
Telanthera   Blue woodruff (*Asperula setosa*)
   (*Alternanthera ficordea* 'Bettzickiana')
English daisy (*Bellis perennis*)   Calendula (*Calendula officinalis*)
Canterbury bells (*Campanula medium*)   Larkspur (*Consolida ambigua*)
Pink (*Dianthus chinensis*)   Annual candytuft (*Iberis umbellata*)
Balsam (*Impatiens balsamina*)   Sweet pea (*Lathyrus odoratus*)
Edging lobelia (*Lobelia erinus*)   Monkey flower (*Mimulus luteus*)
Forget-me-not (*Myosotis sylvatica*)   Baby blue-eyes (*Nemophila menziesii*)
Wishbone flower (*Torenia fournieri*)   Bluelace flower (*Trachymene coerulea*)

ANNUALS THAT WERE ALL-AMERICAN WINNERS IN 1996

Around the country we are fortunate to have experimental stations and testing grounds where new varieties and hybrids can be tested for a year or two before they are placed on the gardening market. Whenever you are near a place such as this, drop in and see what new plant hybrids and types we can expect in years to come. Near Roseburg, Oregon, Jerry Maul and his staff of Master Gardeners have worked a deal where the local boys' ranch provides them with several acres for an experimental and demonstration site. Here are some of their top performers of past years.

Ageratum 'Blue Horizon'   Tall (12-18"), superb dried flower
'Tropical Rose' canna   Seed-grown canna
Celosia cristata 'Tall Chief' Best of all for cut flowers
'Early Sunrise' coreopsis   A perennial that blooms like an annual, should be
                                    considered an annual in PNW
'Ideal Violet' dianthus   Beautiful small flowers, ideal for containers
'Telstar Picotee' dianthus   Red-and-white flower, great for pots
'Mont Blanc' nierembergia   White butterfly-like flower, nearly always in bloom
'Freckles' geranium   Pink with freckles, great from seed
'Purple Wave' petunia   Sprawls over rocks, spreads like ground cover, no
                                    deadheading is required, a must for flower lovers
Rudbeckia 'Indian Summer'   A prolific bloomer, good cut flowers
'Peaches and Cream' verbena   Unique blooms
'Scarlet Spendor' zinnia   Great bloomer, tolerant of overhead watering

"Fertilizing and watering are key management factors that insure your annuals will grow as you want them. For fertilizer, the best choice is triple 16 (16-16-16). Use eight to ten pounds per one thousand square feet of area (one pound per hundred square feet), till it into the soil before planting to give the plants the boost they need for early-season growth. Then, after the plants have set their first flower buds, a sidedressing of ammonium nitrate, about ¼ pound per hundred feet of row, will keep your plants growing and setting flowers all summer."—Jerry Maul, Oregon State University extension agent, Douglas County, Roseburg, Oregon

ANNUALS FOR ALKALINE SOILS

Most annuals seem to do better in soils that are slightly on the acidic side. Begonias for example definitely prefer them and if planted in alkaline soils will either die or look so bad that you wish they would. Here is a list put together by extension agents and nurserymen in central Oregon, where the soil pH ranges from neutral to extremely alkaline.

Snapdragon (*Antirrhinum majus*)
Basketflower (*Centaurea americana*)
Sweet sultan (*Centaurea moschata*)
Larkspur (*Consolida ambigua*)
Baby's breath (*Gypsophila elegans*)
Annual candytuft (*Iberis umbellata*)
Lobelia (*Lobelia erinus*)
Stock (*Matthiola incana*)
Iceland poppy (*Papaver nudicaule*)*
Black-eyed susan (*Rudbeckia hirta*)
Zinnia (*Zinnia* spp.)
* Perennial in warmer regions

China aster (*Callistephus chinensis*)
Bachelor's button (*Centaurea cyanus*)
Clarkia (*Clarkia unguiculata*)
California poppy (*Eschscholzia californica*)
Sunflower (*Helianthus annuus*)
Summer cypress (*Kochia scoparia*)
Sweet alyssum (*Lobularia maritima*)
Forget-me-not (*Myosotis sylvatica*)
Annual phlox (*Phlox drummondii*)
Painted tongue (*Salpiglossis sinuata*)

ANNUALS THAT WILL CONTINUE BLOOMING IN AUTUMN

With the right sort of circumstances, such as a place in the garden that is protected from wind and early frost, fertile and well-drained soil, and a variety of annuals that is noted for blooming right up to the final minute before killing frost, you can have flowers late into the fall. In fact in some of the PNW regions, where freezing weather may not even occur in three winters out of five, annuals become perennials of a sort, continuing growth and bloom right into the next year. Count your blessings. Here are a few that will give you all their best.

Mask flower (*Alonsoa warscewiczii*)
Browallia (*Browallia* spp.)
Plume cockscomb (*Celosia cristata*)
Cosmos (*Cosmos* spp.)
African daisy (*Gazania* spp.)

Sweet alyssum (*Lobularia maritima*)

Blue sage (*Salvia farinacea*)
Marigold (*Tagetes* spp.)
Zinnia (*Zinnia* spp.)

Fibrous begonia (*Begonia semperflorens*)
Calendula (*Calendula officinalis*)
Crown daisy (*Chrysanthemum carinatum*)
Dahlia (*Dahlia* spp.)
Common heliotrope
    (*Heliotropium arborescens*)
Flowering tobacco
    (*Nicotiana alata* 'Grandiflora')
Scarlet sage (*Salvia splendens*)
Black-eyed susan (*Rudbeckia hirta*)

ANNUALS THAT BRING FRAGRANCE TO THE GARDEN

For some gardeners, fragrance from plants is an added benefit, for others who might be allergic or who are bothered by aromas, fragrant flowers are a mixed blessing. Most annual flowers have some aroma, sometimes so slight that you have to stick your nose into the flower to find it. Others have fragrances that they give to passing breezes, which are then carried for some distance before they dissipate. If you like flower fragrance, plant some of these near where you will sit in the garden. If you don't like the perfumery, plant accordingly, perhaps in a viewing garden away from where you like to sit.

Basketflower (*Centaurea americana*)
China pink (*Dianthus chinensis*)

Moonflower (*Ipomoea alba*)
Sweet alyssum (*Lobularia maritima*)
Flowering tobacco
    (*Nicotiana alata* 'Grandiflora')
Mignonette (*Reseda odorata*)
* Perennial in mild winter

Sweet sultan (*Centaurea moschata*)
Common heliotrope
    (*Heliotropium arborescens*)
Sweet pea (*Lathyrus odoratus*)
Stock (*Matthiola incana*)
Petunia (not all—sniff them out!)

Sweet violet (*Viola odorata*)*

ANNUALS THAT ARE TALL ENOUGH TO PROVIDE BACKGROUND INTEREST

Generally, when designing a garden the designer seeks out plants that have characteristics that will serve several functions. Sometimes you need plants that grow tall enough to screen a view or to serve as background for shorter plants. For viewing from one direction, put the tall types on the back side of the flower garden. For viewing all around, a circular garden for example, put the tall plants in the middle, where they will enhance shorter plants. A design with plants shows off the gardener's artistry. Here is your chance to make your own mark on the world. In this list are annuals that will easily grow to be three to four feet tall.

Tassel flower (*Amaranthus caudatus*)
Plume cockscomb (*Celosia argentea*)
Spider flower (*Cleome hasslerana*)
Foxglove (*Digitalis purpurea*)(biennial)
Moonflower (*Ipomea alba*)

Hollyhock (*Alcea rosea*, selected vars.)
Basket flower (*Centaurea americana*)
Cosmos (*Cosmos* spp.)
Sunflower (*Helianthus annuus*)
Castor bean (*Ricinus communis*)

ANNUALS THAT VINE

Annual vines are great fun. They grow so quickly, if you obey their growth needs, such as mostly full sun, good soil, and something they can vine upon. You can almost watch them grow! Grown from seed, they can be used to decorate trellises, walls, or most anything that rises above the ground surface. Some, such as the gourds, will need to be trained up on a trellis. (Left to themselves they will simply scramble around on the ground.) If your region is one where warm weather doesn't come until early June, find these plants already growing at your nearest nursery or retail greenhouse. (For others see the chapter on vines.)

Climbing snapdragon (*Asarina* spp.)
Cup-and-saucer vine (*Cobaea scandens*)
Hyacinth bean (*Dolichos Lablab*)
Cardinal climber (*Ipomoea quamoclit*)
Sweet pea (*Lathyrus odoratus*)
Scarlet runner bean (*Phaseolus coccineus*)
Climbing nasturtium (*Tropaeolum majus*)

Love-in-a-puff (*Cardiospermum halicacabum*)
Ornamental gourds (*Cucurbita pepo ovifera*)
Moonflower (*Ipomoea alba*)
Morning glory (*Ipomoea tricolor*)
Luffa sponge (*Luffa aegyptiaca*)
Black-eyed susan vine (*Thunbergia alata*)
Canary bird flower (*Tropaeolum peregrinum*)

ANNUALS FOR GARDENS IN COASTAL AREAS

Gardeners who live in coastal areas must contend with a nearly constant ocean breeze (which sometimes becomes a gale). Successful growing of annual flowers then becomes a matter of careful selection of plants and of planting sites. First, find the kinds of plants that will tolerate the salt air, then find a place in the garden where you can give these annuals protection, either by larger perennial plants or by garden structures that baffle the wind. Here are some that we think will do well for you. In some of the coastal regions where winters are mild, some of the following may become more perennial in their growing habits, sweet violet for example.

Snapdragon (*Antirrhinum majus*)
Bachelor's buttons (*Centaurea cyanus*)
Godetia (*Clarkia amoena*)
Dahlia (*Dahlia* spp.)
African daisy (*Gazania* spp.)
Lobelia (*Lobelia erinus*)
Lupine (*Lupinus hartwegii*)
Shirley poppy (*Papaver rhoeas*)
Sweet violet (*Viola odorata*)*
* Perennial in mild winter

Calendula (*Calendula officinalis*)
Shasta daisy (*Chrysanthemum maximum*)
Clarkia (*Clarkia unguiculata*)
China pink (*Dianthus chinensis*)
Impatiens (*Impatiens wallerana*)
Sweet alyssum (*Lobularia maritima*)
Flowering tobacco (*Nicotiana alata*)
Geranium (*Pelargonium domesticum*)

 Coastal soils range from sand dunes to silty clay, and tend to be very acidic due to the leaching effect of winter rains. Consequently, landscapers should add lime to the soil at planting time. Also, organic matter should be added to improve the water-holding capacity of sandy and air-retention ability of heavier soils.

ANNUALS NOT TO BE PLANTED UNTIL WARM WEATHER ARRIVES

Many annuals that Pacific Northwesterners like to use in their gardens require warm planting soils. And most of us like to plant just as soon as the rain clouds move elsewhere and the sun begins to shine again. Planting while the soil is still down around 45 degrees F means that the poor little plant sits and shivers until the soil warms, often seems to shrink in size, and may actually turn purple in color. Hold on, dear gardener, until at least two or three weeks after the last frost. Here are some that we definitely need to wait for the soil to warm before planting. Of course there are many ways of warming the soil, such as using row covers, landscape cloth, walls of water, and so forth, but good-sense gardening means understanding when to plant and when to forget it for another week.

Sand verbena (*Abronia umbellata*)
Basketflower (*Centaurea americana*)
Spider flower (*Cleome hasslerana*)
Calliopsis (*Coreopsis tinctoria*)
African daisy (*Gazania* spp.)
Strawflower (*Helichrysum bracteatum*)
Cardinal climber (*Ipomoea quamoclit*)
Statice (*Limonium* spp.)

Plume cockscomb (*Celosia argentea*)
Sweet sultan (*Centaurea moschata*)
Coleus (*Coleus blumeii*)
Snow-on-the-mountain (*Euphorbia marginata*)
Sunflower (*Helianthus annuus*)
Busy Lizzie (*Impatiens wallerana*)
Burning bush (*Kochia scoparia*)
Ice plant (*Mesembryanthemum crystallinum*)

Four o'clock (*Mirabilis jalapa*)

Poppy (*Papaver* spp.)

Scarlet runner bean (*Phaseolus coccineus*)

Nasturtium (*Tropaeolum majus*)

Cup flower (*Nierembergia* spp.)

Petunia (*Petunia* spp.)

Scarlet sage (*Salvia splendens*)

Zinnia (*Zinnia* spp.)

ANNUALS THAT WILL TOLERATE POOR SOILS

If you are not blessed with loamy, rich, fertile soil in your garden, develop a plan for soil building that will extend over your gardening lifetime. Such terms as composting, cover cropping, soil amendments, deep digging, raised beds, incorporation of organic matter, and soil testing all may become a part of your vocabulary as you make your soil better. Most annuals will grow in poor soil if you follow good plant management procedures, like watering and fertilizing, controlling weeds, and protecting the plant from extremes of weather. The care you give to the plants will determine whether or not they grow successfully. Here are some that are more tolerant of poor soil conditions.

Corn cockle (*Agrostemma githago*)

Blue woodruff (*Asperula setosa*)

Basket flower (*Centaurea americana*)

Sweet sultan (*Centaurea moschata*)

Spider flower (*Cleome hasslerana*)

Cosmos (*Cosmos* spp.)

California poppy (*Eschscholzia californica*)

Summer cypress (*Kochia scoparia*)

Blazing star (*Mentzelia* spp.)

Four o'clock (*Mirabilis jalapa*)

Poppy (*Papaver* spp.)

Portulaca (*Portulaca grandiflora*)

French marigold (*Tagetes patula*)

Verbena (*Verbena hybrida*)

Joseph's coat (*Amaranthus tricolor*)

Plume cockscomb (*Celosia argentea*)

Bachelor's button (*Centaurea cyanus*)

Farewell to spring (*Clarkia amoena*)

Larkspur (*Consolida ambigua*)

Chinese forget-me-not (*Cynoglossum amabile*)

Morning glory (*Ipomoea* spp.)

Sweet alyssum (*Lobularia maritima*)

Ice plant (*Mesembryanthemum crystallinum*)

Cup flower (*Nierembergia* spp.)

Beefsteak plant (*Perilla frutescens*)

Pincushion flower (*Scabiosa atropurpurea*)

Nasturtium (*Tropaeolum majus*)

ANNUALS THAT WILL TOLERATE A DRY SHADE GARDEN

Dry shade is more common to the Pacific Northwest region than most gardeners realize. Often the condition is caused by trees in the area that use much of the groundwater and that provide either filtered sunlight or complete shade. One option of course is to remove the trees, but most of us like to keep them for various reasons. Some plants that can tolerate the shade and the intense competition for water are included in the following list. Keep in mind that you as the gardener can cause a lot of things to happen by providing the proper care of the seedlings or transplants you have placed in dry shade. Annuals are temporary at best, but you can make the difference between a short life in your garden and a season-long one. By using the following you will probably have better luck.

Floss flower (*Ageratum houstonianum*)

Spider flower (*Cleome hasslerana*)

Twinspur (*Diascia barberae*)

Annual candytuft (*Iberis umbellata*)

Four o'clock (*Mirabilis jalapa*)

Bachelor's button (*Centaurea cyanus*)

Dwarf morning glory (*Convolvulus tricolor*)

Globe amaranth (*Gomphrena* spp.)

Money plant (*Lunaria annua*)(biennial)

ANNUALS THAT WILL GIVE CONTINUAL BLOOM IF DEADHEADED

Deadheading is the process of taking off the old flowers when they have faded or withered. Most plants will grow, develop blossoms, bloom, and then spend the rest of their summer growing seeds. You can change this sequence and keep the plants in a vigorous state so they will come back with some more blooms. By deadheading you not only provide the impetus to the plant to grow more flowers, but you also remove a possible problem, that of fungus diseases such as botrytis blight. Here are some that will do wonderfully well if you tend them.

Floss flower (*Ageratum houstonianum*)
Snapdragon (*Antirrhinum majus*)
Calendula (*Calendula officinalis*)
Cosmos (*Cosmos* spp.)
Blanket flower (*Gaillardia pulchella*)
Annual mallow (*Lavatera trimestris*)
Monkey flower (*Mimulus hybridus*)
Petunia (*Petunia hybrida*)
Scarlet sage (*Salvia splendens*)
French marigold (*Tagetes patula*)

Hollyhock (*Alcea rosea*)
Begonia (*Begonia semperflorens*)
Spider flower (*Cleome hassletana*)
Chinese pink (*Dianthus chinensis*)
Busy Lizzie (*Impatiens wallerana*)
Sweet alyssum (*Lobularia maritima*)
Geranium (*Pelargonium* spp.)
Painted tongue (*Salpiglossis sinuata*)
African marigold (*Tagetes erecta*)
Pansy (*Viola* spp.)

ANNUALS FOR EARLY SPRING BLOOM

Depending on where you live in the Pacific Northwest, some of the annuals listed below could live through your winter and be ready to bloom in the spring. However, that particular microclimate is a rarity for most of us who live away from the warmer coastal areas. In any case, if your garden can be prepared in early February for planting, you could have bloom on these plants by mid to late spring, depending on the variety and the microclimate that you have arranged for your garden. Slugs will be out early as well, so make sure you protect the young seedlings or transplants that you plant outdoors. A slug-bait station works well.

Calendula (*Calendula officinalis*)
Clarkia (*Clarkia* spp.)
Globe candytuft (*Iberis umbellata*)
Baby snapdragon (*Linaria maroccana*)
Money plant (*Lunaria annua*)(biennial)
Baby blue-eyes (*Nemophila menziesii*)
Pansy (*Viola* spp.)

Bachelor's button (*Centaurea cyanus*)
California poppy (*Eschscholzia californica*)
Sweet pea (*Lathyrus odoratus*)
Sweet alyssum (*Lobularia maritima*)
Forget-me-not (*Myosotis sylvatica*)
Poor man's orchid (*Schizanthus pinnatus*)

ANNUALS FOR SPILLING OVER THE EDGE

Flower gardens can be anything from flat plots of ground to raised beds and containers. When you build your beds upwards, you might need something that will trail downwards, and here is a list of plants that may fill your needs. Trailing plants allow you to develop a sweep of foliage and bloom. By mixing upright types with trailing types, you make the picture even more beautiful, as well as functional. Add to this list as you run across others that fit the situation.

Climbing snapdragon (*Asarina* spp.)
Licorice plant (*Helichrysum petiolare*)
Lobelia (*Lobelia erinus*)
Lotus (*Lotus berthelotii*)
Ivy geranium (*Pelargonium peltatum*)
Moss rose (*Portulaca grandiflora*)
Nasturtium (*Tropaeolum majus*)

Amethyst flower (*Browallia* spp.)
Lantana (*Lantana montevidensis*)
Sweet alyssum (*Lobularia maritima*)
Cup flower (*Nierembergia* spp.)
Petunia (*Petunia* 'Purple Wave')
Creeping zinnia (*Sanvitalia procumbens*)
Verbena (*Verbena hybrida*)

Trailing plants should be planted near the sides of containers so they can gracefully flow over their edges. Use trailing plants in hanging baskets to help give a vertical effect. Trim them as needed to remove yellowed, crowded, or dead foliage and stems.

ANNUALS SUITABLE FOR GROWING IN CONTAINERS

Not all plants are compatible with most planting containers. Mostly it is a matter of size. Some have long, spreading roots while others confine themselves easily to the pot parameters. Containerizing plants gives the gardener more latitude and options for where to place them. If yours is a semishaded yard, containers can be moved to take advantage of where the sun is shining. During winter the annuals are frozen down and we can prepare our containers for the coming year. Always put fresh potting mix in the containers. If you want to hold over the old potting soil, put it on the compost for a year. (Sometimes this soil builds up fertilizer salts, and it may take some time for the salts to dissipate.) Here are some annuals that work wonderfully well for growing in containers.

Floss flower (*Ageratum houstonianum*)
Flowering cabbage, kale (*Brassica oleracae*)
Dusty miller (*Centaurea cineraria*)
Coleus (*Coleus hybridus*)
Busy Lizzie (*Impatiens wallerana*)
Sweet alyssum (*Lobularia maritima*)
Petunia (*Petunia hybrida*)
Moss rose (*Portulaca grandiflora*)
Marigold (*Tagetes* spp.)
Verbena (*Verbena hybrida*)

Wax begonia (*Begonia semperflorens*)
Calendula (*Calendula officinalis*)
Cup-and-saucer vine (*Cobaea scandens*)
Pinks (*Dianthus* spp.)
Lobelia (*Lobelia erinus*)
Geranium (*Pelargonium* spp.)
Ornamental pepper (*Piper* spp.)
Mealy-cup sage (*Salvia farinacea*)
Black-eyed susan vine (*Thunbergia alata*)

Selected annuals provide excellent color for window boxes and hanging baskets, both in sun and shade. Keep in mind, however, that these containers have a limited amount of soil, and it dries out quickly on hot days. Daily watering may be necessary to keep the plants alive. Also, with the regular watering, don't forget to feed them regularly as well.

ANNUALS THAT WILL SUPPLY COLORFUL FOLIAGE

Annual plants can supply more than flowers to the garden decor. Many of them have colorful, unusual, and even exciting foliage, which, unlike flower blossoms, will be present throughout the growing season. The colors can be used in your scheme of landscaping to blend, contrast, or perhaps to enhance different colors and plants. Watch though that the white or yellow variegations and leaf color patterns are not placed in the direct, hot afternoon sun, for they may sunburn easily. Start with this list and add to it as you begin looking around for the colored foliage types.

Love-lies-bleeding (*Amaranthus tricolor*)
Flowering kale (*Brassica oleracea* vars.)
Snow-on-the-mountain
  (*Euphorbia marginata*)
Summer cypress (*Kochia scoparia*)
Castor bean (*Ricinus communis*)

Flowering cabbage (*Brassica oleracea* vars.)
Coleus (*Coleus blumeii*)
Bloodleaf (*Iresine herbstii*)

Beefsteak plant (*Perilla frutescens*)

ANNUALS FOR NATURALIZING A PART OF YOUR GARDEN

This is a list of annuals that will reseed themselves easily, and that also provide something for wildlife, such as seeds for birds, dense growth to hide in, and so forth. Some of us just let Mother Nature take care of things, and she does a good job of growing grass and letting weeds move in from surrounding vacant land. If you don't like Nature's way, here are some to plant. Give them the care needed to grow, bloom, and set seed, then next year watch for their emergence and keep the weeds from overcoming them.

Bachelor's button (*Centaurea cyanus*)
Deerhorn clarkia (*Clarkia pulchella*)
Calliopsis (*Coreopsis tinctoria*)
Common sunflower (*Helianthus annuus*)
Tidytips (*Layia platyglossa*)
Sweet alyssum (*Lobularia maritima*)
Shirley poppy (*Papaver rhoeas*)
Catchfly (*Silene armeria*)

Godetia (*Clarkia amoena*)
Larkspur (*Consolida ambigua*)
Cosmos (*Cosmos bipinnatus*)
Annual mallow (*Lavatera trimestris*)
Baby snapdragon (*Linaria maroccana*)
Baby blue-eyes (*Nemophila menziesii*)
Phlox (*Phlox drummondii*)

 If you are wanting to attract wildlife to your yard, remember that like humans they have four basic needs: food, water, cover, and space. Determine the kind of animals you want to attract and plant accordingly. Most city yards have niches where songbirds can adapt quite nicely.

ANNUALS THAT WILL AND WON'T WITHSTAND HEAVY RAIN

Many of the annual flowers get beaten into the ground with the hard, heavy rains of spring. Usually within a day or two they are up and growing again. But, if you could plant the more tender types where they will receive protection overhead, then some of your worries could stop. Here are a few that stand up nicely against all but hail storms (after all you can't guarantee everything in this world!), along with others that keel over at the first sign of a rain cloud.

These *will* withstand heavy rain

Snapdragon (*Antirrhinum majus*)

English daisy (*Bellis perennis*)

Flowering cabbage (*Brassica oleracea* vars.)

Flowering kale (*Brassica oleracea* vars.)

Calendula (*Calendula officinalis*)

China aster (*Callistephus chinensis*)

Crested cockscomb (*Celosia* 'Cristata')

Livingstone daisy (*Dorotheanhus bellidiformis*)

Sunflower (*Helianthus annuus*)

Strawflower (*Helichrysum bracteatum*)

Sweet alyssum (*Lobularia maritima*)

Forget-me-not (*Myosotis sylvatica*)

Ivy geranium (*Pelargonium peltatum*)

Purple Wave petunia (*Petunia* 'Purple Wave')

Storm petunia (*Petunia* 'Storm')

Moss rose (*Portulaca grandiflora*)

Castor bean (*Ricinus communis*)

Indian Summer rudbeckia
    (*Rudbeckia hirta* 'Indian Summer')

French marigold (*Tagetes patula*)

Zinnia (*Zinnia* 'Scarlet Splendor')

These won't

Amaranthus (*Amaranthus* spp.)

Plumed cockscomb (*Celosia* 'Plumosa')

Bachelor's button (*Centaurea cyanus*)

Sweet sultan (*Centaurea moschata*)

Coleus (*Coleus hybridus*)

Cosmos (*Cosmos* spp.)

Accent Impatiens (*Impatiens wallerana*)

Annual mallow (*Lavatera trimestris*)

Poppy (*Papaver* spp.)

Martha Washington geranium
    (*Pelargonium domesticum*)

Geranium (*Pelargonium hortorum*)

 "To protect tall-growing annuals from wind damage, I place a tomato frame over a clump of young seedlings, like bachelor's buttons, and secure a piece of chicken wire over the top. As the young plants get tall enough, I thread them through the chicken wire so they are supported through our spring storms."—Dorothy Christenson, Oregon State University Master Gardener, Beaverton, Oregon

ANNUALS SUITABLE FOR ROCK GARDENS

Rock garden plants should be selected on the basis of size, form, and whether or not they seem to fit into the garden properly. Rock gardens that are not carefully planned, especially for scale, often become nothing more than a heap of plants, each going its own way, and nothing looks quite like it fits. Here are some that could give you a start on things.

African daisy (*Dimorphotheca sinuata*)

California poppy (*Eschscholzia californica*)

Annual baby's breath (*Gypsophila elegans*)

Lobelia (*Lobelia erinus*)

Sweet alyssum (*Lobularia maritima*)

Forget-me-not (*Myosotis sylvatica*)

Cup-flower (*Nierembergia* spp.)

Annual phlox (*Phlox drummondii*)

Moss rose (*Portulaca grandiflora*)

Creeping zinnia (*Sanvitalia procumbens*)

French marigold (*Tagetes patula*)

Wishbone flower (*Torenia fournieri*)

Nasturtium (*Tropaeolum majus*)

Verbena (*Verbena hybrida*)

Lilliput zinnia (*Zinnia* spp.)

ANNUALS SUITABLE AS EVERLASTINGS

Some flowers dry nicely after they have matured and start to die; others seem to wither away, leaving not enough behind to remind you of what they were. Some that would be suitable as everlasting decorations are listed below. Cut them when the flower head is fully mature. Hang them in a dry, dark storage place until all moisture is gone from the flower head and they are completely dry. Then store them in a cool, dry, dark storage area until you are ready to use them.

Globe
Amaranth

Winged everlasting (*Ammobium alatum*)
Crested cockscomb (*Celosia cristata*)
Chinese delphinium
    (*Delphinium grandiflorum*)
Strawflower (*Helichrysum bracteatum*)

Statice (*Limonium* spp.)
Bells of Ireland (*Moluccella laevis*)
Mealy-cup sage (*Salvia farinacea*)
Immortelle (*Xeranthemum annuum*)

Quaking oats (*Briza maxima*)
Bachelor's button (*Centaurea cyanus*)
Globe amaranth (*Gomphrena globosa*)

Pink-and-white everlasting
    (*Helipterum roseum*)
Money plant (*Lunaria annua*)
Love in a mist (*Nigella damescena*)
Pincushion flower (*Scabiosa atropurpurea*)

> **When drying flowers, remember that they continue opening while they are drying. Some flowers may shatter during drying, dropping the petals that lend beauty to the final product. This is most often due to harvesting the flowers after they have passed their prime condition.**

WATER-WISE GARDENING WITH THE USE OF ANNUAL PLANTS

Throughout the country, people are becoming more concerned about the supply of groundwater. Groundwater supplies most cities' drinking water, the water that we use to hose down the driveway, the water we use to water our new plants after planting, and so forth. Water has many uses. To us the most important uses are to keep our bodies supplied with moisture and to keep our plants alive and healthy. In the garden we can do a lot to conserve water, including doing less cultivation, planting at the proper time, eradicating water-robbing weeds, and using mulches on the ground surface to slow loss through evaporation. Another water-wise thing to do is consider plants that use less water than others and build a landscape or garden using these plants. Here is a list that we believe will provide a good garden even during periods of water stress.

African daisy (*Arctotis hybrids*)
Calliopsis (*Coreopsis tinctoria*)
Blanket flower (*Gaillardia* spp.)
Strawflower (*Helichrysum* spp.)
Morning glory (*Ipomaea nil*)
Poppy (*Papaver* spp.)
Black-eyed susan (*Rudbeckia hirta*)
Verbena (*Verbena hybrida*)

Spider flower (*Cleome spinosa*)
California poppy (*Eschscholzia californica*)
Globe amaranth (*Gomphrena*)
Annual baby's breath (*Gypsophila paniculata*)
Sweet alyssum (*Lobularia maritima*)
Moss rose (*Portulaca grandiflora*)
Sage (*Salvia* spp.)

To maintain annual flowering plants during periods of water shortages, protect them by using mulches. An inch layer of organic mulch covering the row and between plants will cut the loss of water from evaporation by nearly one third.

ANNUALS THAT WOULD ADD COLOR TO A SMALL SPACE GARDEN

If your garden space is a small one, carefully choose plants that will supply your needs, yet not grow so large that they take over the space. If you like bulbs, grow them in containers so they can be moved elsewhere when their beauty is finished. Here are a few to consider.

Coleus (*Coleus hybridus*)
Busy Lizzie (*Impatiens wallerana*)
Sweet alyssum (*Lobularia maritima*)
Nemesia (*Nemesia strumosa*)
Marigold (*Tagetes patula*)
Verbena (*Verbena hybrida*)
Zinnia (*Zinnia* spp.)

Annual candytuft (*Iberis sempervirens*)
Lobelia (*Lobelia erinus*)
Stock (*Matthiola incana*)
Petunia (*Petunia* spp.)
Nasturtium (*Tropaeolum majus*)
Pansy (*Viola* spp.)

In gardens and landscapes, for summer-long enjoyment, gardeners often rely on annual flowers which bloom quickly and, if groomed, will bloom for a long time. If you are handy with seeds and pots and have a place to start them, grow some of your own transplants. Because not all of us are adept at growing seedlings, our local retail nurseries and garden centers will have available for us flats or individual containers of established plants or seedlings when the appropriate season arrives.

GROUND-COVERS

Turf-type grass is the best of all groundcovers because it can be walked upon. No other plant quite fits that use. The groundcovers that we list in this chapter are those plants that can be expected to grow close enough together to form a dense cover over the soil. They are too high for play or traffic areas, but not so high that they become a barrier. For example, a mass planting of Pfitzer juniper would become large enough to deter charging buffalo, therefore we would not list them with our groundcovers. On the other hand a mass planting of *Cotoneaster dammeri* 'Lowfast' would grow together and make a cover only about a foot deep, thus qualifying nicely as a groundcover. Some in the following lists are woody-type plants, others are herbaceous perennials. Members of both groups can be found in their respective chapters elsewhere in this book to help you learn more about the use characteristics of a plant that catches your interest.

The groundcover lists are not to be considered complete. In fact we encourage you to visit retail nurseries and garden centers, arboretums and experiment stations, where a constant stream of new plant types can be found. Look at established landscapes, parks, and municipal plantings for examples of groundcover plantings. As you find others, add them to our lists. That is what will make this book most useful to you.

Before trying to establish a groundcover, do some careful planning. Generally the nurseryman who sells the plants can tell you how far apart to plant them so you know how many are needed for the square footage of your site. Look at the site you are planting with a critical eye. How about perennial weeds, like perennial thistles or quackgrass, or horror of horrors, horsetail rush (*Equisetum arvense*). These need to be dealt with before planting your first groundcover plant. They are very difficult to control after the groundcover plants are in. Tilling and raking out roots will help a little, or use glyphosate (Roundup) before starting to prepare the soil, while the weeds are tall and leafy. After several weeks, till and rake out as many roots as possible. Mulching will help to keep annual weeds from taking over before the groundcover gets established.

Planting in the higher elevations is best done in spring when the ground warms. In the lower areas you can plant in spring or early fall. After planting, keep the new plants well watered, fertilize them several times through the year while they are actively growing, and you will be surprised at how fast they fill the gaps and become a true groundcover.

GROUNDCOVERS FOR SUN AND SHADE

In some landscape situations you will need plants that can tolerate the extremes of full sun or full shade. An example would be if you are planting an area that extends across the yard from shade trees to open space and back again to the microclimate of shade trees. Both conditions may exist in any garden, and in varying amounts. Luckily, we have a lot of plants for our use that are very adaptable. As you travel through the Pacific Northwest, watch for the succession and occurrence of groundcovering plants and how they relate to the light. This list is only a starter that you can add to as you run across others.

Carpet bugle (*Ajuga reptans*)	All PNW
Kinnikinnick (*Arctostaphylos uva-ursi*)	All PNW
White bishop's hat (*Epimedium youngianum* 'Niveum')	All PNW
Pink bishop's hat (*Epimedium youngianum* 'Roseum')	All PNW
Winter creeper (*Euonymus fortunei*)	All PNW
Wild strawberry (*Fragaria chiloensis*)	C, LV, LM, DV
English ivy (*Hedera helix*)	All PNW
Salal (*Gaultheria shallon*)	C, LV, LM, DV
Ground ivy (*Glechoma hederaceae*)	All PNW
Soapwort (*Saponaria ocymoides*)	All PNW
Creeping blueberry (*Vaccinium crassifolium*)	C, LV, LM, DV

GROUNDCOVERS THAT CAN QUICKLY GET OUT OF CONTROL

Usually, we like to cover the ground quickly, so we use groundcovers that grow quickly. Some must be noted as ones that could easily get out of control. Those listed below should be planted in areas where they can do their own thing, where you will dedicate yourself to pulling them out within a given length of time, or in areas where you can restrict their roots in some manner. Remember, too, that the climbers can go up tree trunks or cover structures where you might not want them.

Bishop's weed (*Aegopodium podagraria*)	All PNW
Meadow anemone (*Anemone canadensis*)	All PNW
Crown vetch (*Coronilla varia*)	All PNW
English ivy (*Hedera helix*)	All PNW
Chameleon plant (*Houttuynia cordata* 'Chameleon')	All PNW
Hall's honeysuckle (*Lonicera japonica* 'Halliana')	C, LV, LM, DV
Mint (*Mentha* spp.)	Varies
Silver lace vine (*Polygonum aubertii*)	All PNW
Periwinkle (*Vinca major* 'Variegata')	C, LV, LM, DV

It is wise to check with other gardeners to see what their success has been with groundcovers that are suggested here. Invasiveness of plants can vary with climate and soil, but some plants are notorious everywhere. Hall's honeysuckle is an above-ground invader of any structure or plant that will give it vertical support.

GROUNDCOVERS FOR FULL SUN

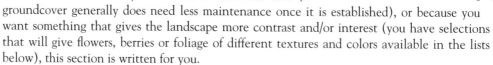

Juniperus horizontalis

If you are planting a site that lies in full sun, you have probably decided that grass is a chore to care for. You will find that in the western region of the Pacific Northwest, one of the problems encountered when trying to grow a lawn is that the trees get in the way. They provide shade which encourages moss and discourages grass. However, if a ground-cover sounds better to you because it takes less care (a groundcover generally does need less maintenance once it is established), or because you want something that gives the landscape more contrast and/or interest (you have selections that will give flowers, berries or foliage of different textures and colors available in the lists below), this section is written for you.

Prostrate white abelia (*Abelia grandiflora* 'Prostrata')	C, LV, LM, DV
Sheep bur (*Acaena* spp.)	C, LV, LM, DV
Wooly yarrow (*Achillea tomentosa*)	All PNW
Bishop's weed (*Aegopodium podagraria*)	All PNW
Carpet bugle (*Ajuga reptans*)	All PNW
Mountain rockcress (*Arabis alpina*)	All PNW
Kinnikinnick (*Arctostaphylos uva-ursi* vars.)	All PNW
Silver spreader (*Artemesia caucasica*)	All PNW
Carpet heather (*Calluna vulgaris* 'Nana')	C, LV, LM, DV
Mrs. Ronald Gray heather (*Calluna vulgaris* 'Mrs. Ronald Gray')	C, LV, LM, DV
Point Reyes ceanothus (*Ceanothus gloriosus* varieties)	All PNW
Squaw carpet ceanothus (*Ceanothus prostratus*)	LM, DV, HD
Chamomile (*Chamaemelum nobile*)	All PNW
Creeping cotoneaster (*Cotoneaster adpressus*)	All PNW
Cranberry cotoneaster (*C. apiculatus*)	All PNW
Bearberry cotoneaster (*C. dammeri*)	All PNW
Lowfast cotoneaster (*C. dammeri* 'Lowfast')	All PNW
Rock cotoneaster (*C. horizontalis*)	All PNW
Euonymus (*Euonymus fortunei* varieties)	All PNW
Blue fescue (*Festuca ovina* 'Glauca')	All PNW
Salal (*Gaultheria shallon*)	C, LV, LM, DV
Genista broom (*Genista pilosa*)	C, LV, LM, DV
Ground ivy (*Glechoma hederaceae*)	All PNW
Creeping baby's breath (*Gypsophila repens*)	All PNW
St. Johnswort (*Hypericum calycinum*)	C, LV, LM, DV
Blue Pacific shore juniper (*Juniperus conferta* 'Blue Pacific')	All PNW
Emerald Sea shore juniper (*J. conferta* 'Emerald Sea')	All PNW
Blue Chip juniper (*J. horizontalis* 'Blue Chip')	All PNW
Blue rug juniper (*J. horizontalis* 'Wiltonii')	All PNW
plus many other *Juniperus* spp. and vars.	
Pheasant berry (*Leycesteria formosa*)	C, LV, LM
Grace Ward lithodora (*Lithodora diffusa*)	C, LV, LM
Creeping Jennie (*Lysimachia nummularia*)	All PNW
Rosemary (*Rosmarinus officinalis*)	C, LV, LM, DV
Stonecrop (*Sedum* species)	All PNW

Creeping thyme (*Thymus praecox arcticus*)   All PNW
Purple clover (*Trifolium repens* 'Atropurpureum')   All PNW
Creeping blueberry (*Vaccinium crassifolium*)   C, LV, LM, DV

While there are few rules to landscaping, low plants of a relatively fine texture should be the main groundcover in close-up situations. Taller groundcovers give a good effect at a distance and in heavier shade. Contrasting textures draw the attention, much as a variegated foliage groundcover will.

GROUNDCOVERS FOR DEEP SHADE

Where trees form dense canopies or tall shrubs cause the ground surface to be completely shaded during the day, you must search for something that will tolerate such conditions. Keep in mind, however, that for these hardy plants to survive you must supply water and fertilizer as needed to keep them from being starved out by the larger shading plants.

In the deep, cool and moist shade of the western part of the Pacific Northwest, the normal groundcover is moss, lots of it. If moss is already growing in your space, enjoy!

Bishop's weed (*Aegopodium podogruria*)   All PNW
Lady's mantle (*Alchemilla mollis*)   C, LV, LM, DV
Wild ginger (*Asarum caudatum*)   C, LV, LM, DV
European ginger (*Asarum europaeum*)   All PNW
Bunchberry (*Cornus canadensis*)   All PNW
Kenilworth ivy (*Cymbalaria muralis*)   C, LV, LM, DV
Sweet woodruff (*Galium odoratum*)   All PNW
Wintergreen (*Gaultheria procumbens*)   C, LV, LM, DV
Box huckleberry (*Gaylussacia brachysera*)   C, LV, LM, DV
Ground ivy (*Glechoma hederacea*)   All PNW
Chameleon plant (*Houttuynia cordata* 'Chameleon')   All PNW
Dead nettle (*Lamium maculatum* varieties)   All PNW
Princess pine (*Lycopodium clavatum*)   All PNW
Oregon oxalis (*Oxalis oregana*)   C, LV, LM, DV
Japanese spurge (*Pachysandra terminalis*)   All PNW
Blue star creeper (*Pratia pedunculata*)   C, LV, LM, DV
Lungwort (*Pulmonaria* spp.)   All PNW
Creeping buttercup (*Ranunculus repens* 'Pleniflorus')   All PNW
Baby's tears (*Soleirolia soleirolii*)   C, LV, LM, DV
Piggy-back plant (*Tolmiea menziesii*)   C, LV, LM
Periwinkle (*Vinca minor*)   All PNW

When selecting a groundcover, consider three factors—the height of the plant, the soil type you are planting into, and the exposure to sun or shade. Depending on your selection, height can range from a few inches to several feet. Some groundcovers can tolerate poor drainage, some can take alkaline soils, some demand a particular soil type. Choose shade-tolerant groundcovers for planting beneath shrubs and those that require full, open sunlight for planting exposed banks.

GROUNDCOVERS TO STABILIZE A SLOPE

A slope presents both a problem and a challenge. Often we avoid the challenge by simply letting Mother Nature grow whatever grows naturally on slopes, given its soil type and climate. The problem is one of trying to blend the slope into the planted landscape, make it sort of fit the picture in your mind, and also prevent erosion. Erosion can happen either gradually, as soil particles wash away, or suddenly, when the entire hillside slides down. In the western part of the Pacific Northwest in January and February, 1996, many gardens were lost because of saturated soils that wanted to slide to the rivers. Not all plants will prevent erosion. In fact even trees that have grown for twenty years on the hillside may slide away during periods of excessive rainfall on silty-clay soils. However, the following groundcover plants are suggested for stabilizing average slopes. There are many other members of the species listed, but we list those that we deem the best for this purpose because of their deep-rooting capability. Add to the list as you run across others.

European beachgrass (*Ammophila arenaria*)	C
Marlberry (*Ardisia japonica*)	C, LV, LM
Feather reed grass (*Calamagrostis acutiflora* 'Karl Foerster')	All PNW
Crown vetch (*Coronilla varia*)	All PNW
Cranberry cotoneaster (*Cotoneaster apiculatus*)	All PNW
Bearberry cotoneaster (*C. dammeri*)	All PNW
Spreading cotoneaster (*C. divaricatus*)	All PNW
Ceanothus (*Ceanothus gloriosus* varieties)	All PNW
Bunchberry (*Cornus canadensis*)	All PNW
Winter creeper (*Euonymus fortunei*)	All PNW
Creeping wintergreen (*Gaultheria procumbens*)	All PNW
Salal (*Gaultheria shallon*)	C, LV, LM, DV
English ivy (*Hedera helix*)	All PNW
St. Johnswort (*Hypericum calycinum*)	C, LV, LM, DV
Sunburst St. Johnswort (*Hypericum calycinum* 'Sunburst')	All PNW
Sargent juniper (*Juniperus chinensis sargentii*)	All PNW
Andorra juniper (*J. horizontalis* 'Plumosa')	All PNW
Savin juniper (*J. sabina*)	All PNW
Hall's honeysuckle (*Lonicera japonica* 'Halliana')	C, LV, LM, DV
Creeping Oregon grape (*Mahonia repens*)	All PNW
Japanese spurge (*Pachysandra terminalis*)	All PNW
Fountain grass (*Pennisetum alopecuroides*)	All PNW
Lowboy pyracantha (*Pyracantha coccinea* 'Lowboy')	All PNW
Gro-Low fragrant sumac (*Rhus aromatica* 'Gro-Low')	All PNW
Lingonberry (*Vaccinium vitis-idaea*)	C, LV, LM

On steep slopes, often the planting soil is thin or of a high clay content, making it difficult to establish plants quickly. Cutting pockets where composted manure or prepared potting soil can be worked into the existing ground will help the new plants to root quickly. Deep watering will be essential during droughty summer weather. A complete fertilizer, either chemical or organic, will help.

GROUNDCOVERS FOR LIGHT SHADE

Some groundcovers will grow and thrive in shade, others will live only in full open sunlight. The shade-tolerant plants vary in their degree of ability to sustain growth in the absence of full sunlight. That is why we have divided the shade plants into two groups; those that will take just enough to prevent a shadow, and those that will survive under a deck or among the trees and undergrowth of forest environs. Those that are vines in this list, even though they will live in shade, will tend to grow upward to whatever light exists and on whatever is handy (for example, English ivy will head for the sun, up the trunks of trees or the supports of decks).

English Ivy

Prostrate abelia (*Abelia grandiflora* 'Prostrata')	C, LV, LM
Sheep bur (*Acaena* spp.)	C, LV, LM, DV
Wooly yarrow (*Achillea tomentosa*)	All PNW
Bishop's weed (*Aegopodium podagraria*)	All PNW
Carpet bugle (*Ajuga reptans* varieties)	All PNW
Dwarf bog rosemary (*Andromeda polifolia* 'Nana')	All PNW
Kinnikinnick (*Arctostaphylos uva-ursi*)	All PNW
Astilbe (*Astilbe chinensis* 'Pumila')	C, LV, LM, DV
Sedge (*Carex conica* 'Marginata')	C, LV, LM, DV
Snow-in-summer (*Cerastium tomentosum*)	All PNW
Dwarf plumbago (*Ceratostigma plumbaginoides*)	C, LV, LM, DV
Chamomile (*Chamaemelum nobile*)	All PNW
Corydalis (*Corydalis* spp.)	C, LV, LM
New Zealand brass buttons (*Cotula squalida*)	C, LV, LM, DV
Indian mock strawberry (*Duchesnea indica*)	All PNW
Bishop's hat (*Epimedium grandiflorum*)	All PNW
Pink Queen bishop's hat (*Epimedium rubrum* 'Pink Queen')	All PNW
Pink bishop's hat (*Epimedium Youngianum* 'Roseum')	All PNW
Winter creeper (*Euonymus fortuneii* varieties)	All PNW
Ground ivy (*Glechoma hederaceae*)	All PNW
English ivy (*Hedera helix*)	All PNW
Plantain lily (*Hosta* selected spp. and vars.)	All PNW
Chameleon houttuynia (*Houttuynia cordata* 'Chameleon')	All PNW
Creeping lily turf (*Liriope spicata*)	All PNW
Grace Ward lithodora (*Lithodora diffusa* 'Grace Ward')	C, LV, LM
Creeping mahonia (*Mahonia repens*)	All PNW
Forget-me-not (*Myosotis scorpioides*)	All PNW
Japanese pachysandra (*Pachysandra terminalis*)	All PNW
Oregon boxwood (*Paxistima myrsinites*)	All PNW
Spring cinquefoil (*Potentilla tabernaemontanii*)	All PNW
Blue star creeper (*Pratia pedunculata*)	C, LV, LM, DV
Crinkle-leaf creeper (*Rubus pentalobus*)	C, LV, LM, DV
Purple clover (*Trifolium repens* 'Atropurpureum')	All PNW
Creeping blueberry (*Vaccinium crassifolium*)	C, LV, LM, DV
Inside-out flower (*Vancouveria planipetala*)	C, LV
Common periwinkle (*Vinca minor*)	All PNW
Barren strawberry (*Waldsteinia fragarioides*)	C, LV, LM, DV

GROUNDCOVERS THAT DRAPE AND TRAIL

Plants that spill over the edge of a wall, trail down a slope, or cascade over rocks soften the overall landscape and help to give it a completed look. There are many situations in the average landscape where a trailing groundcover can add beauty and interest or lead the eye to another feature. Some can be used to scramble on the ground among taller plants. Vinca, for example, will grow and flow like a green stream with blue flowers. Some, like *Polygonum*, might get out of hand unless you give it reasonably constant attention and guide or restrict its normally robust growth pattern.

Rock jasmine (*Androsace* spp.)	All PNW
Bearberry cotoneaster (*Cotoneaster dammeri* vars.)	All PNW
Dorset heath (*Erica ciliaris*)	C, LV, LM, DV
Common winter creeper (*Euonymus fortunei radicans*)	C, LV, LM, DV
Pink Panda strawberry (*Fragaria* 'Pink Panda')	C, LV, LM, DV
Creeping baby's breath (*Gypsophila repens*)	All PNW
English ivy (*Hedera helix*)	All PNW
Beacon Silver dead nettle (*Lamium maculatum* 'Beacon Silver')	All PNW
Creeping Jennie (*Lysimachia nummularia*)	All PNW
Ground ivy (*Nepeta hederacea*)	All PNW
Trailing phlox (*Phlox nivalis*)	C, LV, LM, DV
Creeping phlox (*Phlox stolonifera*)	All PNW
Silver lace vine (*Polygonum aubertii*)	All PNW
Soapwort (*Saponaria ocymoides*)	All PNW
Periwinkle (*Vinca major* 'Variegata')	C, LV, LM, DV
Dwarf periwinkle (*Vinca minor*)	All PNW

GROUNDCOVERS FOR DRY SHADE

This category of plants is for those areas that are planted under the canopy of shade trees, or among the native trees that exist in your landscape. Trees remove a lot of water during the growing season. And, for those of you who have gardened in the Pacific Northwest for a year or more, you know that the summer growing season is also the dry season of this region. So, if you plant anything beneath your established trees, or within their system of roots, plan to water periodically during the summer. It also helps if you select plants that can tolerate shade and dryness. The following list will get you started. Keep in mind that even though these groundcover plants will tolerate dryness, they need supplemental water during their first growing season to become established.

Bellflower (*Campanula takesimana*)	All PNW
Lily-of-the-valley (*Convallaria majalis*)	All PNW
Bunchberry (*Cornus canadensis*)	All PNW
Bishop's hat (*Epimedium grandiflorum*)	All PNW
Salal (*Gaultheria shallon*)	C, LV, LM, DV
English ivy (*Hedera helix*)	All PNW
Japanese spurge (*Pachysandra terminalis*)	All PNW
Soapwort (*Saponaria ocymoides*)	All PNW
Dwarf periwinkle (*Vinca minor*)	LV, LM, DV, HD

GROUNDCOVERS FOR DRY SITES

If your landscaping plans include trying to make the garden one of low maintenance, replace some of the more water demanding plants with some of these groundcovers that can tolerate dryness. Water these well through the first growing season so they can become established in your soil. Once they are established they will endure long periods of dryness, yet still retain their beauty and interest.

Blue star bellflower (*Campanula poscharskyana*)	All PNW
Dwarf plumbago (*Ceratostigma plumbaginoides*)	C, LV, LM, DV
Bearberry cotoneaster (*Cotoneaster dammeri* vars.)	All PNW
Sheep fescue (*Festuca glauca*)	All PNW
Creeping juniper (*Juniperus* spp. and vars.)	All PNW
Emerald carpet (*Rubus pentalobus* 'Emerald Carpet')	C, LV
Stonecrop (*Sedum* spp.)	Varies
Germander (*Teucrium chamaedrys*)	All PNW

GROUNDCOVERS FOR MOIST, POORLY-DRAINED SITES

Low, poorly-drained areas in the landscape can be most frustrating. This sort of challenge is one in which you must match resistance or tolerance to root-infecting diseases with the ability to grow and succeed in a wet soil environment. Poor drainage here does not mean that the soil remains swampy throughout the entire year, but does indicate that during the rainy season in the western part of this region you would expect the roots of your plants to be wet. Here are a few that we have observed throughout the years and found to be surprisingly successful in this sort of situation. We suggest them to you for trial. Add to the list—if wet soils are the nemesis of your garden—so it will become more valuable as your garden matures. One additional consideration is to develop a drainage system for your yard, or for those particular spots that remain wet for long periods.

Bog rosemary (*Andromeda polifolia*)	All PNW
Japanese ardisia (*Ardisia japonica*)	C, LV, LM
Corsican sandwort (*Arenaria balearica*)	C, LV, LM, DV
Wild ginger (*Asarum* spp.)	C, LV, LM, DV
Sedge (*Carex conica* 'Marginata')	C, LV, LM, DV
Bleeding heart (*Dicentra formosa*)	All PNW
Cross-leafed heath (*Erica tetralix*)	C, LV, LM, DV
Algerian ivy (*Hedera canariensis*)	C, LV, LM
Chameleon plant (*Houttuynia cordata* 'Chameleon')	All PNW
Bird's-foot trefoil (*Lotus corniculatus*)	All PNW
Pennyroyal (*Mentha pulegium*)	All PNW
Spring cinquefoil (*Potentilla tabernaemontanii*)	All PNW
Blue star creeper (*Pratia pedunculata*)	C, LV, LM, DV
Dwarf periwinkle (*Vinca minor*)	LV, LM, DV, HD

GROUNDCOVERS FOR CRACKS AND CREVICES

This is a list of those nifty little plants that can be tucked into a spot between stepping stones or beneath a rock or in spaces between flagstones. Look also at the list of herbaceous perennial plants for rockeries for additional plants that suit this category.

Woolly yarrow (*Achillea tomentosa*)	All PNW
Rupture-wort (*Herniaria glabra*)	All PNW
Pennyroyal (*Mentha pulegium*)	C, LV, LM, DV
Requiem mint (*Mentha requienii*)	C, LV, LM
Raoulia (*Raoulia australis*)	C, LV, LM, DV
Rock breaker (*Saxifraga* spp.)	All PNW
Stonecrop (*Sedum* spp.)	Varies
Creeping thyme (*Thymus praecox arcticus*)	All PNW
Foamflower (*Tiarella cordifolia*)	All PNW
Soapwort (*Saponaria pumilio*)	All PNW
Speedwell (*Veronica oltensis*)	All PNW

GROUNDCOVERS FOR THE BEACH

Plants selected for the seacoast part of this region must survive elements like winter gales along with the normal salt-laden winds. Additionally, there are differences in growing conditions, such as cool summer temperatures accompanied by fog. And there is a wide range of soil types, ranging from sand to clay, often within the same landscape site. Here are some suggestions for plants that will survive such conditions. Keep your eyes open for other plants that fit your needs as you travel within the coastal areas.

European beachgrass (*Ammophila arenaria*)	C
Kinnikinnick (*Arctostaphylos uva-ursi*)	All PNW
Point Reyes ceanothus (*Ceanothus gloriosus*)	All PNW
Ceanothus (*Ceanothus griseus horizontalis* vars.)	C, LV, LM, DV
Beach strawberry (*Fragaria chiloensis*)	C, LV, LM, DV
Lydia broom (*Genista lydia*)	C, LV, LM, DV
Genista broom (*Genista pilosa*)	C, LV, LM, DV
English ivy (*Hedera helix*)	All PNW
Horseshoe vetch (*Hippocrepis comosa*)	C
Creeping St. Johnswort (*Hypericum calycinum*)	C, LV, LM, DV
Creeping juniper (*Juniperus horizontalis* vars.)	All PNW
Lithodora (*Lithodora diffusa*)	C, LV, LM
Japanese honeysuckle (*Lonicera japonica*)	C, LV, LM, DV
Silver lace vine (*Polygonum aubertii*)	All PNW

Arctostaphylos uva-ursi

"*The major factors that a landscaper should consider when planning a coastal landscape include the distance that a garden site is from the ocean, the amount of exposure the site is subject to as a result of prevailing northwest winds, the amount of sunlight the site receives, and the quality of soils found at that site.*"—Bill Rogers, Oregon State University extension agent, Newport, Oregon

PLANT SOURCES

Some nurseries charge a fee for their catalogs, and some have a minimum order, so please inquire first. In most cases, the nurseries listed carry more than we have indicated. We mention only those that have plants that are relevant to this book. Nurseries vary in size from big operations that offer full-color catalogs, to firms who are working with single species enterprises. All of them have plants to fill your needs. This is by no means a comprehensive list of plant sources. It is only meant to get you started. There are wonderful nurseries, both speciality and general, that are tucked away all over the the Pacific Northwest.

American Ornamental Perennials
29977 SE Weitz Lane
Eagle Creek, OR 97022-9633
503-637-3095
(ornamental grasses)

Bear Creek Nursery
4999 Samish Way
Bellingham, WA 98226
360-733-1171
(rare and unusual plants)

Bonsai Village
PO Box 327
Wilsonville, OR 97070
503-678-1216
(bonsai plants, supplies)

Caprice Farm Nursery
15425 SW Pleasant Hill Rd
Sherwood, OR 97140
503-625-5588
(hostas, daylilies, herbaceous perennials)

Christianson's Nursery & Greenhouse
1578 Best Rd
Mt. Vernon, WA 98273
360-466-3821
(general nursery plants)

City People's Garden Store
2939 E Madison
Seattle, WA 98112
206-324-0963
(garden center)

Edmund's Roses
6235 SW Kahle Rd
Wilsonvlle, OR 97070
503-682-1476
(roses)

Forest Farm Nursery
990 Tetherow Rd
Williams, OR 97544-9599
541-846-7269
(natives, shrubs, herbaceous perennials)

Garland Nursery
5470 NE Hwy 20
Corvallis, OR 97330
541-753-6601
(general nursery plants)

Greer Gardens
1280 Goodpasture Island Rd
Eugene, OR 97401-1794
800-548-0111
(rhododendrons, azaleas, general nursery plants)

Heirloom Old Garden Roses
24062 Riverside Dr NE
St. Paul, OR 97137
503-538-1576
(heritage roses)

Heronswood Nursery Ltd.
7530 288th St NE
Kingston, WA 98346
360-297-4172
(general nursey plants)

Honeyhill Farm
5910 SW Hamilton St
Portland, OR 97221
503-292-1817
(herbaceous perennials)

Hughes Water Gardens
25289 SW Stafford Rd
Tualatin, OR 97062
800-858-1709
(aquatic plants)

Joy Creek Nursery
20300 NW Watson Rd
Scappoose, OR 97056
503-543-7474
(shrubs, perennials, alpines)

Justice Miniature Roses
5947 SW Kahle Rd
Wilsonville, OR 97070
503-682-2370
(miniature roses)

Kimberly Nurseries, Inc.
2862 Addison Ave E
Twin Falls, ID 83301
208-733-2717
(general nursery plants)

Klamath Basin Perennials
30242 Hwy 97 N
Chiloquin, OR 97624
541-783-2042
(hardy perennials)

Larsen Farm Nursery
25935 SW Stafford Rd
Wilsonville, OR 97070
503-638-8600
(perennials, general)

Lee's Nursery
1650 Hwy 200 E
Sandpoint, ID 83864
208-263-1411
(general nursery)

Log House Plants
78185 Rat Creek Rd
Cottage Grove, OR 97424
541-942-2288
(herbaceous perennials)

Molbaks Greenhouse and Nursery
13625 NE 175 St
Woodinville, WA 98072
206-483-5000
(florist, nursery, display gardens)

Naylor Creek Nursery
2610 West Valley Rd
North Bend, WA 98045
360-732-4983
(shade-tolerant perennials)

Nichols Garden Nursery
1190 N Pacific Hwy
Albany, OR 97321
541-928-9280
(seeds and herbs)

Northwoods Nursery
27635 S Oglesby Rd
Canby, OR 97013
503-266-5432
(edible ornamentals, variety)

Porterhowse Farms
41370 SE Thomas Rd
Sandy, OR 97055
503-668-5834
(dwarf conifers)

Protime Lawn Seed Co.
1712 SE Ankeny
Portland, OR 97214
503-239-7518
(wildflower seed mixtures)

Raintree Nursery
391 Butts Rd
Morton, WA 98356-9700
360-496-6400
(general plant materials)

Robyn's Nest Nursery
7802 NE 63 St
Vancouver, WA 98662
360-256-7399
(herbaceous perennials)

Siskiyou Rare Plant Nursery
2825 Cummings Rd
Medford, OR 97501
541-772-6846
(dwarf conifers, alpines)

J. Frank Schmidt Nursery
PO Box 189
Boring, OR 97009
503-663-4128
(wholesale, shade trees)

Sky Nursery
18528 Aurora Ave N
Seattle, WA 98133
206-546-4851
(general nursery plants)

Sterling Nursery
9797 Fairview Ave
Boise, ID 83704
208-376-3737
(general nursery plants)

Swanson's Nursery
9701 15th Ave NW
Seattle, WA 98117
206-782-2543
(general nursery plants)

Tsugawa Nursery & Water Gardens
410 Scott Ave
Woodland, WA 98674
360-225-8750
(general nursery plants)

Valley Nursery
20882 Bond Rd NE
Poulsbo, WA 98370
800-797-2819
(general nursery plants)

Van Veen Nursery
PO Box 86424
Portland, OR 97286-0424
503-777-1734
(rhododendrons)

Wells-Medina Nursery
8300 NE 24 St
Bellevue, WA 98004
206-454-1853
(general nursery plants)

CONTRIBUTOR LIST

The following gardeners, nurserymen and women, landscape designers, extension personnel, master gardeners, plant society members, and others helped us put this book of lists together. Their contributions are very much appreciated.

1. Jane Anders
Oregon State University
Master Gardener/Portland Rose Society
5253 SW Vermont Ave
Portland, OR 97219-1029

2. Barbara Ashmun
Creative Garden Design
8560 SW Fairway Dr
Portland, OR 97225

3. Emogene and Clint Atherton
Master Gardeners
1251 NW Jefferson
Roseburg, OR 97470

4. Michael Bauer
Oregon State University
Extension Agent, Deschutes County
PO Box 756
Redmond, OR 97756

5. Jan Behrs
Pacific Northwest Gardener
PO Box 19638
Portland, OR 97280

6. Tom and Inger Burns
Klamath Basin Perennials
30242 Hwy 97 N
Chiloquin, OR 97624

7. Sam Benowitz
Raintree Nursery
391 Butts Rd
Morton, WA 98356

8. Linda Beutler
Floral designer/Master Gardener
1145 SE Linn
Portland, OR 97202

9. John Biewener
Oregon State University

Master Gardener/Portland Rose Society
2740 NW 144 Ave
Beaverton, OR 97006

10. Van Bobbitt
Washington State University
Extension urban horticulture specialist
7612 Pioneer Way E
Puyallup, WA 98371-4998

11. Jolly Butler
Oregon State University
Master Gardener
3723 NE 21
Portland, OR 97212

12. Steven Carruthers
Carruthers Landscape Design
8124 SW 56th
Portland, OR 97219

13. Dorothy Christensen
Oregon State University
Master Gardener
12955 SW Hillsboro Hwy
Hillsboro, OR 97123

14. Carolyn Clark
Garden writer
5327 SE 115th
Portland, OR 97266

15. Louise Clements
Heirloom Old Garden Roses
24062 NE Riverside Dr
St. Paul, OR 97137

16. Dr. Michael Colt
University of Idaho
Horticulturist, Idaho Extension
29603 UI Lane
Parma, ID 83660

17. Ruth Donovan
31 NE 76th
Portland, OR 97213

18. Myrna Dowsett
Landscapes & Accents
3045 SW 66 Ct
Portland,OR 97225

19. Toni Fitzgerald
Washington State University
Extension Agent
N 222 Havana
Spokane, WA 99202-4799

20. Mary Fran Fryer
Garden writer/Master Gardener
2301 Wooded Knolls Dr
Philomath, OR 97370

21. Jorge Garcia
Latin Landscapes
3163 SE 165 Ave
Portland, OR 97236

22. Gail Gredler
Oregon State University
Extension Agent, Yamhil County
945 Grandview Pl NW
Salem, OR 97307

23. Harold Greer
Greer Gardens
1280 Goodpasture Island Rd
Eugene, OR 97401

24. Lucy Hardiman
Perennial Partners
1234 SE 18th
Portland, OR 97214

25. Ernest and Elsie Hayes
7 NE 76th
Portland, OR 97213

26. Maurice Horn
Joy Creek Nursery
20300 NW Watson Rd
Scappoose, OR 97056

27. Keith and Christy Hopkins
Pro-time Lawn Seed Co.
1712 SE Ankeny
Portland, OR 97214

28. Don Howse
Porterhowse Nursery
41370 SE Thomas Rd
Sandy, OR 97055

29. Elizabeth Howley
Horticulture Department
Clackamas Community College
19600 S Molalla Ave
Oregon City, OR 97045

30. Eamonn Hughes
Hughes Water Gardens
25289 SW Stafford Rd
Tualatin, OR 97062

31. Jerry Justice
Justice Miniature Roses
5947 SW Kahle Rd
Wilsonville, OR 97070

32. Patt Kasa
Washington State University–Kitsap County
Master Gardener program coordinator
2543 California Ave E
Port Orchard, WA 98366

33. Maureen Larsen
Larsen Farms
25935 SW Stafford Rd
Wilsonville, OR 97070

34. Marje Luce
Oregon State University
Master Gardener
180 Timberlake Dr
Ashland, OR 97520

35. Dr. Ray Malieke
Washington State University
Extension horticulturist
Western Washington Res. and Extension Center
Puyallup, WA 98371

36. Ed Markham
Horticulture advisor
26418 Yale Court
Kent, WA 98032

37. Jerry Maul
Oregon State University
Extension Agent, Douglas County
PO Box 1165
Roseburg, OR 97470

38. Jim and Audrey Metcalfe
Honeyhill Farms
5910 SW Hamilton
Portland, OR 97221

39. Vern Nelson
A New Leaf
3000 SE 115th
Portland, OR 97266

40. Phil Pashek
Oregon Dogwoods Nursery
1332 W 10th
The Dalles, OR 97058

41. George Pinyuh
Washington State University
Extension Agent Emeritus
612 Smith Tower
Seattle, WA 98104-2394

42. Ray and Peg Prag
Forest Farm Nursery
990 Tetherow Rd
Williams, OR 97544

43. Paul Ries
Urban Forestry Coordinator
Oregon Deptartment of Forestry
2600 State St
Salem, OR 97310

44. Linda Robinson
Naturescaping for Clean Rivers
1115 NE 135 Ave
Portland, OR 97230

45. Dorothy and Al Rogers
Caprice Nursery
15425 SW Pleasant Hill Rd
Sherwood, OR 97140

46. William Rogers
Oregon State University
Extension Agent, Lincoln County
29 SE 2 Street
Newport, OR 97365

47. Steve Schmidt
American Ornamental Perennials
29977 SE Weitz Lane
Eagle Creek, OR 97022-9633

48. Scott Christy
Joy Creek Nursery
20300 NW Watson Rd
Scappoose, OR 97056

49. David Stockdale
Center for Urban Horticulture
University of Washington
5260 35 Ave NE
Seattle, WA 98105

50. Ted Swensen
PCC botanist, retired
9325 SW 3rd
Portland, OR 97219

51. Gray Thompson
Oregon State University
Extension Agent Emeritus
5254 SE Oakland
Milwaukie, OR 97267

52. Ted Van Veen
Van Veen's Nursery
PO Box 86424
Portland, OR 97286

53. Keith Warren
J. Frank Schmidt & Son Co.
PO Box 189
Boring, OR 97009

54. Ed Wood
Bonsai Village
PO Box 327
Wilsonville, OR 97070

INDEX